LIBERATION THEOLOGY:

LIBERATION IN THE LIGHT OF THE FOURTH GOSPEL

LIBERATION THEOLOGY:

LIBERATION IN THE LIGHT OF THE FOURTH GOSPEL

Frederick Herzog

 THE SEABURY PRESS · NEW YORK

ACKNOWLEDGMENTS

Grateful acknowledgment is made to the following authors and publishers for permission to use copyrighted material from the sources listed:

Doubleday and Company—Lewis Alexander, "Transformation," *The Poetry of the Negro 1746–1970*. Copyright 1970 by Doubleday and Company.

Farrar, Straus & Giroux, Inc.—Owen Dodson, "Jonathan's Song: A Negro Saw the Jewish Pageant 'We Will Never Die,' " in *Powerful Song Ladder*. Copyright 1946 by Owen Dodson.

Harcourt Brace Jovanovich, Inc.—T. S. Eliot, "The Hollow Men" and "Choruses from 'The Rock,' " *Collected Poems 1900–1962*. Copyright 1964 by Harcourt Brace Jovanovich.

Alfred A. Knopf, Inc.—Langston Hughes, "A Dream Deferred." Copyright 1951 by Langston Hughes. In *The Panther and the Lash* (Knopf).

The Macmillan Company—Vachel Lindsay, "Why I Voted the Socialist Ticket," *Collected Poems*. Copyright 1913 by The Macmillan Company.

October House, Inc.—Robert Hayden, "Frederick Douglass," *Selected Poems*. Copyright © 1966 by Robert Hayden.

Copyright © 1972 by Frederick Herzog
Library of Congress Catalog Card Number: 72–81026
ISBN: 0–8164–0241–8
756–972–C–4.5
Design by Nancy Dale Muldoon
Printed in the United States of America

. . . this freedom, this liberty, this beautiful and terrible
thing, needful to man as air, usable as earth. . . .

—ROBERT HAYDEN

The significant distinction is coming to be not between
"good" people and "bad" people, but between the "open"
and the "uptight."

—JAMES A. PIKE

FOR THE
OPEN GENERATION

PREFACE

In 1970 a strange coincidence made me take a new look at theology as I had viewed it thus far. In October, 1970, James H. Cone published A *Black Theology of Liberation*. In April, *Continuum* had brought out my essay on the "Theology of Liberation." That in a time of particular racial stress both a black and a white could hit upon a common theme gave me pause for thought. Apparently as the sixties drew to a close the mandate of liberation appeared as the center of those challenges that drew us out of our privacy into a wider community than we had known before—into a community of open confrontation. This book is an expansion of my exploratory essay, drawing upon my work in the Fourth Gospel of a goodly number of years.

Crucial to my argument is the judgment of the oppressed on our white affluent ways. There will be violent disagreement with the idea that we must "become black": the demand of the hour is for whites to become white; we cannot become what we are not! But I do not know how else to call attention to the need for theology to begin with a radical *metanoia*. As

long as we predicate Christian existence on our old white ways
we will be denying our Lord.

What blacks and other oppressed minorities will think
of our efforts to come clean with our history as oppressors we
cannot control. Just so whatever we try to do does not look
like an attempt to ingratiate ourselves with the wretched of the
earth! But we must take the risk. If we do not turn our theological attention to the oppressed we will never understand the
Gospel. Our white view of society shuts our minds to it. Without this liberation of consciousness that will empower us to
identify with the oppressed, yet without diaconic condescen-
sion, the Gospel will continue to escape us. It will be a tre-
mendously painful process to go through, with many mistakes
on the way. But where so much pain has been inflicted we
cannot hope to reach clarity at a theological picnic.

Whatever needs to be thought through in regard to black
theology forces us to raise questions of the very foundations
of theology. By the time we have understood what it is all
about we will have realized that the whole structure of Christian theology will have to be rethought. Exegesis will have to
be revamped, church history as well. Systematic theology especially so, but practical theology too.

Someone is sure to put up a smokescreen intimating that
it is difficult for anyone not a member of an oppressed minority to represent the oppressed. To which I can only reply
that it is not my intention to represent the oppressed. Exactly
the opposite! We should get off their backs and give up our
white pride. That's in part what the book is about.

One point I need to underscore from the beginning. The
reader will want to gird himself for the form in which the
argument has been cast: liberation theology *in the light of
the Fourth Gospel*. White Christian America has to be confronted point-blank with the biblical word. Otherwise—with-

out any Christian court of appeal—we will continue to wade in the morass of complete subjectivity and privacy. There will not be any meeting of whites and blacks theologically until this basic point has been grasped. The WASP mind that controls everything—including religion—has to be changed.

One could endlessly discuss the wisdom of using this particular segment of biblical thought. There would always be the possibility that another segment would seem more appealing. The basic issue is whether we whites want to bow before a "rock that is higher than I" or go on endlessly dreaming our private religious dreams.

The problem with white Christianity is not that it does not do enough (remember how many of us rushed off in the sixties to find "where the action is"!), but that it does not have power enough to do effectively whatever it does. Does not this power come from the Word that liberates us for action? The book is an invitation to search for an answer. So this is not a "black theology"—how could it be?—but a groping toward the truth the black knows just because he is black.

It would be repulsive if we were to try to outblack the black. Anyone looking for repeated invocation of the black God, the black Christ, etc., throughout this book will look in vain. The test of our thesis is that at every step of the way we will be found to be struggling with the same issue as black theology: a new grasp of history as liberation history. The historical space in which we stand is the space of liberation. This much black theology has made manifestly clear. Even the most "racist" American should have realized it by now.

The Fourth Gospel in this book functions as interpretive key to liberation history. Liberation—this is not a segment of the theological subject matter, but our historical space. As "historical" documents the Synoptic Gospels might seem preferable as the interpretive key. But in the Fourth Gospel we can almost touch with our hands the first full-fledged theological wrestling with Jesus of Nazareth as liberator. The pristine movement of Christian thought becomes important for us, so that our theological thinking might become more primal too.

Could one perhaps read the Fourth Gospel as a poetic statement, a poem, rather than a chronicle—and with a sense of humor? Must not the man who compelled Nicodemus to wonder whether he could get back into his mother's womb have had a sense of humor, and a poetic one at that? Might not "becoming black" express the same sense of humor today?

Several companions have helped my work along in encouragement and critique. My sister, Mrs. Hannah Neugaard, of Tampa, Florida, proved a most faithful companion from the very beginning. Ann and Brevard Childs of Yale never wavered in their confidence of the outcome. Jürgen Moltmann kept urging me on, occasionally quipping that the book was being written too early. Professor Paul Lehmann of Union Theological Seminary was sterling in his support, as in all things that pertain to my theological odyssey. And a number of discussions with James H. Cone, also of Union Theological Seminary, made much of the material jell exactly at points where it needed abrasive contact with the black counterpart. I know what it means to have encountered black integrity. Mrs. Alfreda Kaplan combined meticulous care with knowledge and insight rare in typists. But without my wife's assistance the manuscript would not have been liberated for print. I am grateful for good companions.

F. H.

CONTENTS

INTRODUCTION

"In this society one cannot be a decent human being" (Ernst Bloch). In this church one cannot be a decent Christian. These are two premises on which I must begin my theology. No longer can we sit back, as it were, and discuss the question of God in the TV chair. As though this question could be decided in leisurely discussion! And as though it were the task of theology to decide it by discussion!

This is a book on the reordering of theological priorities. Too often in our generation have we made peripheral things central. In the sixties the so-called death-of-God theology stood in the limelight of popular and scholarly interest in theology. But did it clarify the primal challenge of theology? It is not difficult to see why it triggered so much talk. It expressed a widely felt uneasiness about the loss of the sense of the divine. Said William Hamilton, the earliest spokesman for this position: "It is not just that a capacity has dried up within us; we do not take all this as merely a statement about our frail psyches, we take it as a statement about the nature of the world and we try to convince others, God is dead." [1] Which

1

God is dead? That question was never squarely faced. It was simply assumed that God was who the death-of-God theologians said he was. And Thomas Altizer could declare: "The message the Christian is now called to proclaim is the gospel, the good news or the glad tidings, of the death of God." [2] Meanwhile a radically countermanding position has appeared. James H. Cone, representing black theology, ventures the opinion: "Some present-day theologians, like Hamilton and Altizer, taking their cue from Nietzsche and the present irrelevancy of the Church to modern man, have announced the death of God. It seems, however, that their chief mistake lies in their apparent identification of God's reality with the signed-up Christians. If we were to identify the work of God with the white church, then, like Altizer, we must 'will the death of God with a passion of faith.' " [3] It is in the dialectical tension between black and white theology and in their confrontation that today we must take up again the task to describe what theology is all about.

The death-of-God theology did not argue its claims in regard to the oppressed and their oppressors. It did not tell us that the God of exploitation and war was still very much alive, that the white God was still sanctioning our bloody American scene. What is more, it did not at all see that the oppressed are still very much hoping for a God who will liberate them for a more decent life. The question of God is still alive as the quest for the power of liberation among the oppressed. If the affluent middle-class American denies the reality of God, that does not undo theology. For God is a live issue only where life is not secure, where man is unable to become complacent, and where we realize that we are not in control of life.

Theology today must begin with an identification with the wretched of the earth, the *marginales*, the marginal figures of life who are still struggling for personhood and dignity. Whether "God" immediately plays a role here is not the primary question. The first decision a man must make is how he wants to regard himself as a human being. Is he ready to discount his status, privilege, and success, and to identify with the wretched, the lost, the damned?

WHY NOT A NEW NATURAL THEOLOGY?

First of all, theology today asks you what kind of a man you are. That calls for hard reflection. Except for the black theologians, there are precious few who point to the wretched of the earth as the orientation point for the theological enterprise. Unfortunately, this is also true of those who in one way or another still wish to cling to the reality of God.

A summary of the argument for God is found in John B. Cobb's essay "Speaking About God," [4] in which the author also immediately points to the significance of the death-of-God theologians: "What is new in our situation is that, as a result of the courageous insistence of the 'radical theologians,' the proposal that God language be abandoned is being taken with great seriousness in theological circles as well." The point of reference here remains the modern subject, the advantaged intellectual who seeks to express his bourgeois ideology in a number of ways, and, as Cobb believes, not necessarily as a denial of God. According to Cobb, there are at least two acceptable ways in Christian history of speaking about God as a relevant reality: "First, God is thought of as personal, and that means as being somehow similar to human beings. Second, God is thought of as transcendent in a sense that has meant *radically* different from man and all other creatures." The second view was largely determined by the spirit of modernity. The modern view of the world (for those who could afford it!) made the old idea of God problematical. Theologians therefore tried to dissociate the concept of God from "crude personalistic conceptuality." The purpose was to clear away intellectual obstacles. Perhaps God could still be understood "not as a transcendent person but as transcendence itself." It is understandable that this kind of reasoning leads Cobb to ask whether the word "God" has any meaning whatsoever: "If God is in *no* specifiable way similar to anything else and *a fortiori* if there is no way of thinking what he is in himself, then it seems difficult to claim that the language we use about 'him' is cognitively meaningful." If every *concept* of God is rejected, if God is purely transcendent, the idea of God is emptied of content. Does this, then, not mean that God is dead?

From the perspective of the identification with the wretched of the earth the argument is largely academic. The oppressed will hardly ask whether or not he can discover some concept of transcendence. What he wants to know is whether there is a power that will liberate him. The question of God for him is not a matter of the right idea, but of the right power for new freedom.

Cobb believes it crucial to affirm that God lives. He wishes to introduce what he calls "the resurrection of God." God has to become credible again. Since God as absolute transcendence has lost credibility, "the time has come to consider the alternative response to the crisis of credibility. This approach is that of making univocal affirmations about God in spite of the fact that every assertion demands justification and runs counter to prevailing skepticism. In *our* situation no language about God is possible at all unless it is univocal language." Such language Cobb believes to have been developed in process philosophy. The theological task now becomes the transferring of concepts from modern philosophy to theology.

The one who knows how to hone his intellectual tools will be able to cut ice with modern man. Cobb is convinced that the theologian will succeed, if he masters the art of transference. But what if modern philosophy is misconceived, so that what one is transferring into theology does not ring true even on its own grounds? "Philosophy is not *Besinnen* but struggle. And this struggle has no end and will have no end" (Shestov).

No one ever believed in God because of an argument. Arguments for the reality of God are *ex post facto* insurance policies for those who can afford them. The *marginales*, the wretched of the earth, have only struggle to contend with. And for them God must make sense in the actual struggle, or he will make no sense at all. This does not exclude thinking; in fact, it involves the most radical thought, the logic of experience, not with primary concern for the successful, however, but for the lost.

Schubert Ogden, as articulate as Cobb in the argument for the reality of God, takes the human self as the basic referend for understanding God: "I know myself most immediately only as an everchanging sequence of occasions of experience, each of which is the present integration of remembered past and anticipated future into a new whole of significance." [5] On grounds of the analogy of being, God is viewed as a genuinely temporal and social reality. God thus understood is obviously different from the timeless and unrelated Absolute of the modern type of theism referred to by Cobb. God is here viewed as eminently social and temporal, related to everything and participating in everything. But while temporal, he also transcends temporality: "If God is the *eminently* temporal and changing One, to whose time and change there can be neither beginning nor end, then he must be just as surely the One who is also eternal and unchangeable." God, in this understanding, is both relative and absolute. Even so, the point of reference for the basis of univocal language about God is always man's self: "The traditional attributes of God are all reconceived on the analogical basis provided by our own existence as selves."

For Ogden, all these things are not guesses, but absolutely real and ultimate reality, the way Hartshorne and Whitehead have determined it, and the way process theology appropriates it. Ogden is also concerned about "the understanding of faith in God to which witness is borne in Holy Scripture." But the whole point of the method is to begin with *modern man's understanding of himself* as prelude to scriptural faith in God. Modern man's self is the model on which God is being patterned. Ogden realizes quite well that "theology speaks of God as well as man." [6] But is the *anthropological* model of God's reality valid as starting point of theology? Can we really find God *in the image of modern man's* experience of himself?

It would be pointless to claim that some theologians do not find a God that looks like Hartshorne and Whitehead's God. The fact is that Ogden and other new natural theologians find such a God. And in the present situation of general malaise about the reality of God this is not insignificant. What remains to be asked is whether the God of new natural theology is the God of the Christian faith. Ogden is helpful in pointing out that the reality of God is not found in some dream castle, but is anchored in the reality of human experience. The crucial issue is: in *which* human experience is he found? Ogden immediately speaks of God as relative-absolute in Hartshorne's sense, after he has proved to himself for his own satisfaction that faith in God is unavoidable. While this does not mean for him that all men are religious, he does claim that all men have confidence in the ultimate significance of life and this functions as the basis of their religious questions and answers. Even a man who thinks that life is absurd cannot escape some acknowledgment of a ground of meaning. For example, Camus claims that "the only fitting response to this absurdity is heroic resistance against it." [7] For Ogden, heroic resistance to absurdity points beyond itself to some ground of meaning we may call God: "If we exist as selves at all only because of a confidence in the final worth of our existence, the more consistently and emphatically we affirm that worth, as is the wont of secularity, the more clearly we evince our faith in that to which the word 'God' refers."

Ogden's new natural theology confronts us with two poles for understanding God: (1) Man's search for a ground of meaning. (2) The relative-absolute that is modeled on man's experience of the self. As both poles are brought into contact with each other a spark crosses the gap and the experience of God is born. This is not in any sense a full experience of the Christian God, but its rational basis. What mandate is there, however, to demonstrate a point of contact between the search for a ground of meaning and the relative-absolute God? Is it not rather that we must point to the *actual event* of God's reality making men human in the face of their next-to-futile attempts to overcome an absurd oppression? Does not Ogden's formula claim too much? It is a brilliant academic argument. But is it clearly in touch with the rough-and-tumble of life?

Leslie Dewart, on the Roman Catholic side of the debate, duplicates some of the dilemmas of Cobb and Ogden. It is not fully clear where the center of his thinking lies. Occasionally he speaks as though in reconceptualizing God in Christianity we must begin with the data of the Christian community. For example: "Unless we retain the Greek metaphysical outlook, the ordinary facets of Christian experience are sufficient to establish that we do *experience* God." [8] At other times he seems to suggest that we must begin with human experience in general: "The reality of human transcendence discloses the presence of a reality beyond all actual and possible empirical intuition." From this latter perspective Dewart introduces what he calls the only valid proof for the existence of God. The reality of God appears "*if* in the presence of myself to myself I find that over and above my own agency . . . there is a presence which 'reveals me to myself' in a supererogatory and gratuitous way, that is, by making me 'more fully myself than I should be if I were not exposed to the impact.' "

While Dewart would seem completely opposed to an ontologically ascertainable God, a God of Being, his access to God, formally at least, is the same: *man finds in himself* the reality of God. For Dewart, this is not a God who exists, a being, or Being itself, but presence: "Unlike the reality of being, God is a transcendent reality. He is not merely present to us; he is both present and absent. . . . What needs to be 'proven' is not that a God-being objectively exists. What requires 'a demonstration,' for it is not immediately obvious, is God's *presence:* whether, in what sense, in what way, and with what consequences, God is present." Dewart, of course, is convinced—as we all are—that his way of conceiving God is preferable to others. Unlike Cobb and Ogden, he does not seek a rational argument that can lead to God. He seems merely to point to an immediacy of God's presence—in man. But this does not differ substantially from the Cobb-Ogden new natural theology argument of the accessibility of God. Dewart, too, wants to arrive at the reality of God through an analysis of man's self. Apparently no other experience needs to be involved in order to encounter God except the grasp of the self.

But do men generally grasp some "presence" in themselves corresponding to the God of the Christian faith? Hardly. Much of what Dewart has done has been to describe the actual dialectic between God's presence and absence. But this dialectic seems not to be a universal experience. It relates chiefly to a *particular* historical experience, the Christian faith. *Directly* accessible to us is the dialectic of life, the questioning we are involved in when we realize that we have to *be*, and that we probably *will be* tomorrow. But this does not confront us with the cutting edge of the event of God's vindication of the most wretched of men, the ghetto-dwellers, the powerless, the poor.

Common to new natural theology is the neglect of the concrete reality of the power that liberates oppressed man to greater humanity. All the arguments noted are chiefly analyses of man's present experience of his self. It is, of course, also possible to move from present to future experience of the self, and yet not to change the basic orientation to self-analysis. Harvey Cox has tried to speak of God in futuristic terms. He points to the fact that man has responsibility for shaping the future. Especially in our day, when it has come within the reach of man to destroy civilization, his responsibility for shaping his future has become extremely pressing. Cox regards man as "that point where the cosmos begins to think and steer itself." [9] This has definite implications as regards the concept of God: "Man, seen as the steersman of the cosmos, is the only starting point we have for a viable doctrine of God." Needless to say, here God also does not in any sense appear related to a present misery from which man needs to be liberated before he can become the steersman of anything. Cox simply shifts gears from present self-orientation to future self-orientation: "If we can affirm anything which both defines and transcends history it will be the *future* as it lives in man's imagination." And so a new view of God arises on the horizon of the future: "If theology can leave behind the God who *is* and begin its work with the God who *will be*, or, in biblical parlance, 'He who cometh,' an exciting new epoch in theology could begin." But is anything gained in reshuffling the chrono-

logical scale? Man's future self is as empty as his present self
if it is not related to the quest of the oppressed to liberate
themselves.

Harvey Cox inadvertently shows that he cannot solve the
problem completely by abstract philosophical analysis of the
future. In order to give content to the future he, too, has to
introduce biblical categories: "Unrequited hope produces cor-
rosive cynicism unless the future is experienced as present now
in a significant way. We need not just the idea of future hope
but also something very much like the Johannine idea of
'eternity,' the present presence of the future, if such cynicism
is to be avoided." But also this is ultimately oriented in the
needs of the private self. A radical orientation to the real agony
of the wretched of the earth is not forthcoming.

Christianity usually knew of definite limitations in its
language about God. It realized it was speaking of God in
view of a particular historical event, the appearance of Jesus
of Nazareth. And here God was certainly not directly available. The event pointed to a radically unique experience of
God. Jesus of Nazareth identified with the wretched of the
earth and compelled others to do the same. Instead of speaking immediately of God in man's self we first need to be confronted with this radical change in the history of man.

LIBERATION THEOLOGY VERSUS
LIBERAL THEOLOGY

Today we are compelled to choose between the bourgeois
self and the longing of the wretched of the earth to be free.
In first turning to the modern self the theologian does not
even ask the question why there are countless multitudes who
do not have the time and the freedom to reflect on their
precious, private white selves. The usual starting point of lib-

eral theology is a truncated view of human existence. The liberal focuses first of all on his private self. But are we even free enough to reflect adequately on our self? "You have not as yet considered the weight of your sin!" *Nondum considerasti, quanti ponderis sit peccatum!* (Anselm) As long as the modern middle-class self, the self of secular man, contributes directly and indirectly to the misery of untold millions throughout this country and the world, it may not be worthy of much concern. Is not the secular self part of the ideological glamorization of capitalist society? Who else but the leisure class can today afford the luxury of focusing on the private self?

Suggested in the analysis of the self as starting point of theology is an adjustment to things as they are. They may happen to be *in process* in the self. Even so, what is expected of us is that we adjust to this process.

I am not implying that the raising of a different type of question will result in a widely accepted demonstration of the reality of God. But the reality of God as introduced into the world by Christianity probably cannot be appreciated at all if it is immediately related to the quest of the modern subject for self-certainty. This modern quest begins with the stance of Descartes: "Today, then, having freed my mind of all care and assured myself of untroubled leisure in peaceful solitude, I shall apply myself earnestly and freely to the general overthrow of all my former opinions." [10] Descartes' intention is understandable within the cultural and philosophical milieu of his day. The question is only whether we are not still aspiring theologically to "untroubled leisure in peaceful solitude" for the analysis of our precious little self. How could we ever think that Christianity and Descartes' primary intention had something in common? "Noting that this truth: *I think, therefore I am,* was so firm and assured that all of the most extravagant suppositions of the skeptics were incapable of shaking it, I judged that I could accept it without misgivings as the first principle of philosophy which I had been seeking." [11]

In the modern age, in America as well as in Europe, Descartes became more and more determinative of the basic theological approach. Schleiermacher's entire methodology, for example, is an adjustment to his stance: self-certainty comes first, and God-certainty is based on self-certainty. The problem of modern atheism, within the bounds of Protestantism at least, emerged exactly at this point: the more self-certainty could be had, the less God-certainty was necessary. And of course one had to have leisure and privacy to find self-certainty. So the loss of God had much to do with the gain of leisure and wealth. All the anthropological proofs for the existence of God had this difficulty built right into them from the beginning. God-certainty based on self-certainty was thus a very tenuous enterprise, subject to the whim of the thinker. To try to study the vicissitudes of this whole development as it catapulted into the death-of-God syndrome in Europe and the United States and to argue its pros and cons becomes a waste of time as soon as we see through the flaw of its first principle. Why should theology be based on the flimsy grounds of bourgeois self-analysis?

Karl Barth raised this question in his own way, but seeing the issue as an expression of the self-contradiction of the Christian faith in German culture-Protestantism and its political consequences in the Hitler Reich, he gave an answer more pertinent to the European situation. Today we must view the matter in our American context in terms of the quest for radical freedom: how is the self-contradiction of the Christian faith in our culture an expression of a radical denial of humanity? In what way is man's manhood contradicted? The basic objection to the Cartesian presupposition of God-certainty remains the same. We must remember that the argument for God in Descartes grows out of the analysis of the self: "Reflecting on the fact that I doubted, and that my being was therefore not entirely perfect, for I saw clearly that it was a greater perfection to know than to doubt, I decided to try to determine how I had learned to think of something more perfect than myself, and it became obvious to me that I must have learned it from some nature which was in fact more perfect." [12] New natural theology, of whatever provenance, makes the mind move toward the divine on the same grounds —as basic premise. The self here operative is the mind *freed of all care and assured of untroubled leisure in peaceful solitude* (Descartes).

The wretched of the earth turn our attention toward another factor. They are no *proof* of God. But they press us to ponder the character of the Christian view of the self which never relates primarily to untroubled leisure in peaceful solitude, but to the identification of a man with the *marginales*, the marginal figures of life. What theology at present needs to learn on the primal level is to acknowledge this unique dimension of the originating event of Christianity and to tie it to the question of radical freedom the *marginales* are raising today.

There is of course nothing intrinsically wrong with the self-in-leisure. What I wish to point out is that, theologically viewed, the self-in-leisure can as easily slip into answering the question of God with the atheist catchwords as with the orthodox catchwords. It is not at all a matter of *not* thinking, or of right (orthodox) thinking, but of thinking about what is worthwhile.

Does the self encounter God in encountering process (Cobb-Ogden), presence (Dewart), or future (Cox), *or* in a man's identifying with the wretched of the earth? The latter is not something we can decide at leisure. It imposes itself upon us, and only in being grasped by it do we know it as truth.

Obviously the self is involved in all that theology is about. The question is, *what kind* of self we focus on, and whether the self-certainty of a particular kind of self, the Cartesian self, is capable of carrying the whole weight of theology, as it were, on its shoulders. If I turn from the private self to the oppressed as part of the self, I am subjecting myself to a more primary hermeneutical or interpretive presupposition operative in my theological thought, more primary because it has placed itself there *before* I begin to reflect on it in terms of my bourgeois self. *The oppressed as part of the self*, this is a compelling factor because of the power of the originating event of Christianity over us. And this happens within a corporate self—the community of the church. Here I learn that there are injustices I cannot forget. That the self is in fact isolable and that it makes for some interesting leisure thinking—the Cartesian self proves this without a doubt.

As soon as one rejects the Cartesian self as starting point of theology and turns to the originating event of Christianity within the context of Christian community, the next interpretive step is a fuller appropriation of the import of this event for a new corporate life.

That in a pluralistic society there are countless ways of being pluralistic in the church and thus also as regards the starting point of theology, should be clear. The issue today is whether in a secularized church we are still talking about Christian faith at all when we do theology. Naturally one can imagine countless ways of continuing to linger with the self as private self. The problem is whether this is really the task of theology in the light of what Christianity stands for in its crucial originating event.

So I am trying to say two things. (1) We have to learn to "think black" theologically. To "think white" is to turn in upon the Cartesian self, to engage in "navel-gazing." The black self over against the white self is the compassionate self (*"compatior, ergo sum"*). It is the corporate self in which the "I" shares. I believe this is a more adequate corrective (from the Christian perspective) of the *cogito, ergo sum* than the "I rebel, therefore we exist" (Camus). To "think black" means to be able to think from the perspective of the underdog. We could also suggest "thinking Indian"—the underdog has many colors in this country and the world over. (2) To think from the perspective of the oppressed, however, is not as yet to think theologically. "Thinking black" ("thinking Indian") has to be radically tied to the originating event of the Christian faith in order to be theological. In fact, ultimately we can "think black" only if we are bound to the originating event. This does not mean leaving reason out of the picture. While the theologian cannot be the man "who is led by reason alone" (*qui sola ratione ducitur*), he is a man who is *also* led by reason, a "black reason" that has been tied to the Incarnation. But reason as an agent here is not primary. It does not control the theological endeavor.

To speak of this theology as liberation theology is to imply that the identification of Jesus Christ with the wretched of the earth not merely brought freedom of the individual, but also gave him public space for freedom to become operative. Naturally many objections to this position are imaginable and will be raised. For some it will seem merely another dogmatic assertion or a camouflage of orthodox ideas. The revulsion against a put-on is strong in us all. Why should we orient ourselves in a Jew of nearly two thousand years ago? A billboard sign read: "Christ is the answer." Someone wrote underneath: "But what is the question?" It should be quite clear that in the following the theme is: Christ is *the* question. But we cannot always talk in hypothetical language. We need to make certain affirmations as we become certain of certain things. Even the question needs a formulation, a very articulate formulation. It cannot remain just a vague feeling. An articulate faith affirmation is involved in asking a question. At least some confidence is presupposed that it might make sense to ask a question. And one had better be clear about the content or nature of this confidence lest talking in questioning language turns out to be no more than mumbo jumbo, or mere shooting off of the mouth.

Liberation theology, then, in terms of asking questions, begins with the supposition that through the Christ-event liberation has taken place for being free to see reality in terms of a new question. That the nature of asking the question is qualified by the Christ-event is of course true. So whoever wants to stay with self-analysis, with the pain of self-torture, or the threat of impending suicide must stay there. But whoever wants to ask: what has *Christ* got to do with self-torture or suicide? must first ask: what has Christ got to offer *anyway?* It seems that too many who are, for example, asking the question: what has Christ got to do with suicide? are unwittingly injecting the expectation that Christ is *the* answer, or at least a partial answer. Thus many close their minds immediately to the possibility that Christ might have something *new* to say to them, something they have not known before.

Liberation theology as distinct from liberal theology begins not with *any* question, but with Christ as *the* question. It presupposes a community that has experienced the liberating effect of the question. Liberation theology is a function of the liberation church. An event has taken place in the history of mankind that has not been forgotten. A unique configuration of history is remembered in a community that asks *the* question over and over again.

THE FOURTH GOSPEL AS CATALYST
OF LIBERATION THEOLOGY

It is useless to try to introduce one or the other biblical term as a stopgap, as it were, when our lofty theological reasoning runs into snags. We must get our field of vision focused on the basic originating history of the Christian faith. There is little promise, for example, in reasoning about the "God of hope" unless we recall immediately "Christ Jesus our hope" (I Tim. 1:1). Nothing is gained today by speaking of the God of the future unless we experience how Jesus Christ liberates man from the misery of the present. It is *his life* that we must understand in order to discover our theological task for the present. Our choice of the Fourth Gospel as basis of our reflection is mainly due to the fact that it is the most reasoned out of all the Gospels, carefully articulating a theology of Jesus' identification with men who had no identity in the eyes of the established church and society of his day.

The primitive Christian writings do not expect us to understand their thought forms on their grounds alone. They invite us to find new forms for our time. The ancient words press us on to find our own words and to discover the Word that liberates us today. In terms of Bengel's exegetical rule, *apply yourself completely to the text, apply the subject completely to yourself,* the "to yourself" becomes more and more pressing today. The past presses us toward the present. We are compelled to think our own thoughts.

In working with the text of the Fourth Gospel I gradually learned that I was searching for a focus of present-day the-

ology. It did not burst upon me suddenly. It grew out of the
taxing process of reading and rereading, translating and re-
translating, interpreting and reinterpreting passage after passage.

The focus that gradually showed itself is God's liberation
of man. God liberates in a twofold way: in serving and in waiting. He serves in giving life and renewing life. And he waits
on us to respond to him by realizing freedom in personal relationships and public structures.

God's waiting creates liberation. Man is freed from bondage to his oppressed self not by the mighty sound of a trumpet
or revolutionary rhetoric, but by the lowly ministry of a man
called Jesus. His life is accessible to us only in the words of
the Gospels. His presence for us is a presence in words, a
Wordpresence. Beyond these words there is nothing we can
ascertain about him. And whatever is said about God in Christian terms is mediated through words about Jesus of Nazareth.
In one respect the Fourth Gospel is merely a piece of literature. In another respect, however, it is God's Word, as it liberates us to a new life. It has the power of creativity that is
"other" than human creativity.

God's Wordpresence in the words about Jesus proves to
be a claim upon us to find its reality in our own experience.
Again and again we must search for its truth in our own lives.
The issue is not that we must immediately find an adequate
philosophy which would help us to interpret a reality called
"God." We must discover this reality where it first was found:
in a human being battling against human misery. Biblical
stories are not props for pious schemes already thought out
beforehand. God's Word is a power that pries open reality
and questions the philosophies that seek to interpret it. Reality
is asked a new question by God's Word. In fact, it is waiting
to be questioned in the light of the liberation of oppressed

men. Interpretation of reality is merely a corollary of the change in reality that God's liberation effects.

My *readings* in the Fourth Gospel do not present the central thought in a comprehensive analysis of theological concepts. They try to break down the text into separate units of thought. Every unit demands an exposition of a major theological point. Reflection on the various units led me to an articulation of their central theological thrust.

The readings do not treat all facets of the theological spectrum with equal emphasis. All I wanted to find out was how these facets contribute to a grasp of the reality of God. The reader will therefore find at a considerable number of points not as much interpretation of a particular facet of theological thought as he might desire. I hope he can keep the main purpose of the readings in mind throughout.

Occasionally a verse or several verses are omitted in my comments. The omission was deliberate. I sought to concentrate on those "units" of thought that in my view bring out the theological significance for today of a particular passage. This should also explain the brevity of my remarks in places. I wished to draw out the theological gist of a passage relative to our contemporary situation, nothing more.

It should therefore be understood that the present volume is not intended as another commentary on the Fourth Gospel. It contains—besides the introduction and conclusion—readings that reflect the gradually emerging grasp of God as liberator. There are excellent commentaries on the Fourth Gospel today—Barrett, Brown, Bultmann, Dodd, Hoskyns, to mention only a few. It would be naive to think that I could improve on them. What I set out to do was to discover the witness of one New Testament writing to the reality of God in human life.

The language of the Fourth Gospel seems liturgical, as

though it were meant to be read aloud in a great cathedral, which accounts for its repetitiousness and, in turn, reflects itself in my readings. This style is not altogether undesirable. It should be possible to ponder a chapter or several chapters and to get at the basic theological intention of the Fourth Gospel without reading all the other chapters. I should point out that I am not introducing my own translation in order to improve on existing translations, but only to form a unity between text and contemporary understanding.

My division of the Gospel into five parts may seem arbitrary. Many emphases and concerns overlap. For example, in the part on *The Liberator* there are also significant reflections on man, and in the part on *Man* there are important considerations on Jesus as liberator. The titles of the five parts merely highlight major emphases in the respective units of thought. Although the Fourth Gospel is not a systematic theology, its overall thought sequence reveals a definite pattern. I tried to reflect this in working out the five parts.

Critical issues, such as the question of the historical sequence of events recorded in the Fourth Gospel, or the problem of which words of Jesus might be original concerned me greatly in the historico-critical research with the text. But it seemed unnecessary to introduce such reflections in a book that tries to grasp the major theological point of the Fourth Gospel: God's liberation of man.

According to John 20:31 the purpose of the Fourth Gospel is to show "that Jesus is the Christ, the Son of God." The problem runs through the entire Gospel: what is the unique relationship of the history of this man to a reality called God? The problem is already present in Chapters 1–4. But it becomes inescapable in Chapter 5 when Jesus is accused of blasphemy: "Now the Jews tried to kill him because he was not only breaking the Sabbath, but called God his own Father, making himself equal to God." This is at the heart of the witness to the reality of God as the Fourth Gospel saw it for its day. From Chapter 5 on it is the explicit issue until the end of the Gospel: God becomes concrete in the public dimensions and structures of life and makes freedom real.

Before turning to the readings I must emphasize that the Fourth Gospel is deeply rooted in the Old Covenant community. It is *not* written *against* Israel. The author seems to be a Jew who wants to discover in what sense Jesus in his identification with the wretched of the earth is the Christ of Israel, the Son of God. His anger is directed toward the ecclesiastical establishment of Judaism that rejected Jesus, not against Israel, the people of the Covenant. Today his words judge the *Christian* religious establishment. They attack the organization church, which in its yen for success again denies the reality of God.

So the Fourth Gospel is a nonecclesiastical interpretation of the Christian faith, a "nonchurch" interpretation, but "nonchurch" for the sake of the liberation of the church. It offers a relevant response to the problem of a political theology as it is shaping up in present-day theological discussion—which I shall discuss in Part VI.

Contrary to the myth that the Fourth Gospel is mystical and withdrawn, it is a theology of protest, of *protestari*, of affirming truth as counterattack upon the forces of oppression that have established themselves in church and society, robbing man of personhood and dignity. It invites men to join in God's work of liberation in forming the countercommunity of discipleship that as liberation church mirrors the corporate reality of God.

What is thus required is to struggle with the words of the

Gospel and to discover whether or not they are able to release in us a new self-understanding and world view. The test of their truth lies in the liberation they bring.

What follows is an attempt to develop an outline of Christian theology and to identify priorities in its present task. Just what are the pressing issues? How can we tackle them? Why is it that probably one first has to go to prison today in order to appreciate *the Word as liberation* (Daniel Berrigan)? I hope the reader will remember that the Fourth Gospel text merely stakes out the area in which I am attempting to identify present theological priorities. It occasionally turns out not exegesis of the text, but even antithesis to the text. And yet it is reflection on the text. The strange silence of the Bible in the church (James Smart) must be broken. American theology, by hook or by crook, must be compelled again to read the Bible. This has nothing to do with bibliolatry. The point is that liberation history has been at work for a long time. The Bible is its Wordpresence inviting us to share in it and to increase it in history as a whole.

READINGS IN
THE FOURTH GOSPEL

CHRISTIAN THEOLOGY IN A NEW FORM

PART I

GOD

HUMAN DESTINY   1:1–13

THE REALITY OF GOD   1:1–2

¹ _Before the world was, the Word was. The Word shared in God and the Word was God._ ² _He, then, was with God at the beginning._

How does one do theology today? By talking from faith to faith? From faith to doubt? From doubt to doubt?

Strange questions? Not so strange, considering the plight theology is in—across the board, whether we are Protestants, Roman Catholics, Orthodox, or just plain human beings trying to become Christians. The nagging doubt that all this is just "not so" I have known for a long time. New philosophies tempt us. Psychotherapy beckons. Sociology is waiting around the corner. And there is LSD. Should we not venture forth on the newly discovered ocean of self-experience?

I have no particular message from faith to faith. And I noticed that talking from doubt to doubt involves much pre-

tense. Talking from faith to doubt is not my angle. If someone wants to pamper his precious little self in a Cartesian
closet, I feel I should leave well enough alone.

However, I have a suspicion that people today are not
listening carefully to anything, not to each other, not to anyone. Everyone is doing his own thing. And I have an equally
strong suspicion that I am not listening carefully to how it all
came to be—whatever we call the Christian thing. But what's
so good about doing your own thing? What if the purpose of
life were doing God's thing?

So my attempt to do theology, without any pretense, I
hope, is initially nothing more than *an exercise in the disci-
pline of new listening.* Just how did such a world-shaking thing
as Christianity come to be? The Fourth Gospel tells us, it all
began in the beginning—before the world was. It also immediately introduces the three letters G-o-d. I notice I'm being
drawn into speculation. But I also discover, as I read on, it is
not very much speculation, not even a whole chapter. Perhaps
this means that speculation can go just so far, that it has little
prospect of carrying the weight of the whole story. *Perhaps,*
I say to myself, as I try to put the pieces of the Prologue of
the Fourth Gospel (1:1–18) together.

We also read something about the Word—besides what
we read about God. But the reference appears quite abstract.
We cannot immediately picture or, for that matter, grasp
what this Word might mean. So to get on we must try to
understand the composition of the Gospel. The author had
been gripped by the man whose story he wants to write. Only
then does he sit down and write it. In a certain sense, the
Prologue finally enters as an epilogue. The author wants to
tie his story to the most primordial, the ground of all stories,
the Word. It may even have been a non-Christian hymn
about the Logos that the author "baptized" to make his Chris-

tian point. So we cannot understand verse 1 of the Gospel apart from verses 14 and the following. The author wants to say that the beginning of all things is tied to the beginning of the Christian thing—the Word become flesh. The abstract and the concrete here are one. History is here the focus of understanding. If one wants to find out something about the beginning of all things one has to turn to a particular history. "Keep faith with the beginning, whose genesis is still to come" (Ernst Bloch). In view of the Prologue we can say: Keep faith with the beginning, whose true genesis comes in Christ.

Greek and Hebrew thought had developed elaborate views of the Logos. For the translation, the English does not have a more adequate term than "Word," which, however, cannot fully convey the specific shades of meaning involved in the Greek term. Whether the reader thought of the Logos as divine wisdom (an important Hebrew connotation), the divine order of the world (a significant Greek understanding), or as the redemptive mediator between the divine and the human (the Gnostic view), he now had to reconsider his view in the light of the "Word made flesh" and to encounter the beginning in the present. A man called Jesus acted in a unique way. Now life had found a new direction of destiny—different from the one known thus far. And men were directed away from speculation about the beginning to making the present more just and human.

Through words men confront each other. The Word is the expression of radical confrontation. Jesus' life will show what the content of this confrontation is. In him we behold what the first words of the Gospel want to say: "The Word shared in God and the Word was God" (v. 1). The loftiest idea man found of the beginning now will receive a concrete content. And the loftiest idea man can form in any respect, the idea of God, will also be concretely filled.

God is not a private self, an abstract "I think, therefore
I am" (*cogito, ergo sum*). Whatever man's concept of God,
whatever his concept of human destiny, the Word made flesh
focuses and transforms it. Whatever the beginning of things,
whether energy or matter, whether six thousand or ten billion
years ago, human life never had any other point than what
Jesus' life embodied: "He, then, was with God at the beginning" (v. 2).

Ultimate reality is no absolute emptiness or singleness,
but corporateness. An encounter takes place: life together.

CREATION   1:3–4

³ *All things were made through him; nothing that is was
made without him.* ⁴ *In him was life, and life was the light of men.*

Hebrew thought had viewed the origin of all things in
terms of creation out of nothing. Now a new factor is being
introduced. Through the Word, creation is tied to the Word
become flesh. To get a concrete grasp of what creation means
we must look at a historical event. The Fourth Gospel does
not speculate in detail on how things came to be. It offers no
cosmology or theory of biological evolution. All it does is to
preface Jesus' life with the rationale of creative activity as
manifested in his life (v. 3).

Life, the transformation of matter into organism, is a
marvel. It is so marvelous that "reverence for life" can become
a separate religion. But it does not generate its own destiny.
It needs to be liberated for its destiny by the Word which
draws it on.

Human life, however, moves toward its destiny long before men try to comprehend it in philosophical systems of
destiny. Man *can* discover purpose in the processes of intel-
ligence and conscience, mind and will. In the processes of

human history, in determination and self-determination, human destiny is being unconcealed (v. 4). While we are afforded an opportunity to become free for our destiny as the Word draws us on, we do not grasp the full dimensions of our destiny as a matter of course. We understand them only in the one life that grasped freedom in the openness of all things to their destiny.

GOD'S UNCONCEALMENT   1:5

⁵ *The light shines in the darkness, and the darkness never put it out.*

If we compare our life with the Word become flesh it becomes obvious that we do not acknowledge the direction of life toward freedom in unconcealment. Mankind as a whole seems not to notice the openness of life to the direction of its destiny. Instead it creates a pseudo-life. We develop a make-believe world and become phonies. We willingly blind ourselves and do not see unconcealment. This is darkness.

But we cannot defy unconcealment, the light. Darkness can never put it out. We must live by it, in all expressions of life. Although a blind man cannot see the sun, he must live by its warmth. Similarly, man must choose the direction of his destiny as shaped by the Word, whether he likes it or not, admits it or not. He must evolve some expression of free personal and corporate existence. Just as little as man has been able to undo the shining of the sun will he be able to undo the unconcealment of the direction of destiny in his life: "The light shines in the darkness" (v. 5). Jesus' life will bear witness to the shining of the light, the openness of all things.

What has been outlined thus far in the Fourth Gospel is a thumbnail sketch of the "metaphysics" of history and human existence. As we said before, the Prologue seems basi-

cally an epilogue. As is so often the case with a preface, it
may have been written last. One does not get the impression
that these thoughts function like rational premises that un-
derlie the whole endeavor. They seem rather like a prelude
that quickly leads to the theme. What an opportunity for an
author to delve into the complexities of the metaphysical
maze! But if one places the Prologue next to some passages of
speculative philosophy one cannot but admire the economy
of language. For example, the German philosopher Schelling
reflected on the same issue with similar categories. But what
a difference in the use of language! "For the process of creation consists only in an inner transmutation, or revelation in
light what was originally the principle of darkness since understanding, or the light which occurs in nature, is actually
only searching in the depths for that light which is akin to
it and is turned inward. The principle of darkness, insofar
as it was drawn from the depths and is dark, is the self-will
of creatures, but self-will, insofar as it has not yet risen to
complete unity with light." (*Of Human Freedom*) In the
Fourth Gospel there is no reflection on the transmutation of
darkness, or the like. The difference between the philosopher
and the "gospeler" is obvious.

The Prologue cannot be understood apart from the history of the man called Jesus. We are not dealing with some
dark impenetrable depths when we think of God—we are dealing with the shape of a human life. While God may be a
predominantly "metaphysical" problem for some, the Fourth
Gospel seems to say that he can no longer be such a problem
since the Word became flesh.

The Fourth Gospel is not immediately interested in fig-
uring out where the darkness came from. It turns around the
theodicy question, if there be God, whence evil? (*si Deus,
unde malum?*), so that it wonders, if there be darkness, what

can God do about it? The whole thrust of the Fourth Gospel
is not an explanation of the old world, but its liberation for
the new world.

Compare any passage concerned with this issue in Descartes' *Meditations on First Philosophy* or in Schelling's *Of
Human Freedom* with the Prologue, and the Fourth Gospel
concern will stand out in bold relief. The Prologue almost
seems to force the metaphysical into history. In the Introduction I spoke of "thinking black"—as access to the corporate self. In the Fourth Gospel "thinking black" begins with
the premise of the concern for the corporate self: the transcendent is tied to the historical, and order and structure—
in fact, all the universals—are shaped in an encounter with
history, crucially in the encounter with the history of the man
called Jesus.

God is unconcealed. Openness is his métier. Just so men
get straight with the history in which this unconcealment *is*
acknowledged. The worry about the metaphysical keeps men
from coming to grips with the physical, the suffering, the injustice, the unceasing oppression. We dream up a beautiful
metaphysical world and all the while, in the physical world,
we participate in creating suffering, injustice, and oppression.

All this does not mean that the Fourth Gospel is promoting belief in the absurd (*credo quia absurdum*). To the
contrary, "the light shines in the darkness" (v. 5) for the sake
of informing man with sense. The light in the darkness, in
fact, is constantly trying to create a *common sense of truth*
(*sensus communis*, according to Friedrich Christoph Oetinger). And yet the darkness does not know what to do with
the common sense of truth. Man misdirects his insight into
the shining of the light. Instead of glorifying his Maker, he
uses the light of his mind to destroy himself and the earth,
for example, by atomic death or pollution. Of course, there

are countermovements, countercultures. But the real content of the common sense of truth is never grasped. For this reason, the light itself becomes flesh.

GOD'S UNCONCEALMENT AND ISRAEL   1:6–8

⁶ *There was a man named John, commissioned by God.* ⁷ *He came as witness to testify to the light that all might trust through him.* ⁸ *He was a witness of the light, not the light itself.*

So the Fourth Gospel urgently presses on into history. It does not linger very long with abstract concepts. After five verses John the Baptist, forerunner of Jesus, appears. He stands for all those who had realized that it is basic for human life to respond to the light. The light had already made its impact on history before John the Baptist tried to speak of God's unconcealment. Before the shining of the light man must always decide what it means to be a man. Compared with this radical referend, man's other referends for decision-making are illusory.

Although men usually camouflage reality, there had been some in Israel who had caught glimpses of the destiny of life, glimpses that did not originate in their own ingenuity. The unconcealed direction of human destiny had been foreshadowed in Israel's history. In relationship to human destiny Israel's history proved unique.

As compared with the incarnate Word, even the one who is closest to the light (*cf.* Mt. 11:11) appears as one who is only an observer of the light, not the light itself. Nonetheless, because of Israel's partial acknowledgment of the light, the light in history has become identifiable. Events had occurred in Israel that pointed to the light and proved especially capable of discerning the light. Israel's history, as represented by the Baptist, is an invitation to faith in the liberative possibilities of human existence (v. 7). Israel is the example par excellence of the common sense of truth.

The incarnate Word makes it plain, however, that religion, cult, or prophecy is not the light itself. Even Israel is not the light. Human insight into the direction of man's destiny proves fragmentary (v. 8). The common sense of truth fails to liberate man.

GOD'S UNCONCEALMENT DENIED 1:9–11

⁹ The true light was already there—the light that illumines every man born into the world. ¹⁰ He was in the world, but the world, although made by him, did not recognize him. ¹¹ He visited his own, but his own would not receive him.

The author of the Fourth Gospel had encountered the direction of human destiny. While he did not as yet directly name the man called Jesus, we can only assume that according to verses 14 and those following he is the occasion for the talk about the light. He embodied the true life of man, "the light that illumines every man born into the world" (v. 9). What meets man in the incarnate Word is nothing alien to him: his true selfhood, the corporate self unconcealed as the direction of man's destiny.

Since Jesus appeared on the human scene, it has become obvious that God's unconcealment is denied by men. In him, men were confronted with the embodiment of their true selfhood in view of their destiny. While they always had been confronted with it in the process of history, they did not grasp and acknowledge it. In the man called Jesus they are now inescapably confronted with it.

And why are not more men overpowered by this truth? Much of the history of the Christian story tells of *truth forever on a scaffold*. That is something we have difficulty get-

ting into our liberal heads, which like to see truth widely ap-
plauded. The embodiment of true selfhood is not everyone's
thing. The acknowledgment of this truth is difficult and painful for a man who is a sinner—who likes to orient himself
completely in himself.

There are those who by historical circumstance are especially close to God's unconcealment. Israel had the witness of
the law and the prophets, and of John the Baptist. But that
did not induce it as a whole to acknowledge God's unconcealment in Jesus. The rejection of Jesus by many of his people, by his own, mirrors the principal reaction of every man
to God's unconcealment (v. 11).

God's Unconcealment Acknowledged   1:12-13

12 To all who did receive him he gave power to become children of God. They are those who trust in his selfhood, 13 who
were born to a new life of God and not through the natural course
of flesh and blood dependent on man's desire and planning.

Some do acknowledge God. Their unusual stance is a
new beginning in the history of mankind. They are directly
related to God, like children to parents (v. 12). They acknowledge unconcealment. That is, they are directly involved in
hammering out their destiny. All who acknowledge the incarnate Word find a new direction of life. True acknowledgment of God is possible only through trust in the one who
first acknowledged God's unconcealment fully. Responding to
the one who first lived in openness to truth, men can discern
the direction of their destiny.

The new life in response to the embodiment of the direction of man's destiny depends on its self-giving and not on
man's planning or programming of a meaningful life (v. 13).
Direction toward his true destiny is present in every man's

life, drawing him onward to a fuller life. But man must be opened for it—through the grace of the incarnate Word itself.

GOD'S MANHOOD   1:14–18

¹⁴ *The Word became flesh and lived among us. We saw his glory, a glory true to the Father's unique Son, full of grace and truth.* ¹⁵ *John testifies of him and proclaims: "This is he of whom I said, 'After me comes who ranks before me because he was first.'"* ¹⁶ *We all shared his corporate selfhood receiving grace upon grace.* ¹⁷ *Moses gave the law, Jesus Christ grace and truth.* ¹⁸ *No man has ever seen God. God's unique Son, the Father's most intimate, has made him concrete.*

The reason for the new theology, the new vision of God, creation, and man now becomes fully manifest. A man is true when he embodies his words. A man's word is his bond. In Jesus we meet a man in whom the deeds correspond to the words. In fact, his words are deeds, and his deeds are words. His life is therefore characterized as a doing of signs (12:37). His deeds are visible words. For faith, his life is the *visible Word*. He is the *direction* of human destiny incarnate. The Word in which God is unconcealed as light in human life means that God is not our problem. We are our problem. As long as we tend to make God our "problem"—as in the debate about God's death in the sixties—we tend to run away from ourselves and turn into oppressors and exploiters. God, if he be God, can take care of himself. His becoming concrete in the visible Word is not so much for straightening out our problem with God as for sensitizing us to who we are.

Our text affirms: "The Word became flesh" (v. 14). Flesh is the sphere of the verily human. In it the Word is embodied in order that man be redirected in his relationship to what is real. The Fourth Gospel focuses on the totality of the history of the Word made flesh, not merely on his message or his understanding of existence. It seeks to show how one man in his entire life reflects the openness of reality to truth.

One has to see this as best one can against the secular background within which the Fourth Gospel was written. Augustine, in his *Confessions*, remarks that he had found some of the ideas of the Prologue in certain writings of the Platonists: "But that *the Word* was made flesh, *and dwelt among us*, I read not there." Greek thought balked at the idea that the universal Word, the Logos, could be united with a particular man. Athanasius, writing *On the Incarnation of the Word*, already pinpointed the issue as he wondered in regard to his secular Greek opponents: "What is there on our side that is absurd, or worthy of derision? Is it merely our saying that the Word has been made manifest in the body?" He then went on to say that the entrance of the Word into a human body is not unreasonable. He precisely formulates what is at stake: the union of Word and flesh seemed impossible for the Greek. "The Word became flesh"—this is shorthand for: the order of natural necessity has been broken, freedom has entered the human scene. No longer is man subject to the elemental world spirits (Gal. 4:3). Of course, it is *faith* saying this, confessing that the Word became flesh. But what more can faith say?

So the primal point is not at all that in this man God has become historically or psychologically observable. The Fourth Gospel is not interested in an objective "window display" of God. Rather it invites trust in freedom. For sinful man, the breaking of the ironclad laws of metaphysical necessity never become clearly visible. Faith in the incarnate Word, however, believes it grasps what freedom is about.

Those who trusted the man called Jesus, the Prologue says,

saw in him an embodiment of *grace* and *truth*. They knew him as a radically new event that drew them into a new primal thinking. Once more, they had to start from the beginning and create the world of their mind anew. *Grace* was now the gift of man's independence from necessity, the laws of nature, the status quo, and death. It was the gift of a life stronger than death: the gift of divine freedom. No longer need we view the ultimate nature of things in terms of absolute necessity to which we must conform. Divine freedom makes possible human freedom. The unexpected can occur.

Christian faith offers us the insight that divine freedom affords us the possibility of choosing a new direction of life. Freedom, the way man usually understands it, is now superseded. It is now understood as the possibility to act on grounds of transcendent freedom, hoping for the prevailingness of man in the universe and his ultimate control of necessity. "Freedom means to be self-contained, or at home with oneself" (Hegel). Christian faith, however, does not root freedom in self-containment of the private self, but in the openness of creation in the freedom of God. "The idea which a man has of God corresponds with that which he has of himself, of his freedom" (Hegel). Hegel's view has to be turned around for the Christian faith to read: the idea a man has of God's freedom determines the grasp of his own freedom.

This has immediate implications for the question of "created" freedom. Is man created free to choose good or evil? In view of our premise, we can say that man is created free to choose the *prevailingness* of life. The fact that he chooses its destruction or perversion is due to the *risk* involved in freedom. But it is not a predetermined, "programmed" possibility. Freedom is first of all that possibility which can make human life prevail.

If grace is the gift of divine freedom, *truth* is now the

unconcealment of this grace in the bare manhood of a man. Let it be clearly understood in what sense we are here speaking of truth. It is not an obvious thing for every Tom, Dick, and Harry to behold in naive directness. We must remember Kierkegaard. Truth, he believed, is "an objective uncertainty held fast in an appropriation-process, of the most passionate inwardness." Truth thus understood implies a measure of uncertainty for the objective beholder. Christian truth is not something quickly to nod one's head at, but to risk one's life for—with the clear understanding that it might all be different. There is no *security* for Christian faith, only the *certainty* involved in risk. "Without risk there is no faith" (Kierkegaard).

Earlier we stressed that the attempt to do theology in reference to the Fourth Gospel was an exercise in new listening. In *content* the issue turns out to be: how can one become a Christian when everybody is a Christian? Confronted with grace and truth in the man Jesus we discover *the radical difficulty of becoming a Christian,* intellectually and existentially. It is not that the Fourth Gospel *wants* to make it difficult. It simply *is* difficult.

"We have reached in Christendom the point of not knowing what Christianity is" (Kierkegaard). That is still our problem. Kierkegaard tried to state what he thought Christianity was: "Not a doctrine, but an existential communication expressing an existential contradiction." This becomes clearer as we move through the Fourth Gospel. *Doing theology* is not about a doctrine, but about doing God's thing: an existential communication expressing an existential contradiction. A radical reorientation in what Christianity is is still the demand of the hour. "What is needed is nothing more and nothing less than a revision of Christianity; what is needed is to wipe out 1800 years as though they had never been"

(Kierkegaard). So I must begin doing theology in the primal matrix of Christian theology. The 1800 years are apt to brainwash us. Therefore theology here is intended as *primal thinking*, a *mode of action*, a form of existing. It gives expression to the existential contradiction a man experiences in *confrontation* with the truth, a contradiction that can only be overcome in faithful action. Let therefore no one assume that everyone will act the Christian way just because we expect him to do so. Not even we ourselves will act the Christian way, unless *grace* grips us and *truth* convicts us. Too many today expect too many to be Christians. No one is a Christian. The best we can hope for is that we *become* Christians.

So faith must begin again from scratch, with Jesus. Primal Christian faith also saw *glory* in him. Today the word usually connotes glamor. Even consumer products can be glorified. Glory in the Fourth Gospel is the reality of freedom. A man has embodied it, a man embodying the Cross on the way to a cross. It demands a complete rethinking of the criteria by which glory, especially religious glory, is usually measured. In American religion glory implies a glamorization of life. The Word become flesh explodes all phony notions of glory. True glory is the freedom of a man who accepts the Cross and yet is not destroyed.

Jesus is fully glorified in his death (*cf.* 7:39; 12:16). In this death the meaning of *God's* glory is consummated (13:31). The nails that go through the hands of the crucified Jesus go, as it were, through the hands of the Father in the back. This is a new experience of God. God is now present in a man as he comes to terms with the vicissitudes of life in new freedom. The religious glamor in which a man seeks to enjoy the transcendent is exposed as spiritual beauty culture. Religion as man's attempt to make God a problem no longer cuts ice. Man must now come to grips with life in battling through his basic questions in *confrontation* with the manhood of the Word.

Man's problem with God is no longer a matter of *correlation*, of getting some synthesis between the divine and the human. What seemed correlation is now *confrontation*. The incarnate Word confronts man, opposes and negates man, even in his craving for "trips" into the spiritual world. For faith, God is unconcealed. No longer is he the hidden God, the *deus absconditus*. Who is still hidden is man, hidden to himself, *homo absconditus*. The incarnate Word confronts man in his playing hide and seek with God and attacks his waste of time. The issue now is how man can become a Christian, not whether God is dead.

The Word appeared in the flesh *after* John the Baptist—to be chronologically accurate. But he was actually before John, even before Adam. Keep faith with the beginning, whose true genesis is in Christ. Faith *reverses* the chronological order. The man called Jesus is the one who embodies the intentionality of life, that which was always intended as the direction of our destiny: the man unafraid of freedom. He is then ahead of John the Baptist and ranks above every man. Whatever future awaits mankind, it is always this man who points out its direction. He is the human selfhood which informs every man (v. 15).

While Jesus does not answer all our questions, he confronts us inescapably with what we can become. He witnesses to greater fulfillment of the world that knows only fragmentation and piecemeal freedom. Because Jesus conceals himself, man blinds himself to the fullness of the corporate selfhood embodied in him (v. 16).

"Moses gave the law, Jesus Christ grace and truth" (v. 17). Fourth Gospel theology involves a transformation of Israel's religion. Israel's law is not abolished. But it is transcended. Something more appears in its stead. Law was only partial insight into human destiny, the real thing was still missing. There were scores of rules. But there was no possibility for man to find his wholeness. Law only partially afforded true life.

This does not mean that Israel's law was worthless. It was part of the most comprehensive expression of the *sensus communis*, of the concept of God-given truth, of the light shining in the darkness. But man did not comprehend the light through it. He was not liberated by his partial insight into the true nature of human selfhood. The law as insight into the structures of order in nature and history tempts sinful man to use it as vindication of the status quo. Grace and truth in Jesus Christ negate the temptation. There is no metaphysical and historical status quo that could not be transcended in the increase of freedom. In Jesus' bare manhood the true purpose of the law became concrete. Becoming obedient to suffering, defeat, and death, Jesus liberates life for resurrection and truth, for newness beyond necessity and oppression.

Trusting Jesus as the incarnate Word does not mean that now "God" has been packaged or that we can control our destiny. Trust in Jesus is not a magic key that opens all doors to the mystery of life. Mystery remains. But we see a direction toward a lifting of the mystery. We are called to liberate men from oppression. And that should suffice as an "answer" to the mystery of life. We too are caught in the same predicament as all men: "No man has ever seen God" (v. 18). But the incarnate Word sets us on the road that leads us to *see* freedom.

For every man the spokes of his life seem to converge in some hub, some center of meaning that holds the spokes together. We sense that we are somehow connected with it. But we regard it as a void—blind as we are. Some try to fill the void with images derived from experience—often making these images their god. But this tells us more about man than about the void. Man has no clear notion of God. He is blind to his unconcealment.

In view of the incarnate Word, however, we need no longer stare into the empty void. "God's unique Son, the Father's most intimate, has made him concrete" (v. 18). In his concrete form he is the true protest against human oppression, against unfreedom, the chains in which we imprison one another. While there are no routes of escape from the human plight, Jesus has joined us in our misery. He does not pontificate about a distant God. Rather he acknowledges unconcealment in making us free. "God's in his heaven, All's right with the world," says Browning. The truth is that the *direction* of man's destiny is open *on earth*, waiting for man to choose, toiling and suffering with him and—liberating him. In Jesus, the "wholly Other" shares in man's deepest shame in order to set him free. True freedom appears only where at the most rugged edges of human experience the potential for the increase of human life is tapped and its negation is resisted.

Incarnation of the "wholly Other" is not God transformed into man. Rather, the man Jesus embodies God in his manhood by acknowledging God's openness, the fact that God does not hide himself. The incarnate Word witnesses to man's future "not by the conversion of the Godhead into flesh, but by taking the manhood into God" (Athanasian Creed). Charles Williams has paraphrased this very well: "It is the actual manhood which is to be carried on, and not the height which is to be brought down." Manhood is to grow into increased freedom. God's height *is* down—always. This is not the problem. Jesus' witness invites man to turn to greater freedom. This is the issue.

We are confronted here not with a metaphysical conun-

drum, but with a physical protest. Incarnation is confrontation. It convicts man of oppression, of the laws in which he
keeps human life concealed, unable to free it for grace and
truth. Incarnation protests idealist schemes that are strait-
jackets for man's growth. What comes across in much theology today is the threat: if you are not the way I am, you
don't even exist (regardless whether the scheme is atheistic,
expecting me to conform to its universalizing pattern; or the-
istic as a natural theology, expecting me to "get with it" in
process; or whether it is liberationist, expecting me to fit myself into the mold of a revolutionary Messiah). What in the
end counts in theology is not ideology, but witness to Jesus
Christ. In him alone there is no straitjacket or ideology into
which we would have to fit. It is because of him that I dare be,
in spite of myself as sinner. The new works-righteousness of
our modern religionists and ideologists is as vicious as that of
the Roman Church in the time of Luther—even worse, since
it is better able to camouflage its attack upon man's integrity
in making ideological works seem the real fruit of faith.

The incarnate Word thus does not answer all our questions. But it galvanizes us for protest against totalitarian
claims, whether ecclesiastical or political. As to our questions,
many of them still remain with us. Faith still experiences the
limits of understanding. Suffering and death are ever near. But
we are now confronted with a new quality of life. Now we
must battle through the great questions in bare manhood,
radically choosing freedom, no longer protected by the apron
strings of religion.

All men live in a perplexing world. There are more questions than answers. While Jesus did not waste his time con-
templating the puzzle of life, he witnessed to a new quality
of life and thus refocused the direction of man's destiny—
waiting on man. His witness puts most questions to shame.

"When, in all honesty, I've recognized that man is a being in whom existence precedes essence, that he is a free being who, in various circumstances, can want only his freedom, I have at the same time recognized that I can want only the freedom of others" (Sartre). Wanting only the freedom of others, this story began in the man called Jesus. And it was thus that God was known.

PART II

THE LIBERATOR

THE NEW WITNESS TO THE CHRIST 1:19–51

THE WITNESS OF HISTORY 1:19–28

[19] *This is John's witness when the Jews sent priests and Levites from Jerusalem to find out who he was. "Who are you?" they asked.* [20] *He confessed and declared, "I am not the Christ."* [21] *They asked, "Who then? Are you Elijah?" "No," he replied. "Are you the Prophet?" He answered, "No."* [22] *So they asked, "Who then are you? We want to have an answer for those who sent us. Who do you claim to be?"* [23] *He answered, "As the prophet Isaiah said, 'I am a voice shouting in the wilderness: Clear the way of the Lord.'"* [24] *Those questioning John had been sent by the Pharisees.* [25] *They continued asking him, "Then why do you baptize if you are not the Christ, nor Elijah, nor the Prophet?"* [26] *John replied, "I baptize with water, but the one is already among you whom you do not know,* [27] *who will succeed me. I am not even good enough to untie his sandal-straps."* [28] *This happened at Bethany beyond Jordan where John was baptizing.*

The Prologue is followed by the account of the history on which it is based. The first chapter moves toward a cli-

45

mactic word in which Jesus declares even heaven to be open
(v. 51): the "metaphysical" need no longer be speculated
about. This does not mean that it is laughed off. The question is how we relate to its unconcealment in Christ. In him
we are no longer confronted with a new possibility for speculative philosophy, but with a contradiction of existence. He
protests how we live.

Why Jesus is the liberator becomes clear as we tell
and retell the stories that make up the Fourth Gospel as a
primal theology. In a preliminary way we can say that Jesus
is liberator because he effects liberation of consciousness.
Our old ways of looking at things are made obsolete. We are
invited to use all our mental, emotional, and physical energies
to deny the oppression in which immoral society keeps many
in chains.

In the discussion of a Pharisee delegation with the Baptist the longing for the fulfillment of Jewish history is summed
up (vv. 20–22). Longing for the fulfillment of history is a human trait. Man would like to see the concretion that answers
his speculations about history. The investigating commission
examining John mentions names which reflect some of Israel's
expectations: Elijah and the Prophet. But the minds of the
investigators trail off into a distant future while the reality
they are yearning for is quite near.

John the Baptist shows the connection between history
and the history of Jesus. Baptism and ablutions in Israel and
in other religions ("I baptize with water . . ."—v. 26) reflect
the ongoing contradiction of man's life in history in confrontation with the light of the Word, which invites man to exist
responsibly.

As indicated before (cf. interpretation of vv. 6–8), the
Baptist represents those who have partial insight into man's
obligation and who know that men getting a glimpse of this

insight try to offer ultimate fulfillment in religion and culture. In the process, however, man creates the wasteland of his soul instead. Denying his responsibility for existing in the present he escapes into dreams—also dreams about the future. The "Johns" cry out in these wastelands and uncover man's failure of nerve to live responsibly. Many modern painters and poets are such voices, crying out in the modern wilderness.

> This is the dead land
> This is cactus land
> Here the stone images
> Are raised, here they receive
> The supplication of a dead man's hand
> Under the twinkle of a fading star.
>
> —*T. S. Eliot*

But these outcries are not the real confrontation with what contradicts man's ease. At best they can only witness that the one who is man's contradiction is "already among you" (v. 26).

Jesus appears in continuity with the reality of unconcealment that contradicts men throughout history. Man's self-deception as to his responsibility is always negated. Wherever the light of unconcealment breaks into history—for example, in a baptism such as John's—men are confronted with the challenge to exist in corporate freedom. Nevertheless, in confrontation with the one who embodies freedom in corporate selfhood the "Johns" seem unworthy even to polish his shoes (v. 27). Their partial grasp of man's freedom is minimal. Their witness, however, is a prolepsis of the Gospel. The man called Jesus did no more than embody that freedom already promised in history and of which men had already caught glimpses in the workings of the light.

The covenant history out of which the Jesus history emerged has often been viewed as "salvation history" (*Heilsgeschichte*). In focusing on the liberation brought in the Jesus history, salvation history now manifests its basic quality as *liberation history*. And in the light of the covenant history all of human history seems meaningful only as liberation history, that is, to the extent that it helps man better to understand the dynamics of history as converging upon the liberation of man.

THE WITNESS TO THE "LAMB OF GOD"   1:29–34

²⁹ *The next day, seeing Jesus approaching him, he said, "Look, the Lamb of God who bears the sin of the world! ³⁰ He is the one of whom I said, 'A man will come after me who ranks before me because he was first.' ³¹ I did not know who he was; but I came baptizing in water that he might become known to Israel." ³² John testified further: "I saw the Spirit coming down from heaven like a dove and settle on him. ³³ I did not know who he was, but he who commissioned me to baptize in water told me, 'He on whom you see the Spirit coming down to stay is the one who baptizes with the Holy Spirit.' ³⁴ I saw it myself, and I testify that he is the Son of God."*

The man called Jesus manifests himself fully in his death. In Israel, the lamb image suggests itself as an adequate interpretation. Important for redemption in Israel was the Paschal Lamb sacrificed at the Passover. The lamb image was one way of saying why Jesus is the Son of God (v. 34).

As Jesus now appears he is introduced by his most salient characteristics in relationship to other men: his selfhood is corporate. He identifies with the wretchedness of all men (v. 29). Even so, sin does not make of all men "wretched of the earth." To be a victim of oppression is one thing, to be possessed by evil, another. Sin makes of all men not the oppressed, but the possessed (*cf.* Chaps. 18 and 19). With Jesus' coming, sin, man's self-negation or denial of freedom, is no longer dealt with in the sacrifice of an animal. It is now in the struggle of a human being who becomes sin's contradiction that sin is done away with.

Not the symbol of a meek lamb happily alive, but a lamb slaughtered is here the analogy. We meet here the suffering servant of Isaiah, accepting his task "like a lamb that is led to the slaughter" (Is. 53:7). Now it is a man who in the darkness of death defeats man's denial of freedom. In its death an animal cannot defeat sin. So Jesus corrects the ecclesiastical dogma of his day. Only in a man's risk of his life is the human condition righted.

Although his baptism prepared the way for the confrontation of unconcealment with man's self-deception, the Baptist himself did not recognize Jesus as the Lamb of God (v. 31). In referring to the coming of the Spirit the Baptist is looking back upon a prior incident not recorded in the Gospel. Apparently the readers of the Fourth Gospel were familiar with the story of Jesus' baptism. Here the Gospel relates merely the coming of the Spirit at the baptism. The gift of the Spirit qualifies Jesus as the one who identifies with the wretchedness of men. Jesus does not arbitrarily claim "corporate selfhood." It is gifted to him by ultimate reality. But he can share it. The expected eschatological outpouring of the Spirit is now tied to him (v. 33). He makes all men one, in offering to all freedom from wretchedness (v. 29).

It is possible that the Baptist knew Jesus personally. But he had not known him as the Lamb of God. Unconcealment itself had to grasp him, so that he could grasp Jesus' inmost being (v. 33). Together with him we are now able to see why this Lamb of God is the Son of God (v. 34). Jesus is the Son of God as the suffering Messiah—the one who identifies with man's wretchedness. The Son of God image says that this man is the confrontation of the ultimately real with all men. He gives expression to what ultimately counts.

THE SHAPE OF THE NEW EVENT   1:35–39

[35] The next day again John was standing with two of his disciples. [36] Seeing Jesus pass by he said, "There is the Lamb of God." [37] When the two disciples heard this, they followed Jesus. [38] Jesus turned and seeing them following he asked, "What are you looking for?" They said, "Rabbi" (which means "teacher"), "where do you stay?" [39] He answered, "Come and see." So they came and saw where he was staying and spent the rest of the day with him. It was about four o'clock in the afternoon.

In this Son of God a new era has begun among mankind —for faith. In order to signalize the change two disciples of the Baptist begin to follow Jesus. Rather than proving disloyal to him, they understand the point of his work. He has prepared the way for Jesus: "There is the Lamb of God" (v. 36). What this amounts to cannot be known in speculative image-making about the Lamb of God, but only in following him, in existential action.

The Gospel has a specific purpose. It invites men to follow the man called Jesus in his public activity. It makes a man face the difficulty of becoming a Christian. It spares no effort to say *how utterly difficult* it is. And yet also how radically liberating! It does not want to tell everything that can be known about Jesus. It zeroes in on the central controversy over his public activity where the difficulty of becoming a Christian is glaring. Many attempts have been made to recapture the exact chronology of Jesus' life, to write his biography. At least since Albert Schweitzer's critique of the Jesus-biography-craze it has been widely understood that it is impossible for faith to make do with such a picture. While the so-called new quest of the historical Jesus acknowledged the impossibility, it felt that one could get at least at Jesus' selfhood on grounds of those words that are in all likelihood authentic. Time and again men will try to find the authentic Jesus. Therefore the new quest of the historical Jesus plays an important role. But the crucial theological question remains: what is the center of everything that has been recorded of the man called Jesus?

The Fourth Gospel is interested in the *shape* of his public activity. Responding to this shape the disciple learns to understand the point of Jesus' life. It is not chronological or psychological detail that counts, although that is not irrelevant. What invites our faith is Jesus' selfhood embodied in the *shape* of his activity. The *Gestalt* of his ministry mediates his selfhood. The disciple is asked to respond to his *mode of activity*.

Nothing is detailed as yet in the first chapter. But a preliminary understanding is given as to what the Fourth Gospel expects us to focus on. Jesus' first word in the Fourth Gospel is: "What are you looking for?" (v. 38). What do you want? The first two followers want to know where he is staying, concerned to discover the shape of his life. All Jesus does is to ask them to come along and to see for themselves. To become a disciple means to see for oneself the shape of Jesus' life. All words and deeds of the Gospel more fully articulate this shape. Kierkegaard pointed out the principle of reduction when he said: "If the contemporary generation had left to posterity nothing more than the words, 'we have had faith that in such-and-such a year God appeared in the humble form of a servant, lived and taught among us, and then died,' it would be more than enough. . . . This brief notice, this historical *nota bene* provides posterity with sufficient occasion (for faith). For all eternity, the most detailed account can do no more for posterity." The one caveat at this point is that Kierkegaard,

contrary to his intention, was still overly influenced by the
tradition of Christianity *as doctrine*. So he saw the hub of the
matter in God existing as man. But the Prologue of the Fourth
Gospel on which also Kierkegaard depended for his faith-rea-
soning conveys something more than doctrine. It involves
world liberation, freedom defeating necessity. Had the earliest
witnesses taught no more than this liberation, it would have
been more than enough. The *shape* of Jesus' public activity is
the concrete source for the *new* experience of liberation. In
this shape we learn to know our real selfhood and the direction of our destiny.

Today the shape of Jesus' public activity stands squarely
opposed to the civil religion in which much of Christianity
is caught. And one of our major theological tasks is to liberate
Christian thought from its subservience to civil religion. The
liberation of consciousness that needs to take place must first
of all begin among churchmen who think they are already free.

THE CHRIST AS JOSEPH'S SON   1:40–46

⁴⁰ *Andrew, Simon Peter's brother, was one of the two who
had heard what John said and then followed Jesus.* ⁴¹ *The first
thing he did was to look for his brother Simon and to tell him,
"We have found the Messiah!" (which means "Christ").* ⁴² *Then
he led him to Jesus. Jesus, looking at him, said, "You are Simon,
son of John. You shall be called Cephas" (which means "rock").*
⁴³ *The next day Jesus decided to go to Galilee. He met Philip and
said, "Follow me."* ⁴⁴ *Philip was from Bethsaida, like Andrew and
Peter.* ⁴⁵ *Philip found Nathanael and told him, "We have found
him of whom Moses wrote in the law, and also the prophets: Jesus
of Nazareth, Joseph's son."* ⁴⁶ *Nathanael replied, "What good can
come from Nazareth?" Philip said, "Come and see for yourself."*

Staying with Jesus did something to the first two disciples. They found in him what they were "looking for" (v. 38).

One of them calls Jesus the Messiah. Jesus was an "imperious ruler" (Albert Schweitzer). He changed the name of Simon to "Rock" (v. 42). He told Philip: "Follow me" (v. 43). This was utter sovereignty. He ruled over the rigid pattern of human relationships. Freedom broke through. They knew no other name for him than Messiah (v. 41), the one who was going to free Israel. The eschatological liberation of Israel was now present in this man.

It was not obvious that Jesus should be identified with the most lofty office an Israelite could imagine. Jesus of Nazareth was Joseph's, the carpenter's, son, a nondescript, and from a hick town: "What good can come from Nazareth?" To which no more compelling answer can be given than: "Come and see for yourself" (v. 46). Jesus himself belongs to the *marginales*, the forgotten, the nobodies. It is exactly where the glory of humanity is least obvious that it appears in its true power. We dare never forget the identity of Jesus with the marginal figures of life. It is here that corporate selfhood breaks forth. And it is *in the ability to identify with the forgotten, the nobodies, that we can check out the truth as to what Jesus was about.*

THE SON OF GOD AS THE SON OF MAN   1:47–51

[47] *Jesus saw Nathanael coming to him and said, "Here is a true Israelite, a sincere man."* [48] *Nathanael asked, "How can you know me?" Jesus explained, "Before Philip called you, I saw you under the fig-tree."* [49] *Nathanael said, "Rabbi, you are the Son of God; you are the King of Israel!"* [50] *Jesus asked, "Do you trust because I told you I saw you under the fig-tree? You shall see greater things.* [51] *Believe me, you shall see heaven open and God's angels going up and coming down on the Son of Man."*

Jesus confronts the man who wants to know who he is with his grasp of what is in man. A man suddenly finds he is

already known in his selfhood (vv. 47 ff.). He cannot but acknowledge the *novum* of the experience by using the loftiest
titles available: "You are the Son of God, the King of Israel"
(v. 49). Jesus Christ—superstar! He shows who he really is by
making a man realize that he is already known. Ultimate
reality already reaches into human life and directs man's destiny. It is nothing glamorous. It is something real—and strong.

Thus the Son of God is the Son of Man. In fact, his
power reaches beyond mankind. He informs all things with
the direction of their destiny, even those realms hidden beyond
man's ken. In him even heaven is open. That which was hidden to man is now unconcealed—for faith. All things are
made to belong together in striving toward a common destiny.
Jesus acknowledges unconcealment. Angels going up and down
on Jesus represent the creaturely realm hidden from the human eye. It is subject to Jesus' acknowledgment of unconcealment. All things invisible are open to the destiny to which
his selfhood points (v. 51).

TRANSCENDENT FREEDOM   2:1–12

¹ After two days there was a wedding at Cana, Galilee. Jesus'
mother was there. ² Jesus had also been invited with his disciples.
³ When the wine gave out, Jesus' mother said to him, "They are
out of wine." ⁴ "So what?" Jesus answered. "Woman, my hour has
not yet come." ⁵ His mother said to the waiters, "Do whatever he
tells you." ⁶ Six large stone water-jars for purification rites were
standing there. Each could hold twenty to thirty gallons. ⁷ Jesus
told them, "Fill the jars with water." They filled them to the brim.
⁸ Then he said, "Draw some out and take it to the headwaiter."
So they did. ⁹ When the headwaiter tasted the water now turned
into wine, not knowing where it came from (the waiters who had
drawn the water, of course, knew) he called the bridegroom and
said, ¹⁰ "Everyone serves the good wine first and the poor stuff

when they have had plenty. You have kept the good wine until now!"

[11] This deed at Cana, Galilee, was the first of his signs. He made his glory public, and his disciples trusted him. [12] After this he went down to Capernaum with his mother, his brothers and his disciples and visited there for a short time.

The story is basically about how we view reality—either as subject to necessity or as free.

The first *sign* of Jesus in the Fourth Gospel (v. 11) sums up what the other signs spell out in greater detail. It is an introduction to the signs, as it were. A sign in the Fourth Gospel is *a deed that epitomizes the shape of Jesus' public activity*.

The story tells of a wedding, the summit experience of man's natural life. Here man and woman join for the most intimate endeavor. At the wedding at Cana a snag developed in the usual course of the event. The party ran out of wine. The man called Jesus makes the festivities go on. He does not shrug off the created order, withdrawing with his disciples to Qumran or some other "retreat center." He goes to a wedding identifying with humanity. When the difficulty with the wine arises he makes public his glory in transforming what human custom decrees. There was the custom of serving the good wine first (v. 10). But now the customary approach to things gets turned around.

Man's usual way of relating to the neighbor is changed. True relating to the neighbor is waiting on him with the good —always. The end of the story summarizes what Jesus did: "He made his glory public" (v. 11). He made ultimate reality manifest as waiting on man with the good and thus embodied the reality of God. Further signs of Jesus underscore the point.

What usually grips the imagination in the Cana story is the changing of water into wine. Rightly so. While the "mechanics" of the change are not detailed, the radical newness of the "miracle" comes through loud and clear. In this first sign the necessity of nature is broken. Jesus views the natural order in a new way. Nature proves pliable to the one who is truly free. He makes nature serve men in order that men have a new chance to choose freedom. *"Natura facit saltus*, nature does make leaps—this much, at least, the old miracle faith has contributed to a no longer magical and even less transcendentally vaulted world. The idea of the leap first grew in the landscape of apocalyptic miracles, which it still has as its background" (Ernst Bloch).

Here freedom appears in the broadest imaginable context. It is not just a question of how to choose between good and evil, but of having the whole world opened to the purposes of freedom. Human freedom grows out of divine freedom, to which all things are subject. We should remember, however, that wine as compared with water is not something absolutely new. Wine contains water, and men can drink both. Likewise Jesus does not as yet bring the absolutely new, the new heaven and the new earth. He liberates man and nature for a new direction of their destiny and thus functions as an anticipation of the absolutely new: the liberation of the world in which all things serve God.

Jesus' death is also part of the story, since he refers to the hour of his death: "Woman, my hour has not yet come" (v. 4). The change of nature and man brought about by Jesus finds its ultimate ground in what transpires in his death. From the beginning he freely identifies with man's total wretchedness. His Passion is not an extrinsic appendix of his life. Rather it reaches into everything he thinks and does. According to the Fourth Gospel, Jesus' death is part of the *shape* of his public activity from the very beginning. Death for Jesus is not a meaningless debacle. "Predictions" of his death appear immediately in his public activity in the Fourth Gospel and make it a Passion story throughout. As compared with the life that embodies God's waiting on man, the prevailing of freedom over necessity enabling man to choose over necessity, man's own making of freedom is unmasked as pseudofreedom. The reference to the hour of Jesus' death at the beginning of his public activity invites us to see freedom immediately prevailing in this life—prevailing in the face of what most radically threatens it.

COUNTERING THE STATUS QUO   2:13–25

13 *The Jewish Passover was near. Jesus went up to Jerusalem.* 14 *In the temple he found the dealers in cattle, sheep, and pigeons, and the money-changers at their tables.* 15 *He made a whip of cords and drove them, with sheep and cattle, out of the temple. He scattered the coins of the money-changers and overturned their tables.* 16 *To the pigeon-dealers he said, "Take them out. Do not make my Father's house a tourist trap."* 17 *His disciples remembered a word of Scripture: "Zeal for thy house shall consume me."* 18 *The Jews challenged him, "What proof can you give of your right to do such things?"* 19 *Jesus answered, "Destroy this temple, and in three days I will raise it again."* 20 *The Jews retorted, "It has taken forty-six years to build this temple, and you will raise it again in three days?"* 21 *But he spoke of the temple of his body.* 22 *After he rose from the dead his disciples remembered it again, and they trusted the Scripture and the word of Jesus.* 23 *During his stay in Jerusalem for the Passover many believed in his name when they saw his signs.* 24 *But Jesus did not entrust himself to them. He knew them only too well.* 25 *He needed no one to teach him what men are like, for he could see through men.*

Verses 1–12 stress that the world indeed is pliable, so that freedom can break forth. Verses 13–25 point out that for free-

dom to be historically concrete the sanctioning of the status
quo needs to be undone.

The clash between the first and the second half of the
chapter is strong. The man called Jesus has no quarrel with the
good order of life affording an opportunity for freedom (vv.
1–12). But he counters ecclesiastical religiosity (vv. 13–25).
It is the most glaring context for unfreedom. Exactly where
man should have a chance to serve only his Maker and to become human, money-making sanctioned by religion proves the
"real" god and claims man's loyalty. Entangled in penultimate
claims, man cannot attain his freedom. Jesus unmasks the un-
holy alliance between capital and religion. Under the power
of a penultimate god man is not free. Capital is perhaps the
most exacting of the penultimate gods putting man under the
heel of the laws of the market. Wherever religion is allied with
capital man is subservient to alien powers. Although not every
religious person will make money in the sanctuary, he may well
try to profit from the alliance between religion and capital,
hoping to receive financial returns from prayer and worship.

Jesus rejects the alliance between money and religion:
"He made a whip of cords and drove them, with sheep and
cattle, out of the temple. He scattered the coins of the money-
changers and overturned their tables. To the pigeon-dealers
he said, 'Take them out. Do not make my Father's house a
tourist trap' " (vv. 15 f.). Do not make my Father's house a
business enterprise! In ecclesiasticism, religion and capital are
joined. The one who questions the alliance is bound to encounter poker faces and adamant opposition. The church program is a success. The money is rolling in. The sanctuary is
beautiful, the spirit of worship heart-warming. What should
be wrong? In contrast, tables turned upside down and money
rolling through the sanctuary is not an inspiring sight. Ecclesiasticism knows of no "right" (v. 18) that could question it.

Jesus, however, rejects ecclesiasticism and points to the real thing: " 'Destroy this temple, and in three days I will raise it again.' . . . But he spoke of the temple of his body" (vv. 19–21). The human body is the *real temple* in which man is to worship. The incarnate Word has made all temples of religion at best preparatory. Jesus' body as temple means: temples are significant only in relationship to the human body as the temple of God. Sanctuaries or religious rites are not primary in man's relationship to God. What counts is to act in the body, in the totality of our being, in response to God's unconcealment. Only when man does not subject himself to the status quo can the body be free. The alliance between capital and religion is the crassest expression of the status quo that keeps man from grasping his freedom. Man tends to use his temples, even at their best, for purposes lesser than the proper use of his body. But the one who trusts Jesus as the true temple will find in his own body the true context of worship. St. Paul put it succinctly: "Do you not know that your body is a temple of the Holy Spirit within you?" (I Cor. 6:19). The body is the proper context of freedom, man's entrance to a public space where he knows liberation.

This becomes even clearer in reference to the destruction of the temple which implies Jesus' death (v. 19). Already in the beginning of his public activity death was a factor in the choices Jesus made, we said earlier. But *resurrection* was also a factor (v. 19). The man called Jesus was also already living as risen from the dead in the choices he made. Death had no power over him. While the disciples understood this only later (v. 22), Jesus himself was acting as the resurrection and the life (*cf.* Chap. 11) from the very beginning of his public activity. At least this is the way the Fourth Gospel sees him. The man who is not determined by laws of necessity, whether the laws of nature or the laws of human institutions claiming absoluteness, is free. Jesus is the one who is free from the power of death.

It is difficult to imagine that death and resurrection were *both* integral to the life of the man called Jesus. But for the Fourth Gospel cross and resurrection were no longer separate additions to the life. And the life was no longer preface to death and resurrection. As a man, Jesus in his totality is the resurrection who constantly resists death. To believe this is part of the difficulty of becoming a Christian. But it also is to know freedom.

Thus far we have been confronted with two astounding signs. Water was changed into wine, and the temple was cleansed. It is not surprising that there were people who admired the great man (v. 23). But they were caught in mass psychology. Jesus came that man would live in openness. He did not want admirers, but followers, men who would give up the frantic struggle for success and recognition and would join him in living in openness and thus acknowledge their true selfhood. He knew man's self-deception, how little man respects himself and his neighbor as temple of God and how much he loves religious glamor and the alliance between religion and capital as camouflage of his predicament. People might have gone "gung ho" over a glamorous "King of kings," Jesus Christ Superstar. But all he offered was his body as temple, so that man would become concerned about liberation in the body.

Just what man's actual historical freedom is can best be measured against the alliance of religion and capital that puts man in the straitjacket of ecclesiasticism. In our time the Black Manifesto's demand for reparations has stirred up vast opposition in the church because once more the ancient alliance between religion and capital has been exposed. No tables are turned upside down, but there are demands for the sharing of profits. In contrast to the status-quo-alliance between profit and religion, a new freedom is called for. But how can man ever attain it, the man who is an oppressor?

BECOMING BLACK 3:1–21

[1] *Nicodemus, one of the Pharisees, a leader of the Jews,* [2] *came to Jesus by night. He said, "Rabbi, we know that you are a teacher sent from God. No one can do the signs you do unless God is with him."* [3] *Jesus answered, "Believe me, no man can see the kingdom of God unless he becomes black."* [4] *Nicodemus wondered, "How can a man become black when he is white? Can he again enter his mother's body and be born different?"* [5] *Jesus said, "Believe me, if a person is not born of water and Spirit he cannot enter the kingdom of God.* [6] *Flesh creates flesh, and spirit creates spirit.* [7] *Do not be surprised that I told you, you must become black.* [8] *The wind blows where it wills. You hear the sound of it, but you do not know where it comes from and where it goes. So it is with everyone born of the Spirit."* [9] *Nicodemus asked, "How can this be?"* [10] *"You are the teacher of Israel," replied Jesus, "and you do not understand it?* [11] *I assure you, we speak of what we know and witness to what we have seen. But you do not accept our testimony.* [12] *If I have told you about things on earth and you do not trust me, how can you trust if I tell you about things of heaven?* [13] *No one entered heaven except the one whose origin is in heaven, the Son of Man who is in heaven.* [14] *The Son of Man must be lifted up as Moses lifted up the serpent in the wilderness,* [15] *so that everyone who trusts him may have prevailing life.* [16] *For God so loved the world that he gave his true Son, so that everyone who trusts him should not perish but have prevailing life.* [17] *God did not send his Son into the world to doom the world, but to liberate it through him.* [18] *He who trusts him is not doomed, but he who does not is already doomed, because he has not trusted in the selfhood of God's true Son.* [19] *This is doom: Light has entered the world, but men preferred darkness to light because their*

deeds were evil. [20] *Everyone who does wrong hates the light and shuns it lest his deeds be exposed.* [21] *But he who does the truth comes to the light, so that it becomes clear that his deeds are done in God."*

Now we are told how man can attain freedom. He needs to go through the shock of recognition: he does not want to change. It takes liberation of consciousness for man to become free. But this is a gift. Without it there can be no real freedom.

The Fourth Gospel does not say what made Nicodemus come to Jesus. It is not very graphic in portraying the persons who participate in the story. Types are sketched without great concern for their background, motives, or personal characteristics. It is concerned with the shape of Jesus' public activity and how men relate to it. All the Fourth Gospel points out in this instance is that Nicodemus apparently had been impressed by Jesus' signs. While somehow close to sensing the point of the mission of this man, he does not really understand it. He addresses him as God-sent teacher: God is with him. God seems somehow involved in the life of this man; otherwise he would not be such a great teacher (v. 2).

In response, Jesus revamps Nicodemus' world view. He offers a new idea. What it involves in our day is plain: "Believe me, no man can see the kingdom of God unless he becomes black" (v. 3). Doesn't the idea seem absurd? "How can a man become black when he is white? Can he again enter his mother's body and be born different?" (v. 4). Jesus' reasoning is based on another logic: "Believe me, if a person is not born of water and Spirit he cannot enter the kingdom of God. Flesh creates flesh, and spirit creates spirit" (vv. 5–6). Nicodemus is still reasoning on grounds of wanting to retain white superiority, private selfhood. Jesus is concerned about a different self, corporate selfhood, which man controls as little as the wind (v. 8). Here the brutal logic of retaining one's identity as the superior white self or the "private I" no longer prevails.

It is significant that the challenge to man's renewal (3:1–21) is prefaced by events that show how much man distorts his selfhood (2:1–25). Culture and religion contribute to man's enslavement, compelling him to view himself other than he is.

The Fourth Gospel presupposes that man has been enslaved in a false relationship toward himself, a false self, a private self. Jesus' open way of acting confronts man with corporate selfhood. It challenges men to begin anew with being human. But beginning over again is not a matter of course. It calls for a radical change, liberation of consciousness. Man is asked to grasp his selfhood anew. Many ask like Nicodemus: "How can this be?" (v. 9). Nicodemus at least ought to have had a hunch: "You are the teacher of Israel . . . and you do not understand it?" (v. 10). He ought to have had an inkling because of the partial acknowledgment of the light in Israel. As a teacher of the church he had to be aware of it. As a human being, the *sensus communis* should have taught him the truth. But being a theology professor does not mean much when it comes to knowing corporate selfhood.

"No man can see the kingdom of God unless he becomes black" (v. 3). Man needs to go through the shock of recognition that he does not want to change. He needs to know how radical the change required is. "Rebirth" of which Jesus is usually made to speak in this chapter has become something trite. One goes through it in a revival, enjoys it, and comes out of it quite unscathed. The change demanded in confrontation with Jesus is something eviscerating, something that touches the core of our being. It destroys the self-made self, that is, man as self-made man. Today it is usually the successful exploiter who preys upon others and uses their labor to build up his beautiful white front. It is all that "whiteness" stands for in the eyes of the poor, despised, and oppressed. To become black means to give up one's glamorous white self-image. "Blackness is an ontological symbol and a visible reality which best describes what oppression means in America" (James H. Cone). We could also speak of redness as an ontological symbol of oppression. The Indian too is debased. To be freed is always a question of being enabled to identify with the *marginales*, the people on the borders of society, through the power of the one who started doing it. Through Jesus we are able to enter the kingdom of God (v. 3), the realm in which all men are free as the truly free man rules over all. To worship one's beautiful private self is enslavement. To be related to corporate selfhood through Jesus is freedom.

There are a few additional dimensions in Chapter 3 that need to be lifted out. The kingdom of God, the realm of freedom, was embodied in a bruised body lifted up on a cross (v. 14). God rules (as king of his realm of unconcealment) as Jesus freely chooses to take death upon himself in order to identify fully with all the wretched of the earth. Here we meet man reborn. Here is opened up a new direction of human destiny, affirming that man is not "real" in the mask of the "white" pseudoself. Here Jesus, the Son of Man, is "in heaven" (*cf.* 1:51), which is standing in the openness of all things by embodying man's corporate self (v. 13).

In fact, God's very character is embodied in Jesus' freedom on the cross. For faith, God himself waits on man in death, breaking the ironclad law of death. For faith, this freedom prevails in resurrection and offers unoppressed life, free from negation, to all who trust it (vv. 15–16).

Becoming black through Jesus does not mean now to have a handle to identify him with any contemporary figure, group, or power. "Then if anyone says to you, 'Lo, here is the Christ!' or 'There he is!' do not believe it. For false Christs and false prophets will arise and show great signs and wonders, so as to lead astray, if possible, even the elect. Lo, I have told you beforehand. So if they say to you, 'Lo, he is in the wilderness,' do not go out; if they say, 'Lo, he is in the inner rooms,' do not believe it" (Mt. 24:23–26). The blackness or redness of the man reborn is always related to *Jesus'* blackness or redness. It is always *his* kind of blackness or redness that counts. It is not *our* identification, but *his* identification with the wretched of the earth that counts and brings the great change among men. Therefore it is always called a rebirth *through the Spirit*. It is a gift mediated through the Jesus event (v. 5). Man needs to be reminded time and again that of his own accord he does not want to find liberation of consciousness through this event.

Human life is still lived by the law of the jungle. We doom ourselves time and again, taking one another's lives in war and in peace, exploiting one another, rejecting history's true possibilities and producing a state of fear and doom. The design of unconcealment—a new direction of our destiny— is not doom, but liberation, freeing man in the structures of life. If a man trusts freedom as the Son embodies it he is not doomed. God liberates *in Jesus*. Doom is lack of trust in what this man embodies: the new corporate selfhood (v. 18).

Jesus' corporate selfhood is the judgment on man's life. Mankind's doom is that his presence illumines man with the potential of true freedom and we keep rejecting it, dooming ourselves. Doom is, not choosing death freely and thus not rising to life. Loving concealment, camouflage, private success, we do not wish to be openly what we are becoming to be. This

is darkness—pitch darkness. The lily-white deeds are dark because of the cover-up (v. 19). Since we sense that the deeds of
our pseudoself are not in accord with our true selfhood, we go
into hiding before the new direction of our destiny, continuing
to construct a pseudoworld (v. 20).

We go into hiding in myriads of ways. But today it is
especially obvious what the hiding is as white men still conceal themselves from black men and red men—imprisoned in
ghettos and reservations. It is only as we openly face one another as we really are and destroy ghetto and reservation that
truth becomes manifest. Truth is ultimately not known, but
done as men begin to see one another in terms of new corporate selfhood. This is not an easy thing, since it means facing
one another as sinners (v. 21).

Lest anyone think we are talking here about an utopistic
scheme, let him remember the water. The new life is tied to
rebirth by *water* (undoubtedly a reference to baptism as prac-
ticed by the church) and Spirit (v. 5). The water says that the
new life finds external expression. There is a space for freedom.
There is liberation. It is in new corporateness that the new
life is experienced: in the church as liberation church (*cf.*
Chapters 13–17). Since the Spirit is God himself (4:24), it is
God's action that creates the new corporate life. Rebirth by
water and Spirit is therefore the new corporate life wrought
by God himself, outwardly as well as inwardly: identification
with the wretched of the earth. Flesh—desire for make-believe,
false fronts, status, deception, illusion—creates only more of
man's hiding from one another. "Flesh creates flesh" (v. 6).
By nature man is born into the realm of flesh. But the Spirit
draws men into new corporateness.

To be reborn, to become black (or Indian, or Vietnamese peasant, or Soviet Jew), is thus to find a new selfhood.
Jesus offers it: "Light has entered the world" (v. 19). In him
man already is the new man. He who trusts him enters into

new community—which is ultimately the realm of liberation, "the kingdom of God" (vv. 3–5). In the community of the church man receives in liberation a foretaste of the kingdom.

THE NEW DIRECTION OF HISTORY   3:22–30

[22] After this Jesus and his disciples went to Judea. He stayed with them and baptized. [23] John was also baptizing at Aenon near Salim because there was much water in that area, and people kept coming to him and were baptized. [24] John had not yet been imprisoned, of course. [25] A question was raised between John's disciples and some Jews over purification. [26] Then they came to John saying, "Rabbi, the man who stayed with you on the other side of the Jordan, the one to whom you bore witness, here he is, baptizing, and all are flocking to him!" [27] John answered, "A man can have only what is given him from heaven. [28] You yourselves witnessed that I have said, 'I am not the Christ, but I was sent as his advance man.' [29] He who has the bride is the bridegroom. The bridegroom's friend who stands and listens for him is very glad to hear the bridegroom's voice. I now experience the same joy. [30] He must increase, but I must decrease."

A question is raised between John the Baptist's disciples and some Jews. The point about the reference to purification is not really clear (v. 25). Clear is the problem of the relationship between the Baptist and Jesus. If Jesus has followers they can only be regarded as a gift (v. 27). Men do not usually walk the road Jesus takes. Reality itself has to compel a man to get out of his self-seeking and self-serving. In the realm of human self-understanding there is no evidence that could convince men to see history moving on a road different from the road to self-made success.

The Baptist can say no more. Whatever insight into the direction of man's destiny there had been in history, now it found a new focus. In oriental weddings the friend of the bridegroom had an important role to play as "best man." He prepared the wedding. John's position in relationship to Jesus is similar. In Jesus a "wedding" takes place: a new direction of life begins. Whatever insight there had been in directing man toward a definite goal, it must now gladly serve the new direction of life (v. 29). The preparatory task of Israel's history and the history of mankind is finished. Now man's corporate selfhood will increase (v. 30).

Christianity began to chronologize history as B.C. and A.D. It considered Jesus a new beginning of history. So it began counting history anew with the year A.D. 1. If it means anything at all that history begins anew A.D., it is that the old human self disappears, and that a new kind of man appears whose self is that of all men. Today this is most concretely felt in "becoming black." The new history is a protest against the old history. Mankind dare no longer be enslaved.

THE NEW HUMAN CONDITION   3:31–36

[31] *The one from beyond is superior to all. He whose origin is of the earth belongs to the earth, and he speaks in earthly terms. The one whose origin is in heaven is superior to all.* [32] *He testifies to what he has seen and heard, but no one accepts his testimony.* [33] *He who accepts it acknowledges that God is true.* [34] *He whom God commissioned speaks God's own words, for God does not give the Spirit piecemeal.* [35] *The Father loves the Son and has put him in charge of all things.* [36] *He who trusts the Son has prevailing life, but anyone who disobeys the Son will not see life and remains under God's anger.*

If Jesus is as pivotal to man's destiny as verse 30 claims he is, it is inevitable that one should continue to probe why this is so. Everything said thus far in the Fourth Gospel tried to clarify the reaction of faith to the confrontation with Jesus. Verses 31–36 reemphasize Jesus' answer to Nicodemus. In Jesus' words God himself confronts man. They judge man and make him face up to himself. The human condition has been changed. God is near in this man.

Jesus' unique position is intimated by his saying that he is from "beyond" or "above." He lives completely out of the "beyond" which is the innermost "within" of man, the openness in which he stands. Usually we center our lives in hiddenness behind our fronts, our masks. In Jesus there is a different orientation point. Identification with the wretched of the earth creates a realm that transcends hiddenness.

It does not grow out of sheer fantasy. In the newness he introduces Jesus is grounded in "what he has seen and heard" (v. 32). The corporate selfhood of all men is rooted in ultimate reality. Whenever Jesus' testimony is accepted, unconcealment is acknowledged. As soon as this has happened man can act in terms of his new condition (v. 33).

What we get here is nothing piecemeal, but the full truth of the human condition (v. 34). Jesus is God's act of liberating man. In choosing the cross he rises to new life and is thus put "in charge of all things." This is the new human condition (v. 35). Trusting that God's freeing of man through Jesus is the direction of history, man will find his purpose unconcealed and will prevail in unoppressed life. Disobeying the new human condition means to continue in enslavement to hiddenness. God's anger is the way his liberating action is felt by those who exclude themselves from it. To doom oneself to nonparticipation in God's liberation, this is ultimate doom (v. 36).

BREAKING DOWN THE WALL
BETWEEN MEN 4:1–45

¹ When Jesus learned that the Pharisees had heard the news: "Jesus is getting a larger following than John and is baptizing more"— ² although Jesus himself did not baptize but his disciples— ³ he left Judea for Galilee. ⁴ He had to pass through Samaria.

⁵ He arrived in a Samaritan town called Sychar, near the piece of land Jacob gave his son Joseph. ⁶ "Jacob's well" was there. Jesus, exhausted from travel, sat down beside it. It was about noon. ⁷ A Samaritan woman came to draw water. Jesus said to her, "Give me a drink." ⁸ His disciples had gone to buy food. ⁹ The Samaritan woman said to him, "How can you, a Jew, ask a Samaritan woman to give you a drink?" (For Jews do not associate with Samaritans.) ¹⁰ Jesus replied, "If you knew what God offers, and who it is that asks you for a drink, you would have asked him, and he would have given you 'living water.' " ¹¹ The woman said, "Sir, you have no bucket and the well is deep. Where do you get that 'living water'? ¹² Are you greater than our ancestor, Jacob, who gave us the well and drank from it himself, with his family and cattle?" ¹³ Jesus replied, "Everyone who drinks this water will be thirsty again, ¹⁴ but whoever drinks of the water that I shall give him will never be thirsty. The water I shall give him will become in him a spring welling up to prevailing life." ¹⁵ The woman said, "Sir, give me that water that I won't feel thirsty again and have to come back again to draw."

¹⁶ Jesus said, "Go, call your husband and come back." ¹⁷ "I have no husband," she answered. "You are right when you say, 'I have no husband,' " Jesus replied, ¹⁸ "for you have had five husbands, and the man with whom you are now living is not your husband. You are at least honest." ¹⁹ The woman said, "Sir, I see you are a prophet. ²⁰ Our ancestors worshipped on this mountain, but you Jews say that one ought to worship in Jerusalem." ²¹ Jesus said to her, "Woman, believe me, the time is coming when you will worship the Father neither on this mountain nor in Jerusalem. ²² You Samaritans do not know what you worship, but we know whom we worship because liberation comes from the Jews. ²³ The time will come, in fact, it is already here, when the real worshippers will worship the Father in Spirit and truth. The Father seeks people who worship him that way. ²⁴ God is Spirit, and they that worship him must worship in Spirit and truth." ²⁵ The woman said, "I know that Messiah is coming, he who is called Christ.

When he comes he will explain everything to us." [26] Jesus said, "I am he, speaking to you."

[27] Just then the disciples returned. They were surprised because he was talking with a woman, but none asked, "What's the idea?" or "Why are you talking to her?" [28] The woman left her water-jar and headed for town. There she told the people, [29] "Come and see the man who told me everything I ever did! Can he be the Christ?" [30] So they left the town to meet him.

[31] Meanwhile the disciples were begging him, "Rabbi, eat." [32] But he told them, "I have food to eat you do not know." [33] The disciples asked each other, "Did anyone bring him something to eat?" [34] Jesus said, "My food is to do the will of him who commissioned me and to complete his work.

[35] "Do you not say, 'Four months yet and then comes harvest'? I tell you, look at the fields, they are ripe for harvest! [36] He who harvests gets paid, bringing in a crop for prevailing life, so that sower and reaper may rejoice together. [37] For this sort of harvest the proverb fits well, 'One sows, and another reaps.' [38] I sent you to harvest a crop for which you did not work. Others worked hard for it. You have come in where they left off."

[39] Many Samaritans of that town trusted him because of the woman's testimony, "He told me all I ever did." [40] When the Samaritans came to meet him, they asked him to stay with them. So he visited there two days. [41] Then many more trusted him because of his own word. [42] They told the woman, "We no longer trust because of your word, but because we have heard him ourselves, and we know that he is the liberator of the world."

[43] After two days Jesus left for Galilee. [44] He himself declared that a prophet finds no respect in his own country. [45] When he arrived in Galilee, the Galileans welcomed him because they had seen all the things he did in Jerusalem at the festival, having been there that day.

Mankind found its liberator in Jesus (v. 42). This is the core of the story of the Samaritan woman. Historical setting

and key images of the liberating work were provided by Israel:
"Liberation comes from the Jews" (v. 22). But the relevance
of Jesus' work is universal. It pertains to the Samaritan as well
as the Jew, the black as well as the white.

The openness of Jesus enabled him to confront men with
their true condition. He makes men face race, color, class, or
any other distinction between men in their true dimension.
Here they are unmasked as pseudodistinctions. And yet they
first have to be faced in their harsh realism. There is no point
in glossing them over. As whites we are quickly enamored by
biblical resolutions of these tensions. We glibly declare:
"There is neither Jew nor Greek, there is neither slave nor
free, there is neither male nor female; for you are all one in
Christ Jesus" (Gal. 3:28). And here as regards the Samaritan
woman we are quickly moved to proclaim: "There is neither
Jew nor Samaritan!" And, then, by the same token: there is
neither black nor white! It is true, Jesus tore down "the di-
viding wall of hostility" (Eph. 2:14). Where once two were
pitted against each other there is now only one man (*cf.* Eph.
2:15). And yet before we glory in this unity we had better
face each other eyeball to eyeball, which also happened in
Jesus' encounter with the Samaritan woman. Nothing was
glossed over.

We whites usually regard freedom first of all as something
we possess. We might understand that we must change our
image of freedom. We enjoy all sorts of iconoclasm today.
But as long as freedom does not become concrete in corporate
life it is no more than private self-adulation. Freedom must
become concrete in the structures which hold us captive.
Otherwise it is not freedom at all. This is what the remainder
of the Fourth Gospel wants to make clear.

Chapter 2 already stressed what is at stake: divine freedom as historical freedom. In Chapter 3 we heard of the radi-

cal change in man on which liberation is predicated. Now we
should be ready to grasp Jesus' liberating action more fully.
In John 4:1–45 Jesus acts again contrary to social custom, but
now in direct confrontation with another human being who
had been a nonperson to the Jew. Segregation between Jews
and Samaritans had lasted more than four hundred years by
the time Jesus appeared, much like segregation had lasted for
hundreds of years in the United States. What is more, the
woman was not very respectable. Finally, she was a woman.
Women's lib had not made its impact as yet. Strict rabbis did
not speak to women in public, some not even to their own
wives. In the open man, discrimination becomes pointless. The
walls between persons come tumbling down. Women's lib is
as old as the encounter of Jesus with the Samaritan woman.
But here is more than women's liberation. Here is color liberation. Even more, here is human liberation.

The walls of discrimination, the external barriers of national, racial, and class distinctions no longer keep men apart
from each other in the open man. In him personhood is the
final criterion. In speaking to the Samaritan woman, Jesus was
doing what according to man's corporate self is the thing to
do. He simply confronts the other person. And he identifies
with the wretched of the earth, the outcast.

The woman is surprised. Why does this man not act like
everyone else according to established "segregation" practices?
Jesus' answer is somewhat mystifying: "If you knew what God
offers, and who it is that asks you for a drink, you would have
asked him, and he would have given you 'living water'" (v.
10). The woman needs new understanding to overcome the
barriers between her and Jesus. She, too, has distorted her self
and needs "living water." But what is it? The woman does
not get the point (vv. 12 ff.). She thinks of running water,
the water of a river or a spring. This was the way "living wa-

ter" was understood among her people at that time. Jesus gets
back to his point by comparing his "running water" with ordinary well water. Well water does not quench thirst forever
(v. 13). But the one who drinks Jesus' kind of water never
gets thirsty. In fact, it proves to be a spring that feeds him
with unoppressed life, a life that death cannot silence (v. 14).
Later in the Gospel the claim will be made that the unoppressed life is to know God and Jesus Christ (Chap. 17).
Living water that gives eternal life is thus acceptance of the
confrontation with God in his Son. So living water is the open
person, the corporate self for which all men are "thirsting."
As well water sustains the body, participation in the corporate
self sustains a person's entire being.

The woman still does not understand (v. 15). But the
open man understands her (v. 17). The one who stands in
openness is able to see through the distortion of the human
self (cf. 2:25). Jesus' freedom is to confront man with his
dilemmas, so that he grasps how utterly confounded he is in
all he thinks and does and thus stands exposed in his self-
contradiction (v. 18). Without this kind of confrontation
there can be no real solution to any self-contradiction of man.
But men love their self-deception. The woman is typical. She
is exposed. What does she do? She switches the subject and
begins to discuss religion with the "Reverend." Where to worship was a bone of contention between Samaritan and Jew (v.
20). Suppose it was a genuine problem for the woman. But
it is also a phony escape to discuss religion when the disorder
of one's own life is the real issue.

The woman is typical of man's response to the open man.
White theology today also responds by discussing religion,
religious language, metaphysics, or new ways of worship, house
church, underground church, etc., while the real issue is to
realize how much man distorts his self, how screwed up he

is in wrong economic patterns, profit-making, and the whole capitalist scheme of who man is. Much of what happens in the white divinity schools is beside the point. Theology that does not challenge man to participate in the corporate self is wrongheaded.

Jesus objects to man's escape from himself, especially to his escape into religion. He exposes the passé character of religious observances (v. 21). Men shall not worship God the Samaritan or the Jewish way, the Roman Catholic or the Protestant way, but God's way, in participation in man's corporate self.

There are differences in the way God relates to men. The defeat of man's self-contradiction took place within the context of Israel's history. In Jesus' iconoclasm of what Israel had done with the faith images offered it by God, a new grasp of God's relationship to man is introduced. It is in this iconoclasm that the liberation of mankind comes from the Jews (v. 22).

God is Spirit. Thus he does not dwell in temples made by hands. But he dwells in the human body, seeking to free it to be human in corporate selfhood. True worship is the acknowledgment of the presence of God among all men in the body. Worship that is not response to God in the body is pseudoworship (cf. 2:13–25). But human bodies cannot worship truly unless they have been liberated to face the truth.

Truth is unconcealment—which sinful man does not wish to acknowledge. It is mediated to him through the body of the incarnate Word (cf. 14:6). True worship is thus to be open to God—personhood in the body—through Jesus' word. It is the reverse attitude of the first human couple: "And the man and his wife hid themselves from the presence of the Lord God among the trees of the garden" (Gen. 3:8). In the confrontation with the Samaritan woman Jesus is worshipping

God, not hiding behind false fronts that keep men separate from one another and God. So the story as a whole is the best demonstration of worship in Spirit and truth. It is the liberation of man for honest confrontation of his false selfhood and for new selfhood in new corporate relationships.

The confrontation between Jesus and the woman ends abruptly. Men easily yearn for a never-never land where all that now seems confused will be cleared up and the agony of life will come to an end. The woman epitomizes this yearning. Jesus' ideas about worship seemed intriguing. But she would still have to wait for the one who would have all the answers, the Christ.

Jesus terminates the conversation with the brief reply that he is the Christ (v. 26). He is the Christ because he breaks down the wall between men, the false fronts which they regard as the truly real. In the body he fulfills man's hopes and summons him to find the consummation of history (the Christ) in radically new relationships. Of course, man today can grasp the future only in the Spirit, in faith, not in sight. And yet in the Spirit embodied in the man called Jesus the future of freedom reaches into the present and liberates man. Something new is happening—a concrete bouleversement of human relationships—as the open man appears.

Enter the disciples. Returning from town where they had gone to buy food, they are puzzled that their master is speaking to a woman, and a Samaritan one at that. "He isn't a nigger-lover, is he?" But all they dare to say is: "Rabbi, eat" (v. 31). So they are typical of men who think of external needs, but not at all of the one thing needful: the stilling of man's hunger for freedom.

Facing the disciples' puzzlement, he makes them understand that this is the doing of a greater will than his own (v. 34). He has made freedom concrete in relating to a nonperson. Thus a person really receives food (v. 34). This is what truly sustains him: that he can break down the walls that separate men.

The unrestricted confrontation with the incarnate Word implies the missionary task which is bringing liberation to all men (vv. 35–38). God has sought to bring liberation to every person long before the Christian witness appears. The light has been shining in the darkness of man's self-distortion, so that every man has been touched by it. God makes man a conscience, so that all men are aware of the need to experience freedom concretely. They all share in the *sensus communis*, the common sense of truth.

All men have been prepared for the Gospel. "Others worked hard" (v. 38). In our story also the woman! She told of her encounter with embodied unconcealment. Many began to trust her because of her word. But then they were personally confronted with the open man. His own word confirms their trust. The open man is an inclusive event in the history of mankind. It seeks to liberate all men, everyone separated from his neighbor because of the wall built up in his false self. In the story the Samaritan and the Jew are liberated. They find a new freedom in their relationship to each other. Thus the man called Jesus is the liberator of the world (vv. 39–42).

The word of Jesus in verse 44 is a variant of Mark 6:4. After the "success" in Samaria a word of caution is entered lest anyone think that Jesus is universally acclaimed (vv. 43–45). Trust in Jesus is not an obvious thing. In fact, what resembles trust is soon exposed as superficial adulation (*cf.* 6:26 ff.). The person who associates with Jesus because he seems to bring external success is soon unmasked in his shallowness.

What is important to remember in this passage is that the open man brings about a new concrete situation by simply confronting men in their separateness. It is not at all a friendlylike, chatty, backslapping reconciliation that is provided, but a painful examination of one's self-deception.

"The problem of the twentieth century is the color-line," DuBois said decades ago. Here we see what it means. The need for liberation becomes clear at the color-line. Freedom does not break forth in immediate reconciliation. It grows out of the open clash in polarization, as men are liberated to participation in corporate selfhood.

BREAKING DOWN THE WALL IN MAN   4:46–5:15

DEATH CHECKED   4:46–54

⁴⁶ *Again he came to Cana, Galilee, where he had changed the water into wine. There was a king's officer whose son was ill at Capernaum.* ⁴⁷ *When he heard that Jesus had come from Judea to Galilee, he came to him and begged him to go down and heal his son who was dying.* ⁴⁸ *Jesus said to him, "Unless you see signs and wonders, you will not trust."* ⁴⁹ *Said the king's officer, "Sir, come down before my son dies!"* ⁵⁰ *"Go," Jesus replied, "your son lives." The man trusted Jesus' word and went home.* ⁵¹ *On the way his servants met him and told him, "Your son lives."* ⁵² *He inquired what time it was when he began to recover. They answered, "Yesterday, at one in the afternoon the fever left him."* ⁵³ *The father knew that it was exactly the time when Jesus said, "Your son lives," and he trusted him together with his whole household.* ⁵⁴ *This was the second sign Jesus did coming from Judea to Galilee.*

Man, involved in the struggle for life, is anxious to preserve himself. It is perhaps his most vital concern that humankind perpetuate itself and prevail: "Sir, come down before my son dies!" (v. 49).

"Go . . . your son lives" (v. 50). Not every father's son
has been saved from death, no matter how much he prayed
or asked for his son's life. What the father in the story learns
from Jesus is trust in the open man: "The man trusted Jesus'
word and went home" (v. 50). We too can learn—at least
this much the event conveys—trust in the incarnate Word
in the face of death, regardless of the outcome. What man
usually calls trust, however, is based on external assurances,
"signs and wonders" (v. 48). As long as man seeks security
in external things he shows that he is afraid of death and has
built a wall between his true self and the pseudoself he dis-
plays. The new condition in which men live calls for trust in
Jesus' word of life (v. 50). In audacity over Jesus' word a man
can choose a new direction of life, rejecting fear. As little as
man relates openly to God and neighbor does he relate openly
to himself. The fear of death reflects man's self-deception. He
does not admit that he must face death as summons to an
open life, that death is part of true life.

Jesus faces death. In choosing death freely he prevails
over it. And the king's officer's son is healed by the one who
in his free choice is already raised from the dead—as faith
sees it. In Jesus the wall that separates man from his true self
is torn down. The healing epitomizes the rule of man's true
self over death. The "miracle" is that the ironclad laws of
nature are broken for faith. Man is indeed free wherever the
wall that separates him from his true self is broken down. But
he is truly free only in a concrete liberation, here a liberation
in which death loses its actual power. Just like in the story
of the Samaritan woman, freedom does not remain a mere
idea, and man is not only liberated in his relationship to others, but also to himself.

It should be clear, too, that Jesus' identification with the
wretched of the earth is not a mechanically exclusive thing.

The king's officer: that does not sound like the title of someone on the margin of society. And yet the threat of death makes every man wretched. The open man does not refuse to identify with human wretchedness of any kind. There is no point in "outblacking the black" or "outindianing the Indian." The truly oppressed man is concerned about the threat to life wherever it appears.

Also note the inversion of the theodicy question: "If there be God, why evil" (*si Deus, unde malum*)? The Fourth Gospel does not ask this. It is the other way around: "If this be evil, what about God" (*si malum, unde Deus*)? If this be evil, how can we survive? God's reality is assumed—and appealed to as the power that protests man's wretchedness, so that man liberated and unoppressed may find prevailing life.

SUFFERING CURBED   5:1–15

¹ Later there was a Jewish festival and Jesus went up to Jerusalem. ² Near the sheep gate in Jerusalem there is a pool with five porches. Its Hebrew name is Bethesda. ³ Many sick people were lying in these porches, blind, lame, and paralyzed. ⁵* One man had been crippled for thirty-eight years. ⁶ When Jesus saw him lying there he knew he must have been in that state for a long time. So he asked him, "Have you the will to get well?" ⁷ The sick man answered, "Sir, I have no one to put me in the pool when the water is moved. Somebody always beats me to it." ⁸ Jesus said to him, "Get up, take your mat and walk." ⁹ Immediately the man was healed, took up his mat and walked. It was Sabbath that day.

¹⁰ So the Jews told him who had been healed, "Today is the Sabbath. It is against the law to take up your mat today." ¹¹ He answered them, "The man who healed me told me, 'Take up your mat and walk.'" ¹² They asked him, "Who is the man who told you that?" ¹³ The man who had been healed did not know who it was, for Jesus had disappeared in the crowd gathered at that

* Verse 4 does not appear in the most reliable manuscripts.

place. [14] Later Jesus found him in the temple and said to him, "Look, you are well again. Sin no more, lest something worse happen to you." [15] The man went away and told the Jews that it was Jesus who had healed him.

Many men have been sick and have suffered in soul and in body. Even a people or nation as a whole can be sick. Some men seem able, as individuals or in groups, to escape suffering. But will they have regard for the suffering of others?

The open man says to the cripple: "Get up, take your mat and walk" (v. 8). Here again we have liberation becoming effective for the wretched of the earth. Thirty-eight years sick! And now relief—not in soothing rhetoric, but in the ability to throw off the crutches, to walk, to stand up, to be independent.

The man called Jesus claims that suffering could return quickly, even worse suffering: "Sin no more, lest something worse happen to you" (v. 14). A "nexus" between sin and suffering is implied. In this instance Jesus apparently concurs with the Jewish doctrine that sin and suffering are related (but note 9:3, where he takes the opposite view). Sin, the negation of freedom, the yielding to oppression, can lead to unbearable suffering, be it physical suffering or the loss of self. This does not say that all suffering is due to sin. The mystery of suffering goes deeper than human frailty. But human corruption can vastly increase suffering. It is this syndrome that is focused here.

Jesus, not yielding to any ironclad law, heals the man on the Sabbath. Understandably, the organization churchmen are upset. The ecclesiastical code opposes liberation. The space for freedom is denied most where it is most concretely afforded. God, however, has not given man a Sabbath to enslave him in organized rest, but to aid him in finding his freedom. Jesus healing the cripple embodies the meaning of the Sabbath. Here again is freedom made concrete as liberation —liberation from the human restrictions of the Sabbath for its creative purpose.

Jesus shows what the truly world-historical figure is like and how it differs from what men usually call a world-historical figure. "So mighty a form must trample down many an innocent flower—crush to pieces many an object in its path" (Hegel). As loudly as Hegel may speak of freedom he shows how much a man can still miss its point. Only where man refuses to trample under foot a single neighbor and is ready to curb his suffering is man free.

BREAKING DOWN THE WALL
BETWEEN GOD AND MAN   5:16–47

Man's Isolation from God Overcome   5:16–30

[16] The Jews persecuted Jesus because he did this on the Sabbath. [17] Jesus' response merely was, "My Father has never stopped working and I keep working too." [18] Now the Jews tried all the more to kill him because he was not only breaking the Sabbath, but called God his own Father, making himself equal to God.

[19] Jesus told them, "Believe me, the Son can do nothing on his own, unless he sees the Father doing it. The Son responds to whatever the Father does, [20] for the Father loves the Son and shows him all he does. He will show him greater works yet to awe you. [21] As the Father raises the dead and makes them live, so the Son makes alive whom he chooses. [22] The Father dooms no one. He has turned over all judgment to the Son, [23] that all may honor the Son as they honor the Father. Whoever does not honor the Son does not honor the Father who commissioned him.

[24] I solemnly tell you that anyone who listens to my word and trusts him who commissioned me has prevailing life. He will not be doomed, but has already passed from death to life. [25] Be-

*lieve me, the time is coming, in fact, it has already come, when
the dead will hear the voice of the Son of God, and they who hear
will live.*

*[26] As the Father has life in himself, so he has granted the Son
to have life in himself. [27] He has authorized him to judge because
he is the Son of Man. [28] Do not wonder at this, for the time is
coming when all who are buried will hear his voice [29] and come
forth, those who have done right to a resurrection of life, but those
who have done wrong to a resurrection of doom. [30] I can do nothing on my own. As I hear I judge, and my judgment is just because
I do not try to do my own will, but the will of him who commissioned me.*

Those who absolutize the ecclesiastical system will always be prone to destroy him who embodies its true purpose
(v. 16). Man's freedom is not protected by any "system,"
code, or law; and not by the ecclesiastical system, either. Freedom becomes real only where a man obeys the "law" of his
own being as it reflects God's "law" (v. 17), here expressed
in breaking the Sabbath law. A man walled off from his freedom stands in need of external props in a system of cult and
rite to safeguard his legalistic view of the self. Not willing to
presuppose that God is unconcealed in life and that life offers
its own fulfillment, he shapes his actions in terms of the security systems of society. A man who grounds his thoughts
and deeds in the unconcealment of God's waiting seems to be
blaspheming. In fact, the open man seems to be usurping
God's place (v. 18).

In the open man the false wall between God and man
comes tumbling down. Not that God now becomes man's
buddy! But God is no longer far removed from man by the
barrier interposed by man between himself and the transcendent. Here the bent of God's work toward man's freedom
informs the shape of a man's life as he responds to unconceal-

ment (v. 19). Instead of a communication gap there is limit-
less communication. It was the unique impact of unconcealment, its special commissioning of this man, that enabled him
to do his work (v. 30). Transcendent freedom urges this man
on to embody it in historical freedom. The open man breaks
down the wall between transcendent freedom and historical
freedom in living completely out of the power of man's true
self. For him it was impossible to make "law and order" an
absolute. He realized that man had to embody what he learned
from the openness of all things (vv. 19 f.).

Since the open man understands himself as the Son of
true reality, rising through death to life, he rules over death
and is able to offer unoppressed life to others (v. 21). Death
viewed apart from unconcealed freedom separates man from
life. But death viewed in the light of divine freedom in the
open man points to unoppressed life. The impact of the open
life is far-reaching. The ultimate judgment of the value of
human life is now tied to the one who embodies freedom.
Men are judged by their relationship to freedom. Whoever
finds God embodied in Jesus' freedom relates to the openness
of God's freedom in every man's life (vv. 22 f.).

Jesus embodies God. Everyone who participates in Jesus'
freedom through his word shares in God's prevailing life and
finds that his own life also prevails. He need not be afraid of
the doom of death. He has already passed beyond death, man's
negation of the unconcealed reality of all things, into prevailing life (v. 24). As Jesus is the embodied temple (*cf.* 2:13–25)
and the embodied purpose of the Sabbath (*cf.* 5:1–15), he is
also *embodied* eschatology. This does *not* mean that he *is* the
eschaton, *realized* eschatology. But in him the eschaton is anticipated in human form. In him the future reaches into the
present, so the dead can hear the voice of life. In sin all men
are dead to their freedom. The one, however, who obeys the

open man's summons to trust breaks through the wall of death to prevailing life (v. 25).

The freedom-giving power of life is centered in the Son who is empowered with the truly free life (v. 26). The one who lives the unconcealed life is the true man, the Son of Man. In Jewish eschatology, the Son of Man is the final judge, the criterion by which all of history is measured. The open man has now become the final judge because in him the embodiment of man's destiny has become the new direction of human life. The truth of a man's life is judged by unconcealed life (v. 27). In view of open manhood, some men prove to live in accord with freedom, others are exposed as preferring concealed oppression to openness, deception to truth. Jesus' manhood is the measure of whether or not men will work for an unoppressed prevailing life or doom themselves to perish in privatism (v. 29).

The other side of the coin is the constant communication between Father and Son, the intimate union between transcendent freedom and human freedom issuing in the truly "corporate self." There is no private self here, no communication gap, no breakdown of community. There is constant call and response, constant give and take, constant waiting on the other.

The implications are a radically new way of doing theology. It is focused clearly in 5:17: "My Father never stopped working and I keep working too." The theology here expounded is deeply rooted in doing—communicating activity. Who God is is experienced in an act. Truth is primarily not known, but *done*. Already 3:21 made this clear: "He who *does* the truth comes to the light." American theology still suffers from the notion that one can know God in classroom discussions or Sunday-school lessons.

Christology in the Fourth Gospel is not abstract reflection on God and man, but the experience of a new action. It is new in that it claims that God's presence in Christ Jesus opens man for freedom, liberates man in an act. God and man do not relate in Jesus primarily in the mystery of a uni-personality of Godhead and manhood which we would need to view as a great puzzlement. God and man relate in the open man as condition and consequence. God liberates. This is who God is. And as a consequence man can act freely. This freedom becomes the contradiction to man's oppression. Man is attacked in his self-distortion.

Why not casually accept some of the church definitions of Christology? The problem is that Christology is all about God and man *acting* in concert. And our image of man with whom God is to act together is wrong, an idol that must be smashed. God cannot unite with the WASP, the white middle-class self. Our image of man must go.

The reason we oppose liberal Christology is that its image of man is false. If we superficially look at Schleiermacher's view of religious man, there may be little to criticize. But if we consider that a particular view of political and economic man is implicit in his view of religious man, the picture begins to change. Religious man is not as innocent as Schleier-macher makes him out to be. The trouble with liberalism is that it looks at man as mainly a nice fellow. And as a consequence we never come to understand what phonies we are as secular men, hucksters and impostors, exploiting and manipulating one another.

In spite of all the iconoclasm that has gone on as regards the Western image of man, it is still very much ingrained in our basic attitudes. We are still utterly private selves. Christology in terms of the Fourth Gospel is a radical attack upon our isolation. "A new corporate self has been embodied in the life of a man and has become the hinge of history" (Carl Michalson).

UNPRECEDENTED INVOLVEMENT OF GOD AND MAN   5:31–43

³¹ If I endorse myself my testimony is not true. ³² There is
someone else who endorses me, and I know that his testimony of
me is true. ³³ You sent an investigating committee to John, and
he testified to the truth. ³⁴ Not that I depend on man's endorsement. I only mention this that you may be freed. ³⁵ John was a
bright burning light, and for a while you basked in his light. ³⁶ But
the endorsement I have is greater than John's. The works which
my Father gave me to complete, that is, the very actions of my
life, bear out that the Father commissioned me. ³⁷ In fact, the
Father who commissioned me has endorsed me. You have never
heard his voice or seen what he is like, ³⁸ and his word does not
endure in you, for you do not trust him whom he commissioned.
³⁹ You study the Scriptures because you think you find in them
prevailing life, and all the time they are my credentials. ⁴⁰ But you
refuse to come to me to find life. ⁴¹ I do not find status by man's
approval. ⁴² I know you. You do not have God's love in you. ⁴³ I
have come endorsed by my Father and you refuse to associate with
me. If another comes self-endorsed you will associate with him.

The Gospel claims that through the open man human
beings are liberated from their bondage to the private self. Is
there any proof that this is true? There is no proof, but there
is Jesus' life, the life of a fellowman, *which speaks for itself.*
This man does not need public relations to build his image.
And he does not sell himself. Having been put on trial by the
Jews, he replies in effect: if I were trying to sell myself my
testimony would not be true (v. 31). The truth of his message
can be checked out against man's corporate self, to which
every man has access in God's unconcealment.

"We try to make the candidates bigger than life and we
try to do it emotionally. Our job is to glamorize them and hide
their weaknesses" (Robert Goodman). Measure the open man
by the selling of the political candidates in America. The issue

should be clear. A man predicating his acts on God's unconcealment refuses to become bigger than life and to tamper
with reality. "Reality has to be touched up a little, so that it
looks like reality to the simple viewer" (*Newsweek*). Here
the WASP dogma of the self is openly exposed. The real self
does not count. What counts is what *looks* like reality—so
claims the bitch-goddess "success," distorting the real. "You
sometimes have to strain yourself to create reality . . . it
doesn't come naturally" (Robert Goodman). Here the whole
shysterism of our WASP way of achieving selfhood stands revealed. Liberal theology has never radically attacked this deal.

Jesus refuses "hidden persuasion," even open persuasion
to prove the validity of what he offers. If his life and message
are not "self-evident" to man, no amount of "sales talk" will
convince him of God's unconcealment. Freedom informing
man's inner being, making man a conscience, is the "internal"
witness in every man which can check out the Gospel.

For a while apparently the Jews had appreciated the work
of the Baptist. But they were far from grasping what he was
trying to do. What is more, partial insight by a third person
into God's unconcealment is not decisive "evidence" of the
truth of Jesus' work. It depends on no factor other than my
own grasp of openness in Jesus. All the witness of a third person can do is to remind me of my own need for liberation, to
illuminate the darkness of my concealment and self-enslave-
ment (vv. 32–35).

God's involvement in Jesus' life, his commissioning and
endorsing this particular man, is a new event among humankind. It offends the onlooker who is involved in touching up
his self and raising the walls of pseudodistinctions between
men in selling himself. It is revolting to a person who thinks
of God in objectifying terms, who regards God as a being who
hides himself in transcendence, and who can become an ob-

ject of "religious studies." It is repulsive to be confronted with
God in a man edged to a cross. Worse, this man thought of
himself as embodying God. "Now the Jews tried all the more
to kill him because he was not only breaking the Sabbath, but
called God his own Father, making himself equal to God"
(v. 18). The ecclesiastical system that undergirds the WASP
self has good reason for rejecting Jesus as embodier of the
new image of man. Organization churchmen want organized
mystification about God, so men can remain sufficiently confused.

Jesus' word about the churchmen's ignorance of God does
not automatically convict them (vv. 37 f.). Their own conscience must convict them. While the Word of freedom is
present to them, they wall themselves off against it: "His word
does not endure in you" (v. 38). Jesus is appealing to the Old
Testament Scriptures. All along the Word had sought to find
response in Israel. All along had God offered men the opportunity for grasping freedom. All along Israel had been guided
by the power of the Word. And yet it largely refused to acknowledge it in its embodiment. The Scriptures are thus indeed Jesus' credentials (v. 39). Had the organization churchmen not read the Old Testament with a wall between them
and true reality they would have had to realize that the man
called Jesus confronted them with the Word of freedom, the
Word that had been the lifespring of Israel's history. The
same with the organization church today. The Scriptures are
still read, at least in most worship services, even though
preaching is not based on them. Here lies the difficulty. The
Scriptures testify to the true reality of human selfhood. They
point to its embodiment in the man called Jesus. But they
are not understood in this regard. They are only read mechanically.

As men refuse to associate with the man who embodies

freedom they refuse themselves, that is, they refuse their own life (v. 40). Failing to grasp Jesus' real selfhood, men desire to behold God in "signs and wonders" (4:48), in objectively stupendous deeds. While they would seek to develop a mystifying Christological metaphysics, they have no notion of the radical trust to which men are summoned by Jesus' embodiment of God's freedom and his supplanting of religion in nonecclesiastical liberation. For organization churchmen, the criteria of the divine are the sacred rites and the metaphysical dogmas of the ecclesiastical establishment.

Take note of the man who acknowledges the openness in which God makes freedom a present reality for every man, the Gospel wants to say. Here is a man not dependent on the ecclesiastical system. But Jesus' freedom seems unintelligible to men engaged in building their external image, who, though they may ceaselessly be reading the Bible, are blind to its real point. Only the man who is convicted in his conscience by God's freedom embodied in his Son can make sense of Jesus' message.

The proof of man's yen for pseudoreality is his status-seeking (v. 41). Men give themselves and each other "reality" as communists and capitalists, rich and poor. But it is sheer make-believe that the external image of status is the truly real, the permanently valid.

"I know you. You do not have God's love in you" (v. 42). Man does not respond to God's freedom as a matter of course. We manipulate ourselves and others to establish our "real" value by mutual endorsement. Thus we paralyze ourselves as well as our neighbor in our true spontaneity. In view of what happened to the man called Jesus it becomes obvious that we loathe a person who does not want to be endorsed by anything but God's waiting on man and who merely expresses his true self.

The unprecedented involvement of God and man creates the embodiment of true selfhood: the counterself of the private self. This is the core of Christology.

Man's True Self   5:44-47

44 How can you trust as long as you find status by mutual praise and ignore the status rooted in the only God? 45 Do not think that I shall accuse you before the Father. You have already an accuser, Moses, on whom you have set your hope. 46 If you trusted Moses you would trust me because he wrote of me. 47 But if you do not trust his writings, how will you trust my words?

Nothing distinguishes man more as a person than trust. But in order to trust, man must be liberated from his make-believe world of the private self. "We do not content ourselves with the life we have in ourselves and in our being; we desire to live an imaginary life in the mind of others, and for this purpose we endeavor to shine. We labor unceasingly to adorn and preserve this imaginary existence, and neglect the real. And if we possess calmness, or generosity, or truthfulness, we are eager to make it known, so as to attach those virtues to that imaginary existence. We would rather separate them from ourselves to join them to it; and we would willingly be cowards in order to acquire the reputation of being brave" (Pascal).

If we understand Christology on the primal level as the counteroffer of a new self negating man's false self-image, the issue at this point is clearly drawn. For American society, the new self, however, is by no means an immediately viable option. As much as Norman Vincent Peale has been ridiculed by theologians and organization churchmen, he is much more representative of what transpires in our minds and hearts than we probably care to admit. "With sound self-confidence you can succeed. . . . Self-confidence leads to self-realization and successful achievement." And what is successful achievement? It is consummating "the most important business deal of [your] life." It is having "a triumphant thought pattern." It is sitting "on a balcony of one of the most beautiful hotels in the world, the Royal Hawaiian on the famed and romantic Waikiki Beach in Honolulu, Hawaii," writing books. There is no need to go on. Success is the standard of selfhood also for the ecclesiastical establishment. The fabric of the make-believe world determines who a man is. In a sense, of course, the private self is also a "corporate self." But it is corrupted corporateness, a corporateness that is created by illusory endorsement of one another. It determines that the acme of achievement is reached when man is most private, when he sits in one of the most beautiful hotels of the world and the wretched of the earth cannot reach his eye. It is the success-principle carried into the deepest recesses of American religiosity that ultimately makes the wasp-self innocuous and doomed to oblivion.

As long as a person relies on the fickle thoughts of what others determine as success and the image in which others see him as success, his life will be poisoned with distrust—since he is unable to trust the fleeting thoughts of others who are not aware of true selfhood. The success-principle has not contributed to healing the American nation, to breaking down the walls of separation. Since the heyday of Norman Vincent Peale, American society has become more sick, more poisoned with distrust. The cancer of the soul has spread. What creates trust is man's awareness of himself in response to God's unconcealment (not to success) and his participation in God's waiting on man. Jesus does not offer man transient "status," but sensitizes man to the "status" before God, the openness of all things (v. 44).

"Man is obviously made to think. It is his whole dignity and his whole merit; and his whole duty is to think as he ought. Now, the order of thought is to begin with self, and with its end. Now, of what does the world think? Never of this, but of dancing, playing the lute, singing, making verses, running at the ring, etc., fighting, making oneself king without thinking what it is to be a king and what to be a man" (Pascal). Orientation toward the success-principle creates absent-mindedness, so that a man loses himself in trivialities. By contrast, the man called Jesus thinks about what it means to be a man—a real person. And herein he became the self that counters man's forgetfulness of corporate selfhood.

It is difficult for featherbrained man to think of nothing more than being a man. Fragmentary insight into true reality, represented among the Jews by the law of Moses, convicts man of forgetting his true selfhood. His conscience accuses him of not being fully man (v. 45). But men usually do not listen to their partial insight into true selfhood when confronted with one who desires to be no more than a man (vv. 46 f.). They want to continue to be known by their "laws," their pseudoimages as communists, capitalists, Hindus, Christians, Catholics, Protestants, Jews. Some also want to be known as new theologians! Those who are willing to view their fragmentary insight into God's unconcealment critically seem to be able to *trust* Jesus' words that liberate for the Word of freedom. Trusting his words is to learn what it means to be a man, a person. While man believes he must prove himself in an external image, the point of Jesus' life is that man cannot prove himself. Man proves himself only in the trust that he does not have to prove himself. God proves him (v. 44).

It is not until Chapter 5 that we get a full view of who the man was to whom the message of Jesus Christ was ultimately addressed. The organization churchman appears as representative of men who do not put human need first. His world view is subject to ironclad law. Today the Gospel attacks the WASP self, the callous huckster, who puts law first, bolstered by the ecclesiastical establishment. If this is seen, the Gospel is not immediately a matter of apologetics or of faith talking to faith. First of all, a confrontation takes place. And who has ears to hear, let him hear! The issue is whether we are willing to stand the confrontation. If it rings true we are going to listen and others are going to listen. It is a matter of self-evidence, presupposing the *sensus communis*.

What comes across in the Gospel as central is a particular shape of activity, a unique configuration of history. No great chronologizing happens, no great psychologizing. The issue is simple: will the shape of this selfhood compel us to change our own? It embraces cross and resurrection within itself, the freedom to prevail and to live the unoppressed life. But it does so in encompassing community as part of the self.

The question of how we see our selfhood is central in theology. There is no point in getting involved in the pros and cons of contemporary God-talk that *antecede* the question of Jesus' selfhood and our selfhood and the pros and cons of resurrection-talk that *succeed* the question of selfhood. There is an order of priorities. For the view of the self we hold will determine whether the Gospel story can break through to us in the first place. In some respects the God-question is not primary. The Gospel, first of all, compels us to acknowledge a new view of the self. And the question of the resurrection is also answered in terms of a new view of the self.

It is not that reality independently suggests to us what it is like. We shape the world according to how we view our self. Ontology and historiography depend on it. The father of liberal theology, Friedrich Schleiermacher, viewed the whole world in terms of the absolute dependence of the self on an absolute cause. All of reality was thought to fall into this mold. Miracle and freedom were both subject to the primary mold. Here the self is simply part of the causal nexus. Hegel as the philosopher of freedom might be expected to have had a different view of the self. But his self is ultimately dependent on the logical necessity of the deduction of the categories and on how the world process evolves from them. As a consequence, God and Christ become subject to the ironclad logic of historical process and merely symbolize it. Nothing really new can break through, nothing that could run counter to the necessity of the historical process. By contrast, the Fourth Gospel invites us to consider the reality of a self that truly embodies freedom.

OPEN MANHOOD AS
THE COUNTERSELF   6:1–71

REFUSING STARDOM   6:1–15

¹ After this, Jesus crossed the Sea of Galilee (or Tiberias). ² A big crowd followed him because they had seen the signs he performed on the sick. ³ Jesus went up the hill and there sat down with his disciples. ⁴ The Passover, the Jewish festival, was near. ⁵ Jesus looking up and seeing the big crowd coming to him, said to Philip, "Where can we buy bread to feed this crowd?" ⁶ He said this to test him, for he himself knew what he would do. ⁷ Philip answered, "You need more than ten dollars to buy enough bread for them, even if everyone gets only a bite." ⁸ One of his disciples, Simon Peter's brother Andrew, said to him, ⁹ "There is a boy here who has five barley loaves and two fishes, but what is that for such a crowd?" ¹⁰ Jesus said, "Make the people sit down." There was plenty of grass there, and about five thousand sat down. ¹¹ Then Jesus took the loaves, gave thanks, and passed them out to those sitting on the grass; also the fishes, as much as they wanted.

[12] When they had eaten enough, he told his disciples, "Pick up the scraps, so that nothing is lost." [13] They gathered them and filled twelve baskets with the leftovers of the five barley loaves. [14] When the people saw the sign they said, "This must be the prophet who is to come into the world!" [15] Jesus, knowing that they were about to seize him to make him king, withdrew again to the hills by himself.

The Fourth Gospel Christology makes it clear that in this church today one cannot be a decent Christian. The basic premises of our WASP Christianity are false. It is not a matter of touching up this or that point a bit. Religious make-up does not get at the fundamental issue—defined by William Stringfellow in the November, 1970, *Christian Century*: "I had supposed, in the early '60s that the apostasy of white denominationalism in America was an issue of acculturation and secular conformity, but I gravely misunderstood. The apostasy here is not so quaint, but is, in truth, a *generic* apostasy: white Anglo-Saxon Protestantism is radically false. It represents no corruption of the gospel only, it is an aggression against the gospel. And as such its influence in this society and culture has been pervasive, infecting churches outside its nominal precincts as well as dominating the ethics of society."

Chapter 6 is a manifestation of the counterreality of WASP Protestantism. Verses 1–15 rather than mystify the reader intend to destroy his hankering for the religious superstar. The man called Jesus did something astounding. Men were tempted "to make him king" (v. 15), to put him on a throne. We enjoy being one another's "kingmakers." That Jesus was about introducing a new selfhood we can hardly appreciate.

Jesus is not part of the make-believe game. He does not invite the "Crown him with many crowns!" He is a king already. So he withdraws from the featherbrained who want to make him a somebody. Instead of trying to make him king, the five thousand might have thought of what it means to be a king and what to be a man. The free man outwits those who want to capture him in the ironclad laws of success.

Jesus is neither a supernatural king nor a this-worldly king. He is the king as he breaks through the ironclad laws of what men expect of this world. Said Philip: "You need more than ten dollars to buy enough bread for them, even if everyone gets only a bite" (v. 7). The selfhood of Jesus confronts the world with a different possibility: "Jesus took the loaves, gave thanks, and passed them out to those sitting on the grass, also the fishes, as much as they wanted" (v. 11). Viewing the world and its goods in a new way he is king. His selfhood does not bow to natural or logical necessity.

The feeding of the five thousand is the expected Messianic meal as embodied in Jesus' new selfhood. According to Messianic "dogma" the meal belonged to the coming age. In the feeding of the five thousand the dogma is transformed. Jesus' appearance creates a new situation in which the fantastic Messianic hopes are smashed and their true intention is retained in a liberated relationship of men to each other. In Jesus the five thousand share a new selfhood and a new direction of history while simply sharing food. He opens up a new future for them.

Men need no longer program the future in terms of necessity. They can anticipate it in freedom. Jesus' ministry to the five thousand has given the future a new direction. The sharing of the bread among the five thousand forestalls future history: the sharing of bread among all men. The self that believes in necessity fears it can't be done. The crowd in the story reflects man's principal insensitivity to true selfhood. Jesus' sharing of the bread intimates a different outcome.

Do Christians gathering about their communion tables discern more keenly the purpose of the sharing of the bread? It is not a mystifying rite, but the symbol of the new liberation-history: the freedom of man acknowledging unconcealment, sharing possessions rather than hanging on to them, remembering the one whose broken body was the broken and shared bread of the world.

THE FREEDOM OF THE TRUE MAN   6:16–21

16 When evening came, his disciples went down to the sea, 17 got into a boat and began to cross over to Capernaum. It had become dark, and Jesus had not yet returned to them. 18 A strong wind began to blow, and the sea grew rough. 19 After rowing about three or four miles they saw Jesus walking on the sea and coming near the boat. They were scared. 20 But he said, "It is I, do not be afraid." 21 They wanted to take him aboard. Immediately the boat reached the shore they were heading for.

Even though Jesus has come close to men, we cannot manipulate him according to our laws of success. His fulfillment of the Messianic hope is an expression of his waiting on man. It grows out of his concern for the liberation of man and is not the megalomania of a madman. Presupposing God's unconcealment, Jesus realized what otherwise men would not embody. His presence today still depends on the act of his freedom. Today some still seek to build him up as the beautiful religious hero, "God's kind of guy." But whenever we lay our hands on him to make him king, a somebody, he withdraws (v. 15) and returns as the sovereignly free man (v. 19) who rules over the necessity we impose upon nature. "The sight of a man who is ready and capable of directing his own destiny at his own risk and peril and following his own will poisons the existence of our reason" (Shestov). Men are not used to this. In the quiet of the free self a decision has been

made that runs counter to all systems of necessity. A new
freedom breaks through to make the world react on new terms.

THE QUEST FOR JESUS CHRIST SUPERSTAR   6:22–29

22 *The next day the crowd which stood on the other side of
the sea saw that there had been only one boat, and that Jesus had
not embarked with his disciples, who had left without him.* 23 *But
small boats from Tiberias had landed near the place where they
had eaten the bread after the Lord had given thanks.* 24 *When
the crowd realized that Jesus was not there, nor his disciples, they
got into the boats and left for Capernaum to look for Jesus.*
25 *When they found him on the other side they asked him, "Rabbi,
when did you get here?"* 26 *Jesus answered, "Believe me, you are
looking for me not because you understood the signs, but because
you ate your fill of the loaves.* 27 *Do not work for perishable food,
but for food that will keep for prevailing life. The Son of Man
will give you this food because God has authorized him."* 28 *That
made them wonder, "What must we do to be doing God's works?"*
29 *Jesus answered, "The work of God is to trust him whom he
sent."*

Why do men turn to Jesus? In our passage they seek him
because they feel he has satisfied their physical hunger. For
the affluent church today, is Jesus more than a convenient
guarantee of constant supply on the religious supermarket?
Does he not see to it that we continue in spiritual abundance?
By contrast, he himself summons men to work for food supply that brings life eternal, an unoppressed life. Man is to
work for what "the Son of Man will give you" (v. 27).

But how can a man do something that is given him? (v.
28). The answer is: "The work of God is to trust him whom
he sent" (v. 29). Trust is doing what is given to us in Jesus'
selfhood, giving up viewing God as subservient to reason, is
accepting the new freedom embodied in Jesus. Trust is being
audacious in risking everything as Jesus risked everything be-

fore the five thousand—introducing a new logic. Trust is what feeds us with unoppressed life. It is risking a new view of the world where the law of reason does not prevail.

To men seeking a spiritual idol, a stained-glass Christ, all this forebodes frustration. A man edged to a cross is a fool —in terms of the law of success. How can one trust a person who is not a success?

It is not we who have introduced a new selfhood. So what is left for us to do is to trust in what is gifted us in the man called Jesus. But trust in him becomes in our own selfhood doing what he did in his, grasping freedom as the event in history that makes us new men.

The True Man Battling the Superstar Image   6:30–40

[30] They replied, "What sign can you perform that we can see something and trust you? What can you do? [31] Our ancestors ate manna in the desert, as Scripture tells us, 'He gave them bread from heaven to eat.'" [32] Jesus said, "Believe me, Moses did not give you the bread from heaven; my Father gives you the real bread from heaven. [33] God's bread is that which comes from heaven and gives life to the world." [34] They said to him, "Sir, always give us this wonder bread." [35] "I am the bread of life," Jesus replied, "anyone who comes to me will never feel hungry, and the one who trusts me will never thirst. [36] However, I have told you that you do not trust, although you have seen. [37] All that the Father gives me will come to me, and I will never reject anyone who comes to me. [38] For I have my origin in heaven not to do what I please, but to do the will of him who sent me. [39] He who sent me wills that I should not lose anyone of all he has given me, but raise them all on the last day. [40] This is my Father's will that everyone who sees the Son and trusts him shall have prevailing life, and I will raise him on the last day."

Man looks for some brilliant feat that can boggle the imagination, now that Jesus has shown his power—just as the

"captive fan," in the rock opera *Jesus Christ Superstar*, does
when he demands of Jesus an instant miracle. Insensitive to
the real power of selfhood, he wants to see staggering deeds.
The five thousand are a case in point. Having shared the bread,
they have seen true freedom embodied. And yet they do not
grasp what has been done. So they appeal to past miracles—
manna in the wilderness—without understanding the real
point. Receiving manna from heaven without becoming a
truly free man—this is not true food, bread from heaven.

Jesus offers the truly free self: "God's bread is that which
comes from heaven and gives life to the world" (v. 33). We
easily misunderstand. As we today gladly draw on a continu-
ous food supply in the supermarket, men in Jesus' day would
have been more than happy to have had such a constant food
supply: "Sir, always give us this wonder bread" (v. 34). Jesus'
response is: "I am the bread of life" (v. 35). The real food
man needs is a grasp of his true selfhood. Miraculously sup-
plied food does not at all touch upon man's real hunger. Trust
in the new freedom is "bread from heaven" (vv. 32 f.). Here
the world is opened up for what it intimates to man in terms
of freedom.

"You do not trust, although you have seen" (v. 36). Jesus
cannot give more than himself. Men receive no more than
what this self has achieved, an opening up of a new world free
from oppression. The new self appears as a fellowman, in his
word and deed. It is difficult to trust this unassuming man.
A man who thinks black, this is altogether too unimposing.

If a man can trust Jesus it is because of the power of the
light that reaches every man and reminds him of his true selfhood. Man is able to live an unoppressed life. Eternal life is
that life which the ironclad laws of reason and nature do not
permit. "What no eye has seen, nor ear heard . . ." (I Cor.
2:9). This is what man is drawn toward in the man called
Jesus (vv. 39 f.).

The Revolting Truth of the Counterself   6:41-51

⁴¹ *The Jews began arguing about him because he claimed, "I am the bread that came from heaven."* ⁴² *They said, "Is not this Jesus, the son of Joseph, whose father and mother we know? How can he say, 'I have come from heaven'?"* ⁴³ *Jesus replied, "Stop arguing.* ⁴⁴ *No one can associate with me unless the Father who sent me draws him, and I will raise him on the last day.* ⁴⁵ *It is written in the prophets, 'And they shall all be taught by God.' Everyone who has listened to the Father and learned from him associates with me.*

⁴⁶ *"No man has seen the Father except he whose origin is God; he alone has seen the Father.* ⁴⁷ *I assure you, he who trusts me has prevailing life.* ⁴⁸ *I am the bread of life.* ⁴⁹ *Your ancestors ate manna in the desert, and yet they died.* ⁵⁰ *Here is the bread that comes from heaven that a person may eat it and never die.* ⁵¹ *I am the living bread that has come from heaven. If a man eats this bread he will live forever. The bread which I will share that the world may live is my flesh."*

Jesus offends man's natural religiosity—white organization church thinking. Why should a man offer unoppressed life? Why should a man "come from heaven"? Jesus for many Jews was the guy next door whose background was well known (vv. 41 f.). Can the guy next door offer eternal life? The organization churchmen consider the idea obnoxious.

White religiosity is geared to yielding to the world. It is falling in tune with the eternal laws of the universe. We have not as yet rid ourselves from the presuppositions of the liberal view of religion: "The religious sense corresponds not to the masses in the outer world, but to their eternal laws. Rise to the height of seeing how these laws equally embrace all things, the greatest and the smallest, the world systems and the mote which floats in the air, and then say whether they are not conscious of the divine unity and the eternal immutability of the world" (Schleiermacher). The religious attitude seems to have been very much the same in Jesus' day.

White thinking seems not to be interested in radical freedom. Jesus could not expect anyone to trust his new selfhood. Presupposing unconcealment as the condition according to which men in their conscience would be drawn to him, he claims no drawing power for himself (v. 44). The organization churchmen assuming they know him and his father and mother, so that there could be nothing unique about this man, cannot grasp the point of the incarnation: God as the condition of a new selfhood. The incarnation invites us to see God in a completely new light through this particular man who acknowledges God's unconcealment as the condition of a new freedom (v. 45).

Man's new selfhood implies even freedom from the law of death: "I will raise him on the last day" (v. 44). But the new life is already offered to those who have the audacity to trust the new man. Through him man here in time can experience life as prevailing and unoppressed. This is not a merely private experience. It is a matter of sharing in concrete relationships, first in the liberation covenant and then in the broad political and social contexts of society. But the principle has first of all to be grasped. Eternal life is the counterthrust to eternal law (v. 47). In time the sharing in ultimate freedom is tied to the audacity of trust. The "last day" will manifest ultimate freedom. Then men shall truly "all be taught by God" (v. 45).

The eating of the manna did not give eternal life to the ancestors of the Jews. Unoppressed life is not the effect of a miraculous food of immortality. It is experienced in the response to a new self that thinks black. And it is the shape of Jesus' public activity that is shared in this experience: "The

bread which I will share that the world may live is my flesh"
(v. 51). But it is offensive to man that in order to find his true
future he should identify with the one who identifies with the
oppressed—not just in "liberal" ideas, but in his entire life,
whose words act, and whose deeds speak.

The selfhood of Jesus again stands out in stark contrast
to the perspective of the organization church. This is the significant Christological point in this context. The world is not
ruled by necessity, but by the free choice of God to transcend
it and to offer man through resurrection a prevailing and unoppressed life. Jesus finds his historical freedom in embodying
transcendent freedom. "The bread of life" stands for this
reality of freedom. It speaks of making transcendent freedom
concrete.

Obviously the result is *iconoclasm*. The view of manna
held by the organization church was destroyed. The real
"miracle food" is the self that rules over the necessities of
natural food supply. The organization churchmen were still
keyed up over the *physical* miracle *apart* from the one who
wrought it. Important is the miracle of this whole man, this
new self.

IDENTIFICATION WITH THE COUNTERSELF   6:52-58

⁵² *The Jews now began arguing vehemently, "How can this
man give us his flesh to eat?"* ⁵³ *Jesus replied to them, "I want to
assure you, unless you eat the flesh of the Son of Man and drink
his blood you do not have life in you.* ⁵⁴ *Whoever eats my flesh
and drinks my blood has prevailing life, and I will raise him on
the last day.* ⁵⁵ *My flesh is real food and my blood is real drink.*
⁵⁶ *Whoever eats my flesh and drinks my blood shares my life, and
I share his.* ⁵⁷ *As the living Father sent me and I live because of
the Father, so he who eats me will live because of me.* ⁵⁸ *This is
the bread which has come from heaven. It is not like what your
ancestors ate. They died. Whoever eats this bread will always live."*

Jesus' words are hard to take for the white mind wedded to law and order thinking (v. 52). His countermanding offer is quite blunt: "Unless you eat the flesh of the Son of Man and drink his blood you do not have life in you" (v. 53). Obviously we identify ourselves, as Northerners, Southerners, Protestants, Catholics, Jews, etc. We want identity. But do we find it? Transcendent freedom became incarnate in a man in order that a man could identify with what he truly is: the being that is open to freedom. This is what the crude language of the eating of the body and the drinking of the blood symbolizes. In primitive thought, a man is what he eats. So men are here summoned to *be* in terms of who this man is. Too primitive? Perhaps. But who is the man, primitive or modern, who is able to identify with the free man?

Jesus' words do not intend to mystify. All he asks us to do is to give up our make-believe world. In discriminating identifications, man seldom gets a glimpse of the oneness of man in his true freedom. Living behind the masks of manufactured segregation, the image in which we would have others see us, we basically remain phonies. "Unless you eat the flesh of the Son of Man and drink his blood you do not have life in you" (v. 53). As long as man does not identify with real freedom he is dead, although he simulates life. Death means yielding to the immutability of nature. The one who identifies with the Son of Man breaks the ironclad law and breaks through to unoppressed life, the life that prevails (v. 54). The emphasis on the raising of man implies that man is not absorbed in God or Christ. This is not a new pantheism. Man *shares* in a new corporate self in which he becomes himself.

We who in an economy of abundance crave for even greater abundance are invited to listen: "My flesh is real food and my blood is real drink" (v. 55). Nothing makes more sense for man than to be man in response to the free man.

Human flesh and blood are the meat and drink to be concerned about, so that we understand our body as temple of God's Spirit.

Acknowledging freedom as the innermost reality of man identifies all men. To share life in the freedom of a radically new relationship is to bear the glory and the shame of manhood together. This is what the incarnation implies. We are here not offered a new scheme of self-redemption, but man's open reality. Man's unconcealed reality presupposes God's unconcealment: "As the living Father sent me and I live because of the Father, so he who eats me will live because of me" (v. 57). Jesus' flesh and blood are the center around which humanity turns—the hinge of history.

IDENTIFICATION WITH THE GESTALT
OF THE FREE MAN   6:59–65

[59] He said these things while he was teaching in the synagogue at Capernaum. [60] Many of his disciples, when they heard this, said, "These words are hard to take. Who can stand that kind of talk?" [61] Jesus knowing that his disciples were grumbling about it told them, "Does this offend you? [62] What if you would see the Son of Man going where he was before? [63] It is the Spirit which makes alive, the flesh alone is of no avail. The words which I have spoken to you are Spirit and life. [64] However, there are some of you who do not trust." For Jesus knew all along who did not trust and who was to betray him. [65] He went on to say, "This is why I told you that no man can associate with me unless the Father enables him."

The externally observable flesh alone does not liberate man. Liberation relates to the wholeness of the truly free person. What we must understand is that flesh and spirit are interdependent in him and form a unity, a *Gestalt*. We never can get at more of Jesus than this *Gestalt*, the shape of his public activity. And we do not need to know more of him. What we need to see is how in this *Gestalt* freedom unifies flesh and spirit, bringing both together to form a whole man. Flesh as the supple tool of the spirit making freedom break forth is the direction, or *telos,* of manhood. The Gospel expects man to encounter himself in the words that interpret this shape (v. 63). Words without action are cheap. And actions without words are mute. Once again, this calls for trust, for faith. Man is *able* to have the audacity of trust because of the light that unconceals his life and enables him to be free (v. 65). But not everyone overcomes his inability to trust (v. 64). Men love law too much. They are unwilling to expose themselves to God's enabling action.

PERSEVERING WITH THE FREE MAN   6:66–71

[66] After this, many of his disciples withdrew and no longer accompanied him. [67] Then Jesus said to the Twelve, "Are you going to turn your back on me, too?" [68] Peter Simon answered him, "Lord, where should we turn? You have words of unoppressed life. [69] We have trusted and experienced that you are the Holy One of God." [70] Jesus replied, "Did I not choose you as the Twelve? But one of you is a devil." [71] He meant Judas, Simon Iscariot's son, one of the Twelve, who would betray him.

Jesus' liberation of consciousness was obnoxious even to many of his first followers (v. 60). So they eventually turned their backs on him (v. 66). His claims ran contrary to the familiar view of religion. A person confronted with Jesus must soon decide whether he is hankering for security in religion or whether he will take the risk of freedom. Twelve stayed with Jesus acknowledging the liberation of consciousness in him. "Lord, where should we turn? You have words of unoppressed life" (v. 68). But even in the smallest circle of trust distrust appears (v. 70). One in the group was ready to betray the free man. One among the Twelve was unable to wait for the fuller manifestation of the truth that the free man is the Holy One of God (v. 69), who liberates reality, who presupposing God's unconcealment begins to walk in the direction of unoppressed life.

THE OFFENSE OF THE COUNTERSELF 7:1–53

OFFENSIVE TIMING   7:1–13

¹ After this, Jesus went about in Galilee. He wanted to stay away from Judea because the Jews were planning to kill him. ² It was close to the Jewish holiday called "Dwelling in Tents." ³ So his brothers said to him, "Leave here and go to Judea, so that your disciples may see the works you are doing. ⁴ No man works secretly if he wants public attention. If you really do these things, show yourself to the public." ⁵ Not even his brothers trusted him. ⁶ Then he said to them, "This is not the right time for me, but any time would suit you. ⁷ The world cannot hate you. But it hates me because I prove that its deeds are evil. ⁸ You go up to the festival; I am not going because it is not yet the right time for me." ⁹ Having said this he remained in Galilee. ¹⁰ After his brothers had gone to the festival he went anyway, but so as not to be seen. ¹¹ At the festival the Jews looked for him and asked, "Where is he?" ¹² There was much arguing over him in the crowd. Some said, "He is a good man." Others claimed, "To the contrary, he is misleading the people." ¹³ However, for fear of the Jews no one spoke openly of him.

As we reflect on the Christological implications of the preceding chapter, the emphasis on Jesus' selfhood stands out. Here was someone who would not take the nonsense of man's usual view of the world. This self had faith as its center: "If you have faith as a grain of mustard seed, you will say to this mountain, 'move hence to yonder place,' and it will move; and nothing will be impossible to you" (Mt. 17:20). Jesus' miracles were all understood as signs (*sēmeia*). Signs of what? Of the credulity of the primitive mind? If this would have been the case, why so great a selectivity? Only a few signs appear in the Fourth Gospel. Everything else is interpretation. The signs seem not to have been bluntly stupendous happenings. They point beyond themselves to the selfhood of Jesus that is ready to move mountains, willing to break those laws which imprison reality in necessity. Thus the primal Christological affirmation is the freedom of the man called Jesus, not his sheer divinity. Who God is we learn when we know what this freedom is.

For the organization churchmen it was repulsive to be confronted with this freedom as the place where God is known. God seemed to have been unseated from his lofty height, trampled underfoot, and to have become less than God. This was an offense. There are always those who are ready to kill a man in order to get rid of what they consider evil. So the organization churchmen want to kill Jesus (v. 1).

Jesus' brothers are said to have been offended too, only on different grounds. They seem to have sensed the unusual qualities of their sibling and wanted him to make them public. The festivities in Jerusalem would afford a splendid opportunity. Should not a great man try to sell himself when there are crowds around? Also the brothers, valuing man in terms of external status, did not know what to make of true manhood (vv. 3 f.).

Men are usually ready any time to waste time and kill time, to eat and to drink, to make love and to sleep, to dream and to loaf. Almost any time is also expedient for finding success and recognition (v. 6). By freeing himself from man's

view of time, Jesus exposes man's abuse of time. It is not surprising that people hate him (v. 7).

Freedom for the right use of time excludes wasting time
on ostentatious publicity, selling one's image. So Jesus does
not go to Jerusalem with his brothers. The reason why he first
would not go together with his publicity-hungry brothers, but
then goes anyway need not be specifically articulated. His
principal aversion to publicity is quite clear: "He went anyway, but so as not to be seen" (v. 10).

The crowd in Jerusalem understood the free man as little as his brothers. Some appealed to moral maxims: "He is
a good man." Others thought of him more in terms of political expediency: "He is misleading the people" (v. 12). They
did not see that they were challenged by freedom to break
through their naive view of who man is. Even men with high
moral and political aspirations are not without fear. No one
dared to speak openly of Jesus, a mere man (v. 13). Only if
men grasp the reality of personhood rooted in unconcealment
do they find freedom from fear.

OFFENSIVE TEACHING   7:14–18

¹⁴ When the first half of the festivities was over, Jesus went
up to the temple and taught. ¹⁵ The Jews were amazed and said,
"How can this uneducated man read the Scriptures?" ¹⁶ Jesus answered them, "What I teach is not my own doctrine, but his who
commissioned me. ¹⁷ If someone is willing to do his will he will
find out whether my teaching is from God, or whether I speak on
my own authority. ¹⁸ He who speaks on his own authority is a
status seeker. But he who is concerned about the status of the one
who commissioned him is sincere, and there is nothing two-faced
about him."

The confrontation that creates the offense continues.
How can an untrained man teach theology? (v. 15) He did

not attend Divinity School, did he? Jesus teaches as one who embodies what is not foreign to man, what every man should know. Not promoting himself, he invites man to open himself to what is most near to him. His teaching, unverifiable by sophisticated argument, must be checked out by life. Men here must act their way into a new thinking rather than think their way into a new acting. This is a central concern of the Fourth Gospel. Only in action can we find our way into the truth of Jesus' teaching. God's unconcealment is understood in action alone (v. 17). Jesus does not "authorize" himself. He depends on what the process of life itself suggests as true. Seeking status we try to authorize and to commend ourselves, and we forget that our true history is grounded in our having been sent into existence and being empowered to live in this mission (v. 18). The "acknowledgment of the power which sent me into the world and which is called God disentangles the whole thing and gives sense to human life" (Tolstoi).

Offensive Healing   7:19–31

¹⁹ "Did not Moses give you the law? But none of you keeps it. Why do you want to kill me?" ²⁰ The crowd answered, "You are crazy. Who wants to kill you?" ²¹ Jesus replied, "I have done one work (on the Sabbath) and you are all shocked. ²² Moses gave you the rite of circumcision (of course, Moses did not introduce it, it came from the patriarchs) and you circumcise a man on the Sabbath. ²³ If a child is circumcised on the Sabbath, so that the law of Moses is not broken, why should you be angry with me when I completely healed a man on the Sabbath? ²⁴ Do not judge by outward appearance, but be just in your judgment."

²⁵ Then some of the Jerusalem people said, "Is not this the man they want to kill? ²⁶ It is strange, here he speaks in public, and they say nothing to him. Can it be that the leaders really think that this is the Christ? ²⁷ We know where this man comes from. But when the Christ comes, no one knows where he is from."

[28] *While he was teaching in the temple, Jesus proclaimed with a loud voice, "So you know me and where I come from? I have not come on my own authority. The one who commissioned me truly is, and you do not know him.* [29] *I know him because he is my origin, and he has authorized me."* [30] *At this, they tried to seize him, but no one even touched him because his time had not yet come.* [31] *Many of the crowd trusted him and said, "When the Christ comes, will he do more signs than this man?"*

The clash between man's law and order thinking and Jesus' acknowledgment of openness continues. Why did the organization churchmen want to kill a fellowman concerned about the neighbor? Of course, the healing of a man on the Sabbath (v. 23; cf. 5:1–15) was offensive to them. But was the law against concern for the neighbor? Man should judge more in terms of the spirit of the law than its letter.

Captive to their worship of law in regard to all human relationships, the ecclesiastics were unable to view the free man in terms of the essence of the law. They were not looking for freedom, but for the Superstar, the Christ. An unpretentious human being would not measure up to their expectations: "We know where this man comes from. But when the Christ comes, no one knows where he is from" (v. 27). Illusory thinking about man finds the lowly form of Jesus' activity offensive. This should be an embodiment of the ultimate?

The free man does not have much of an answer for those who want Superstar glamor. Jesus is a man. But this is not the whole story (v. 28). The mystery of his life is that he presupposes unconcealment as the precondition of action. Sinful man is unwilling to acknowledge openness as the true presupposition of action. Instead of living openly man puts on the mask of status and prestige and authorizes himself. Over against man's self-deception the free man affirms the reality of unconcealment. Some trust him, and yet they also misjudge him. Not Jesus' feats are the ground for trust (v. 31), but his open manhood.

OFFENSIVE DEPARTURE   7:32–36

³² The Pharisees heard the crowd muttering about him, and the chief priests and Pharisees sent officers to arrest him. ³³ Then Jesus said to them, "I shall be with you only a little longer, and then I shall return to him who commissioned me. ³⁴ You will seek me, but you will not find me, and you cannot come where I am." ³⁵ The Jews asked each other, "Where can he go that we should be unable to find him? Is he planning to go to our emigrants among the Greeks and to teach the Greeks? ³⁶ What does he mean by saying, 'You will seek me, but you will not find me,' and 'You cannot come where I am'?"

Man benefits from the institutions that maintain his society. But he also abuses them as means of manipulating the neighbor (v. 32). Law and order should help man attain a fuller life. But, in the dimension of freedom, man is accountable ultimately to his origin in God and not to man-made institutions. The free man appeals to a transcendent home (v. 33). Society, state, and church cannot claim absolute authority.

Society is so enamored of its distorted criteria of corporateness that it can think of the limits of its power only in terms of neighboring societies that curb it. Will Jesus leave Judea for Greece? The "emigration" from the absolute claims of society to transcendent openness is incomprehensible to those who absolutize themselves, their institutions, and their status (v. 36).

OFFENSIVE DRINKING   7:37–44

³⁷ On the last day, the climax of the festivities, Jesus stood and proclaimed with a loud voice, "If any man is thirsty, let him come to me. ³⁸ Whoever trusts me, let him drink. Rivers of living

water will run from his body, as Scripture says." [39] He was speaking
of the Spirit whom those who trusted him would receive. The
Spirit had not yet been shared, since Jesus had not yet fully embodied God.

[40] When some of the people heard this they said, "This is
really the Prophet." [41] Others said, "He is the Christ." Some asked,
"Does the Christ come out of Galilee? [42] Does not Scripture say
that the Christ will come out of David's family and from Bethle-
hem, the village where David lived?" [43] So the people were divided
over him. [44] Some of them wanted to seize him, but no one dared
to touch him.

Jesus confronts men once more with his new selfhood.
He presupposes that men thirst for it (v. 37). But without
trust, sharing in it is impossible (v. 38). His appeal to the
Spirit underscores once more that free manhood depends on
transcendent openness. The Spirit is the concrete offer of openness, most fully embodied on the cross (v. 39). Through the
cross the heart of ultimate reality is radically brought near.
God gives himself to him who realizes what the cross stands
for (v. 39).

Some, close to overcoming Jesus' offense, conclude that
here is the one for whom they have been longing. Others fall
back again upon the familiar standards of tradition and prestige. The Christ must have a distinguished background (vv.
41 f.). He cannot be a mere man with no distinction other
than being free. In the end, the confrontation with the free
man remains an offense. His enemies try to get rid of him.
But they seem to have an uncanny fear of touching him. And
so he still remains free (v. 44).

OFFENSIVE ORIGIN   7:45–53

[45] Later the officers returned to the chief priests and Pharisees
who asked them, "Why did you not bring him?" [46] The officers

answered, *"No one ever spoke like this man!"* [47] *The Pharisees replied, "Are you also confused?* [48] *Has anyone of our leaders trusted him, or of the Pharisees?* [49] *This mob that does not know the law can go to hell."* [50] *However, one of them, Nicodemus (the man who had come to Jesus before) raised a question.* [51] *"Does our law condemn a man before we have given him a hearing and ascertained the facts?"* [52] *All they could answer was, "Are you also from Galilee? Search the Scriptures, and you will find that no prophet comes from Galilee."* [53] *At this everyone went home.* *

Even though the organization churchmen abuse the law, the officers' treatment of Jesus is a ray of hope which shows that not all men will distort life. The officers who had been sent to arrest Jesus had been struck by the unique stature of the man (v. 46). Those entrusted with the enforcement of the law sense the "higher law" to which the law is subject: freedom. This freedom is not the licentiousness of the mob (v. 49), but the freedom to act in accord with human destiny. So they do not lay their hands on Jesus. But the organization churchmen blind themselves to true life. Could there be a greater hindrance to grasping true manhood than ecclesiastical power and prestige? (vv. 47–49)

The power of the Word to free men can make itself felt by one man's courageous appeal to the law (v. 51). As fragmentary insight into true life the law can witness to unconcealment. But, as before in the Gospel, man's fragmentary insight proves insufficient. Man subjects the law to his yen for illusion. A rigid dogmatism here blinds the organization churchmen to the truth. Searching the Scriptures, they use them to support their dogmatic illusions (v. 52).

What would have mattered, was letting a man speak for himself. If we are willing to listen to the neighbor and to let

* Verses 7:53–8:11 do not appear at this place in some of the manuscripts. Others do not have it at all. 7:53 is probably the beginning of 8:1–11.

him speak for himself, we are already taking a step toward unconcealment. Unwillingness to let a person speak for himself is to deny manhood. "At this everyone went home" (v. 53). Especially the organization church, the ecclesiastical establishment, proves incapable of true communion. Man's true self remains an offense.

PART III

MAN

MAN'S CONCEALMENT AND
THE UNCOVERING OF MANHOOD   8:1–59

OUR IMAGE OF MAN MUST GO   8:1–11

¹ Jesus went to the Mount of Olives. ² Early the next morning he came again to the temple, and all the people flocked to him. He sat down and taught them. ³ The lawyers and Pharisees paraded in with a woman caught in adultery and placed her in the center. ⁴ They said to him, "Teacher, this woman has been caught in the act of adultery. ⁵ In the law Moses commanded such people to be stoned to death. What do you say?" ⁶ They brought this up to trap him hoping to find something to accuse him of. Jesus bent down and wrote with his finger on the ground. ⁷ When they continued pressing the question he sat up erect and told them, "He who is without sin throw the first stone at her." ⁸ Again he bent down and wrote on the ground. ⁹ When they heard what he said they left, one by one, the eldest first. Jesus was left alone with the woman still standing in the center. ¹⁰ Looking up he said, "Woman, where are they? Has no one condemned you?" ¹¹ She answered, "No one, sir." Jesus said, "Neither do I. Go, sin no more."

Many things have already been said about man, at least by implication, in Chapters 1–7. Now we must draw these points together in focusing on the question: who is man? Usually in Christian understanding the answer is centered in the concept of the *imago dei*, the image of God. But what can it really convey? Man is not accessible to us in the state of primal innocence to which the concept refers. We need to take this more seriously than heretofore. If we look at man in his present state we do not have any concrete evidence available that might clearly suggest the *imago dei*. We are quickly able to sense the distortion of humanity, for example, in the act of the woman caught in adultery. But the lawyers and Pharisees express much more radically the human dilemma. It is the pride of self-righteousness, of *being* the *imago dei*, that shows how much man is at odds with himself.

Although the story is not part of the more reliable manuscripts of the Fourth Gospel, it continues the theological argument of the Gospel quite well. Man stands against himself in his concealment and he wants to see everyone drawn into the plight of his condition. The woman's misstep affords an opportunity for the organization churchmen to show their true colors. They also wish to implicate Jesus, their fellowman. Sin here appears immediately as social phenomenon. Men get involved in it corporately, and they want others to get involved in it too. Made for corporateness, we cannot avoid it. Since we do not share true corporateness, our corporate openness before God, we share the consequences of our privatism and isolation.

We need to take into account, however, the differences between the then and the now. Doubtlessly, few churchmen today would drag into church a woman caught in adultery. Today adultery is frequently a badge of courage rather than a badge of shame. What a progressive gal! Churchmen today are apt to judge adultery by Hugh Hefner's law. What they will not excuse is failure to use the pill to avoid the consequences of fornication. For white churchmen, the ones to be blamed are mostly the ignorant females—of the other color.

"This woman has been caught in the act of adultery. In the law Moses commanded such people to be stoned to death" (vv. 4–5). The theology underlying this public reasoning about unrighteousness remains very much the same throughout the ages. Only that from time to time it turns to different fixations. We know who we are: the *imago dei*. We have a right to determine a man's life and death accordingly. *We are* the *imago dei*. Some do not live up to it. So they must be eliminated. But *we* have a right to live. We are the lords of creation.

The story shifts the problem of sin away from the woman to the churchmen. It seeks to nail down our real depravity. We are not sinful just when we are caught in an act of sin. We are sinful in thinking *that we already know who man is* and that we can judge him accordingly. It is the ironclad image of man as *imago dei* that is the real trouble. So our image of man must go.

It is high time that we put a moratorium on our *imago dei* thinking: "He who is without sin throw the first stone" (v. 7). There is not much of an image of God in us as yet that we can be proud of. We should no longer take our eroding white self, exploitative and greedy as it is, as the measure of who man is. The time has come that our white *imago dei* thinking disappear from the center of the stage: "When they heard what he had said they left, one by one, the eldest first" (v. 9).

It is strange how much churchmen are drawn to the hang-ups of sex as the area where the dilemmas of man should be fought out. The man called Jesus, by contrast, is concerned about a boy born blind, a man thirty-eight years sick, or a woman's total well-being: "Sin no more" (v. 11). It seems that we have developed our image of man in order to run away from the real issues. Just as little as the churchmen in Jesus' day saw the problems of life where Jesus saw them, we today, too, fail to turn to the real needs where life hurts.

Man is not as yet what he is supposed to be. Jesus does not lecture the woman on sin. He trusts the power of openness to draw man onward in order that he find himself. We need not wallow in depravity. We can become sensitive to our potential. Jesus did not condemn the woman (v. 11). God sent his Son into the world to liberate the world, not to doom it (3:17). If this waiting of God on man does not bring change, nothing will. Confronted with openness, we ought to realize our possibility for new life. So all we have to be told is: "Sin no more" (v. 11).

Is this not an impossible demand, however? Sin is not an eternal reality. It is man's pseudocreation. Jesus' liberation curbs sin's power. He embodies a new direction of our destiny. And he announces the "dis-empowerment" of sin rather than the fact that we are sinners.

IMAGO FUTURI   8:12–20

[12] Again Jesus spoke to the people: "I am the light of the world. He who follows me shall not walk in darkness, but have the light of life." [13] The Pharisees said to him, "You are witness in your own case, your testimony is not valid." [14] Jesus replied, "Even if I witness in my own case, my testimony is valid because I know my origin and my destiny. You do not know my origin and my destiny. [15] You judge by outward standards, I judge no man. [16] If I do judge, my judgment is valid because I am not judging alone, but together with him who sent me. [17] In your law it is written that the testimony of two persons is valid. [18] Indeed, I am testify·

ing to myself, but the Father who sent me is the other witness."
[19] *They asked him, "Where is your Father?" Jesus replied, "You*
know my Father as little as you know me. If you knew me you
would also know my Father." [20] *Jesus spoke these words in the*
treasury as he taught in the temple. No one arrested him because
his hour had not yet come.

Who man is, is still concealed to him in his sin; he remains hidden man, *homo absconditus*. But in the confrontation with Jesus, manhood is uncovered for faith: "I am the
light of the world" (v. 12). We can now see at least where
we are going as men. We can understand ourselves as Adam
who is the type of the coming one (Rom. 5:14). This is more
clearly focused in I John: "It does not yet appear what we
shall be, but we know that when he appears we shall be like
him, for we shall see him as he is" (3:2). The man called
Jesus is the light of the world in that he opens a new future
for mankind. Man concealing himself is captive to a state of
gloom, darkness, even though he thinks of himself as pretty
white and full of light, having reached the enlightenment and
being able to come to grips with what it means to be a man.
Man's self-concealment expresses itself in the gloom of
the mind, in inner darkness. Sin is the gloom of self-concealment from God and fellowman in the privacy of the private
self. Following the one who lives unconcealed—in terms of
the basic dimensions of life—man will experience the *uncov-
ering of manhood* (v. 12). But this is not something that is
already complete. We are only beginning to take first steps in
this direction. Could we thus think of man as image of things
still to come, as image of the future, *imago futuri?*
Man concealed to himself does not know his origin and
destiny, and thus also not the origin and destiny of his neighbor. The white churchmen could not know from where Jesus

came and where he was going because they remained concealed to themselves. What Jesus knew was the openness of
man (v. 14). The truth of what he brings does not depend
on objectified white criteria, but on what is true in the life of
every man. Jesus' origin and destiny are also the origin and
destiny of every man. They should be self-evident without the
open man having to adduce further witness. In faith in the
man called Jesus we can at least sense what we can be as *imago
futuri*.

We usually judge the importance of a man's life externally, in keeping with white criteria of status (v. 15). We are
ignorant of man's inner certainty of himself as unconcealed.
We consider the value that grows out of illusory white thought
as ultimate truth. Jesus refused to judge by white standards of
illusion. If he judged at all, it was in terms of the truth that
manifests the real in every man.

According to Jewish law the testimony of two witnesses
verified a person's claim in legal matters (vv. 17 f.). Obviously we expect identification of one another, whether we apply for a job, run for an office, or fall in love. Identification
calls for character witnesses. But as to ultimate truth man
cannot be identified by other witnesses. Ultimate truth in one
man must be verified by ultimate truth in the fellowman. Ultimate truth is its own witness (v. 18).

Darkness, man's concealing of himself, does not want to
associate with light, open life. If man would know unconcealed manhood, he would also know God (v. 19). But men
hide themselves from the self-evident truth in the flesh and
blood of a fellowman. Whom should man know better than
man? But when faced with the openness of a fellowman,
man's darkness becomes exceedingly dark.

The rejection of the light took place in the temple.
Churchmen are especially blind to unconcealment as acknowl-

edged by Jesus. They long for the religious hero. Even so,
God's truth asserts itself even within the walls of the organization church. Man's hankering for religious glamor does not
have the last word (v. 20).

Sin and Death   8:21–30

21 Again Jesus said to them, "I am leaving and you will be
looking for me, and you will die in your sin. Where I am going
you cannot come." 22 The Jews wondered, "Does he want to com-
mit suicide because he says, 'Where I am going you cannot come'?"
23 He said to them, "You are from down here. I am from beyond.
You belong to this world, but not I. 24 I told you that you would
die in your sins. For if you cannot trust that I am who I am, you
will die in your sins." 25 Then they said, "Who are you?" Jesus
replied, "What is the use of talking to you? 26 I have much to say
about you and much to judge. But the one who sent me is true,
and I declare to the world what I learned from him." 27 They did
not grasp that he spoke to them of the Father. 28 So Jesus continued, "When you have lifted up the Son of Man, then you will
know that I am who I am, and that I do nothing on my own, but
communicate as my Father has taught me. 29 He who sent me is
with me. He never left me isolated, for I always do what conforms
to his will." 30 As he said this, many trusted him.

Man's self-inflicted fate is that he dies in his sin, his self-
concealment in privatism. Denying corporate life, he does not
acknowledge the light and dies either with the idea that after
death there is no future or that only judgment awaits him.
His life is not directed toward a future that would embody
corporate manhood. This is dying in sin (v. 21).

Jesus invites man to see his end not in the darkness of
finitude. He does not point to his own self as the ultimate.
He is "from beyond" and he points to the beyond: to transcendent freedom as the ultimate. Sinful men are "from down

here" (v. 23). The future of man as man's "beyond" in which
he finds fulfillment is not completely removed from man's
grasp, but it is not as yet identical with man. He can only
reflect it and thus be the *imago futuri*. But sinful man captive
to the "down here" of concealment in his pseudoworld does
not wish to reflect the future and so dies in his sin. Death is
for him his *telos*, his destiny. Since he wants to enjoy the
pleasure of the moment, he has no great interest in reflecting
the future.

"For if you cannot trust that I am who I am, you will
die in your sins" (v. 24). We know who man is in the one
who simply is who he is: the person called Jesus. It takes trust
to put confidence in a man who wants to be no more than he
is. This is not trust in the man Jesus as such, but in what he
embodies: God's waiting on man, transcendent freedom.
Whoever does not trust that God waits on him with transcendent freedom dies in his sin. For him death becomes the
ultimate (v. 24).

It is understandable that the organization churchmen are
puzzled (v. 25). In his response Jesus can only repeat what he
said. He is what he has told them all along. He is what he is
as corporate self, directing man toward a new future.

When men crucified Jesus they would know that for the
open man death was not ultimate. The incarnate corporate
self depends on a reality beyond itself. He never parted from
it. He always relied on it, responding to it in his every deed:
transcendent freedom. So sin is overcome at the point where
it is most blatant. Death is not man's real future (vv. 28 f.).
Death in disobedience to God is the final isolation, the ultimate surrender of man to his privatism. It is dying in sin.
Death with the eyes upon transcendent freedom is trust in the
prevailingness of the corporate self.

FREEDOM   8:31-40

³¹ Then Jesus told the Jews who trusted him, "If you continue to share my word, you are truly my disciples. ³² You will know the truth, and the truth will set you free." ³³ They answered, "We are Abraham's descendants. We have never been anybody's slaves. How can you say, 'You will be set free'?" ³⁴ "Believe me," Jesus replied, "every man who sins is a slave to sin. ³⁵ A slave does not belong to a family forever, but a son does. ³⁶ So if the Son liberates you, you will be free indeed. ³⁷ Of course, I know that you are Abraham's descendants, but you are planning to kill me because you cannot stand my words. ³⁸ I share what I saw in communion with my Father, and you are doing what you have learned from your father." ³⁹ They replied, "Abraham is our father." Jesus observed, "If you were Abraham's children you would do as Abraham did. ⁴⁰ But now you are planning to kill me, a man who has told you the truth he learned from God. Abraham never did that."

What makes man truly human is freedom. In the privacy of concealment man is in bondage. Only as he comes out of hiding (*a-lētheia*), into the truth of the corporate self, is he free.

Of his own accord man cannot be what it is possible for him to be. Only through sharing the Word of the open man does he have freedom (vv. 31 f.). Human freedom is not doing what one pleases but sharing in transcendent freedom. Man is free as he shares in the Word that mediates transcendent freedom.

We often think of freedom as our inherited and inalienable right. "We are Abraham's descendants" (v. 33). No one dare say that "the children of the Reformation" are not free, or "George Washington's children." But true freedom has nothing to do with a mechanical handing on of privileges and rights from generation to generation. We are enslaved to external status symbols of traditional freedoms that actually keep increasing our concealment. Clinging to traditional freedoms often brings about new bondage (vv. 34 f.).

Once man grasps corporate freedom he is on the way to becoming man. On his own, man remains in the state of concealment. It takes an act of liberation—responded to by faith —to unshackle us from our self-contradiction. Only through liberation from the concealment of privatism can we be set on the road to becoming human. This occurs in the unconcealed one who uncovers the new direction of our destiny toward a new future: "So if the Son liberates you, you will be free indeed" (v. 36). As for the *Reformation*, justification by faith was the interpretive key to the Christian life; for the *Liberation* today, liberation by the Son is the key. This is the core thought of the Fourth Gospel for our age. Man can only be grasped through the analogy of liberation (*analogia liberationis*), in accord with his liberation in Christ. Man is not something static, finished, but a process of ever-increasing freedom, a growth into greater freedom.

The white churchmen claiming to be Abraham's (Luther's, Calvin's, the Mayflower's, Wesley's) children think they are free as descendants of the white clan of freedom. But pride in inherited freedom is the opposite of true freedom. Accustomed to illusion, we cannot stand the one who in freedom embodies the Word (v. 37). God as transcendent freedom is offered in Jesus to all men, so that they can become what they are destined to be. But white churchmen prefer to turn to another freedom (v. 38).

All that the white churchmen could think of was that Abraham was their origin. Their freedom originated in the "father of their country," another evidence that men seek their "reality" in the sphere they can control. The center of life here lies in externals, represented by the sacred traditions. But these traditions do not justify perverted freedom. The white churchmen can't really claim Abraham as their father. Abraham, trusting God's Word, prefigured true freedom. While the text does not directly suggest it, may it not have been Abraham's openness to God's Word that kept him from killing his son? Nothing, however, could keep the white churchmen from killing the Son of Man (v. 40). But truly free men do not kill the fellowman. As long as man is ready to destroy the fellowman he is still enslaved, concealed in his manhood, *homo absconditus*.

THE THREAT TO FREEDOM   8:41–47

[41] "You are doing the works of your father." They retorted, "We were not born of adultery. We have one father, God." [42] Jesus replied, "If God were your father you would love me, for God is the origin of my life, and from him I come. I did not authorize myself; he commissioned me. [43] Why do you not understand my language? Because you cannot bear to listen to my words. [44] The devil is your father, and you long to act according to your father's desires. He always was a murderer and never shared in the truth, for there is no truth in him. When he tells a lie he expresses his very nature, for he is a liar and the father of lies. [45] Because I speak the truth you will not trust me. [46] Which of you can convict me of sin? If I speak the truth, why do you not trust me? [47] He who originates in God, can hear God's words. You do not originate in God; therefore you cannot hear them."

Loyal churchmen claim that Jesus is denying them God as their father (v. 41). But had they truly believed in God as their father, could they have hated a fellowman? God had commissioned this man to embody him (v. 42). Churchmen have a hard time understanding Jesus because they cannot see how God gives himself in the words of a man (v. 43).

The plan to kill a fellowman justifies the charge that the devil is the father of the shysters. The devil is the personification of man's evil, of his illusion and concealment. Evil from the beginning, he destroys corporateness. The Fourth Gospel does not explain the origin of the devil. It is enough to experience evil as constant threat to life and to realize that it is not part of unconcealed reality. Nothing of God is in it. It never had part in unconcealment. The personification of illusion does not belong to the good world. It has no origin, no created reality. It belongs nowhere (v. 44).

What underlies human rejection of freedom is metaphysical deception. In the devil, illusion becomes metaphysically personified. But actually this metaphysical evil has no share in created reality. When a lie is told, the true nature of the devil is divulged. A lie is the pretension of the unreal to be real, the attempt to conceal what cannot be concealed. The devil personifies the pretension of the lie. So he is called "the father of lies" (v. 44), that which fathers lies. He is all illusion which cannot be explained from anything but itself. Lacking created reality, it threatens the most really real: transcendent freedom overriding our illusory schemes of reality as necessity. The organization churchmen thought that "of necessity" they belonged to the clan of freedom, that no particular personal decision for freedom was required.

What is more, men are so used to illusion or camouflage that they cannot trust when someone appears on the human scene who does not lie, who lives unconcealed (v. 45). Here appears one who cannot be convicted of illusion, who lives openly who he is (v. 46). He does not put up a front or create an "image." Every man's sense for the counterself must finally help him decide whether this man embodies unconcealment or not. The man who finds his origin and the direction of human destiny acknowledged by Jesus understands Jesus' words

as God's presence. It is not the fulness of God, but an earnest
of the coming presence of God in which he will be all in all.

The free man acknowledges true reality as the corporate
self and unmasks unreality. And yet some do not wish to associate with him. They show how much true freedom remains
threatened by so-called necessity and death (v. 47).

THE GROUND OF FREEDOM   8:48–59

⁴⁸ *The Jews answered, "Are we not right in calling you a
Samaritan and insane as well?"* ⁴⁹ *Jesus said, "I am not insane. I
honor my Father, but you dishonor me.* ⁵⁰ *I am not a status-seeker.
There is someone who gives me status and judges me.* ⁵¹ *Believe
me, if someone obeys my word, he will not see death forever."*
⁵² *At this, the Jews said to him, "Now we know that you are insane! Why, Abraham died, and so did the prophets, and you say,
'If someone obeys my word, he will not experience death forever.'*
⁵³ *Are you greater than our father Abraham? He died, and the
prophets died. Who do you think you are?"* ⁵⁴ *Jesus answered, "If
I were seeking status, my status would be nothing. My Father
gives me status, the one you say is your God.* ⁵⁵ *You never knew
him. I know him. If I should say I do not know him, I should be
a liar like you. But I know him, and I obey his word.* ⁵⁶ *Abraham,
your father, rejoiced that he would see my coming. In fact, he saw
it and was glad."* ⁵⁷ *The Jews protested, "You are not even fifty,
and you have seen Abraham?"* ⁵⁸ *"Believe me," Jesus replied, "before Abraham was, I am."* ⁵⁹ *They picked up stones to throw at
him, but Jesus hid and left the temple.*

You are a "nigger" and crazy to boot! (v. 48). Men, unmasked as phonies, seek to discredit the truth. And how better to discredit it than to make its witness a nonperson. The
white churchmen assume that Jesus is selling himself just as
they would sell themselves. And what he seems to be selling
they do not like. But the man called Jesus was not at all selling

himself. He simply acts as the true man in terms of freedom. A man cannot produce true freedom, for it emerges out of the unconcealment of all things (v. 49).

The person who keeps the Word of him who roots himself in transcendent freedom will not see death (v. 51). If freedom is truly grasped, death cannot terminate man's life. Man in concert with Jesus Christ can point beyond death. Had Jesus said this to give himself status (v. 50), he would have been insane indeed. But he was pointing to the unconcealed reality of every man, the prevailing "pull" from the ground of freedom that beckons man toward a new direction of destiny. A person who shares in the Word of this new direction of life will not see death because he acknowledges his true self as the corporate self grounded in transcendent freedom (v. 51).

Once more men prove their ignorance of true life. Is Jesus greater than Abraham? (v. 53). Even Abraham died, the father of the Jews. Who does the man called Jesus pretend to be? Actually he is not pretending to be anyone. He does not need to. No man does. And yet, though man wants to be a somebody, he sees his self-granted status coming to an end in death. Man, however, cannot be real besides or beyond the reality which God provides for every man in equal measure. And this reaches beyond death. Jesus' reality as a man relies on no other status than the one he has before God (v. 54). It is exactly this reality in which his freedom is grounded as a freedom over death.

Because they cling to their world of pseudovalue, of illusory status, white churchmen cannot know God (v. 55). But Abraham, whom they consider their father also in death, looked forward to a different reality. He did not sacrifice his son and thus had a vision of true life, an *imago futuri* (v. 56; for contrast, see v. 40). The white churchmen misunderstand the point: "You are not even fifty, and you have seen Abraham?" (v. 57). In response, Jesus utters the bold words: "Before Abraham was, I am" (v. 58). Those who trust freedom in Jesus understand. The opportunity for man to experience freedom from death existed before Abraham: "In him was life, and life was the light of men" (1:4). The life Jesus embodies is the freedom from death in every man's life. Gripped by its power, Abraham could see Jesus' day and rejoice. Already Abraham could witness to the new direction of human destiny.

UNBLINDING REASON 9:1–41

¹ As he walked along Jesus saw a man blind from birth. ² His disciples wondered, "Rabbi, did this man sin or his parents that he was born blind?" ³ Jesus answered, "Neither this man, nor his parents sinned. His blindness affords an opportunity to embody God's works. ⁴ While it is day we must carry out the works of him who commissioned me. Night comes when no man can work. ⁵ While I am in the world I am the light of the world." ⁶ Having said this he spat on the ground. He mixed the saliva with clay and spread it on the man's eyes. ⁷ "Go," he said, "wash in the pool of Siloam" (which means "sent"). The man left, washed, and came back seeing.

⁸ His neighbors and others who had seen him before as a beggar asked, "Is not he the one who used to sit and beg?" ⁹ Some said, "That is him!" He himself said, "It is me all right." ¹⁰ So they asked, "How were your eyes opened?" ¹¹ He answered, "The man called Jesus mixed clay, spread it on my eyes and told me, 'Go to Siloam and wash.' I went and washed, and I could see again." ¹² They asked him, "Where is he?" "I do not know," he replied.

¹³ They brought the man who had been blind before the Pharisees. ¹⁴ It was Sabbath when Jesus mixed the clay and opened

his eyes. ¹⁵ The Pharisees, too, asked how his eyes had been opened. He said to them, "He spread a paste of clay on my eyes, I washed, and now I can see." ¹⁶ Some of the Pharisees remarked, "This is not a man of God because he does not observe the Sabbath." Others said, "How can a sinner do such signs?" They were divided over him.

¹⁷ Turning to the blind man again they asked, "What do you say about him? You are the one whose eyes he opened." He answered, "He is a prophet." ¹⁸ The Jews would not believe that he had been blind and now received his sight until they called his parents ¹⁹ and asked them, "Is he your son who you say was born blind? Why can he see now?" ²⁰ His parents replied, "He is our son; he was born blind all right, ²¹ but we have no idea how he can now see, or who opened his eyes. Ask him. He is old enough to speak for himself." ²² His parents fed the Jews this line because they were afraid of them, for the Jews had already agreed that anyone who acknowledged Jesus as the Christ would be excommunicated. ²³ That is why his parents said, "Ask him. He is old enough."

²⁴ They again summoned the man who had been born blind and said to him, "Praise God by being honest! We know that this man is a sinner." ²⁵ He answered, "I do not know whether he is a sinner, but one thing I know for sure, once I was blind, now I can see." ²⁶ They asked him, "What did he do to you? How did he open your eyes?" ²⁷ He replied, "I have told you already, and you did not listen. Why do you want to hear it again? Do you also want to become his disciples?" ²⁸ Then they railed against him and said, "You are his disciple. We are the disciples of Moses. ²⁹ We know that God spoke to Moses, but we do not know where this man comes from."

³⁰ The man replied, "This is the amazing thing, you do not know where he comes from, and yet he opened my eyes. ³¹ We all know that God does not listen to sinners. But if there is someone who is committed to God and obeys his will, God listens to him. ³² It is unheard of since the world began that someone opened the eyes of a man born blind. ³³ If this man were not from God

he could have done nothing." ³⁴ "You are completely born in sin, and you want to teach us?" they answered. Then they threw him out. ³⁵ Jesus heard that they had excommunicated the man, and when he found him he asked, "Do you trust the Son of Man?" ³⁶ He wondered, "Who is he, sir? I would like to trust him." ³⁷ Jesus said, "You have seen him. He is speaking to you." ³⁸ He said, "Lord, I trust," and knelt before him.

³⁹ Jesus said, "My coming has been the verdict on history: That the blind see and those who see are blinded." ⁴⁰ Some Pharisees near him heard this and asked, "Do you mean to say that we are blind?" ⁴¹ Jesus answered, "If you were blind you would be free from sin; but because you claim, 'We see,' your sin remains."

Homo absconditus! Hidden man! We are blind to who we are. We are not the image of God. And we can open ourselves to a new future of man only if our reason is unblinded. The unblinding of the boy born blind must be viewed as part of Jesus' entire mission: "My coming has been the verdict on history: That the blind see and those who see are blinded" (v. 39). The event of the unblinding of the boy is also a sign of liberation, of freedom not remaining abstract but becoming concrete in the public space of a new relationship. A story is taking place here that takes in more than one or two men. Bystanders appear, questioning the liberation, wanting to control the event, callous to its real meaning. The point of the story is found in the total occurrence.

In the man Jesus we see walls broken down, between men, in man himself, and between man and God. If we consider ourselves we note helplessness, in fact, utter blindness to our condition. I am the blind man. "I that am blind, cry out against my blindness" (Vachel Lindsay). Around me are those who claim my humanity, who claim to know who I am, what I ought to do. Our society is racist, and I participate in its racism. I hear the accusation that I am a whitey, that I had better revolutionize church and society, or else I have no right to be regarded human. Our society reeks of militarism. I share in its worship of Mars. I pay taxes. I, too, pulled the trigger at My Lai. I, too, am guilty of the death of Vietnamese peasants. There is no way out of my involvement in corporate guilt. I very well hear the demand that I should demonstrate, picket, and go to jail. But I am blind. Our society is oppressive. I hear very well that I should quote Marcuse and Roszak and Harrington. The white churchmen today appear in all kinds of disguises, even as blacks, demanding obedience to new laws and criteria of manhood. I know what I should do. But I am blind. Around me, too, gather the curious, the powerful, and the callous. What they see is premised on their confidence that they think they see. They say they "see." They know exactly what I should do, how I should behave, and what I should say. I know I should make the world perfect. But—I just can't.

Somehow there seems to be no human predicament for those who "see," for the "knowers." In Christian theology the issue has been discussed time and again as the tension between revelation and reason. It often has been solved by asserting that reason can "see" for a good distance, but that at a certain point revelation takes over. Somehow implied in the concept of revelation is the idea that God is principally hidden to man and must come out of hiding in revelation. But this is a strange misconception. It is sin that blinds man to God's unconcealment, to his presence as light that illumines man in his reason. The revelation that needs to take place is nothing but the *unblinding of reason*, so that a person can truly "see" the direction of his destiny. Man's blindness, not God's hiding, is the problem. And man's blindness is the problem especially in the confidence that he "sees" what ought to be, and what the criteria are for being human.

Jesus' appearance in history creates a crisis. Men find themselves now in two camps, the blind and those who think they see. Does this not contradict his basic intention? Did he not come to unite mankind? He certainly did not appear in order to offer some vague togetherness. The point of his coming is the verdict on history: those who think they see believe they can come to grips with life apart from God's liberation and thus exclude themselves from the true unity of all men. Only those who admit that their reason must be unblinded and who see with the eyes of faith what the boy born blind saw with his physical eyes, free manhood in Jesus, truly see.

Jesus heals the man on the Sabbath contrary to the Sabbath laws. The white churchmen "know" what the Sabbath laws are for. And they "know" that a person who disturbs law and order is a sinner. Their religious code is more important to them than the healing of a person.

In confrontation with Jesus what becomes important is seeing the free man. Although we often would like to know who Jesus is "metaphysically," we too have to be content with knowing what the boy born blind knew: "I do not know whether he is a sinner, but one thing I know for sure, once I was blind, now I can see" (v. 25). What counts is to know the shape of Jesus' life. To Jesus' opponents this does not amount to anything. His public status is obscure (v. 29). But before God only the doing of his will gives status. Jesus is obeying God's will embodying his works (v. 3). He liberates man as he embodies transcendent freedom alleviating suffering. This does not give an answer to the question: Why suffering? (v. 2). But in liberating those who suffer man "knows" the answer in action. Only in concrete experience of the corporate self will the intellectual wrestle come to rest. The opportunity afforded by Jesus to find a new grasp of oneself must be used (v. 4). In liberating man, man's true condition is unconcealed. Thus Jesus is the light of the world (v. 5).

"My coming has been the verdict on history: That the blind see" (v. 39). The blind see what the blind man saw when his eyes were opened: Jesus, a man waiting on man. Nothing more. To see manhood unconcealed in Jesus is what counts. Jesus told the healed man that he had seen the Son of Man. The man trusted. And whom did he trust? God himself waiting on suffering man in Jesus, liberating man for true life. God is the ultimate subject of trust.

Since the churchmen claim to see, their sin remains (v. 41). Captive to illusion, they presume life to be transparent to them. Can the real point of life consist in the waiting of a nobody on a nobody? But God's criteria are different. Those who trust their external criteria of success exclude themselves from humanity as it is unconcealed and remain separate from eternal life. Unwilling to acknowledge corporate selfhood, their sin remains. "If you were blind you would be free from sin" (v. 41). Only those who do not pretend to see are ready for true manhood.

> I am unjust, but I can strive for justice.
> My life's unkind, but I can vote for kindness.
> I, the unloving, say life should be lovely.
> I that am blind, cry out against my blindness.
>
> —Vachel Lindsay

AT THE INTERSECTION OF ANTHROPOLOGY AND CHRISTOLOGY

With the emphasis on *unblinding reason* a massive continental shift is taking place right now in theology, a moving away from the hang-ups of modern man to an identification with oppressed man. The movement is away from thinking white to thinking black. White theologians have never taken a good look at themselves in the mirror since Puritan days.

For generations, theology in the United States has assumed that its basic landmarks remain fixed. No longer so. Whirl is king. What becomes clearer and clearer is that the sure image man had of himself has been eroding. And whatever of the old image is still around must go: *our image of man must go.*

In this regard theology is compelled to dig down to bedrock, to begin over again at the beginnings and to consider what the foundations were and what they still might be for us. Here theology needs to be involved in *storytelling,* trying to retell one story of the Gospel after the other in order to discover something of the bedrock of faith. The one who retells the story must view himself as a "poet," that is, he must be creative as well as faithful to the original. It is like translating a poem from another language. The original must still be there, and yet it must be there in another form!

In the retelling Jesus appears as the counterself, the true self, the open man. One has to understand this primally, for example, in terms of John 9:39–41. The remark refers of course to the healing of the boy born blind who represents mankind. Man does not as yet see what he is supposed to become. But we white churchmen have claimed that we see. And we have promulgated an image of man that is supposed to give us direction. It is exactly this hybris that has led us astray. And so Jesus must first of all be appreciated by us as the verdict on history: that the blind are unblinded and those who see are blinded.

We modern theologians have said: we see. We know who modern man is. He is the steersman of the cosmos, "the point where the cosmos begins to think and to steer itself" (Cox). Man has begun to understand life and to control it in technology. Along comes David Rockefeller at Senate hearings concerned with poverty in the ghetto and claims: "As a banker, I invest money in order to make money; and if you want private enterprise to go into the slums, you have got to make it profitable." So what is left when the cosmos begins to steer itself? Rockefeller's kind of reasoning. We theologians, of course, still have some pragmatic inhibitions. But truly secular men have long drawn out the consequences of Cox's steersman principle. The exploiter image of man is the real referend of theological concern, even if only for making the writing of theological books profitable. If the theologian got into the slums he was writing about—again it was to make his work profitable. There is a remarkable passage in William Styron's book on Nat Turner, clarifying our white problem. After Nat's master has sold some slaves in order to salvage his farm with the money received in return, he cries out: "Surely mankind has yet to be born. *Surely* this is true! For only something blind and uncomprehending could exist in such a mean conjunction with its own flesh, its own kind. How else account for such faltering, clumsy, hateful cruelty? Even the possums and the skunks know better! . . . In the name of money! *Money!*" Underlying the profiteering is an image of man that today is still being promoted also by the church. This image of man must go.

There has been a hardening of man's self-image as exploiter. Probably many influences have shaped the present image. At the core today is perhaps a fusion of the Puritan and the Cartesian. But the principle of the fusion seems nothing new. In the context of theological thought in the New Testament, we are also confronted with such a hardened self-image of man. The man called Jesus appears on the scene to confront this self-image. Jesus is the Christ (and thus Christology begins) because he meets man with the offer of a new self.

Christian anthropology and Christology *intersect* at this

point. In fact, Christian anthropology is merely the other side of the coin of Christology. As we talk about man's self we also need to take into account the counterself. This must be understood in terms of John 9:39–41. This self is the verdict on history, the judgment on corrupted human selfhood. Jesus did not bring all the conditions the Christ was expected to bring in terms of the fantasizing about the future of Israel. But as the counterself he gave a nonecclesiastical interpretation of the Messiah. His self-offering in confrontation with the white churchmen of his day became the primal Christological stumbling block. Man as a prideful white self is not concerned about a new self. And as a *religious* white self he is mainly concerned about building up a glorified self that he can use as escape mechanism from his social responsibility—which happened in part in the development of Christological dogma. Christ against culture as liberator of culture stands at the beginning of Christology, not the "acculturated" Christ. If we forget John 3, the motif of the liberation of consciousness, then as we get to John 6 and John 9, we cannot develop an adequate contemporary Christology or anthropology. What is at stake in the new selfhood Jesus confronts us with is radical freedom that can liberate us from the ironclad necessity in which we are caught. At its core lies transcendent freedom, not just abstract otherness. The real Christological and anthropological issue is how transcendent freedom and human freedom can be fused.

The difficulty arising in many contemporary Christologies lies at the point where it is assumed that what is necessary is merely a rearranging of the metaphysical or doctrinal "toys." But that is a cop-out. What is here assumed is what can be assumed the least: that man in his present state can be the *measure* of who God and Christ are. The Christ-event in the New Testament is first of all a radical questioning of all of man's self-images. God liberates: this is the sum of the Fourth Gospel. Of course, we must ask: liberates from what? The answer is: first of all from a false image of man.

It is exactly this insight which is not a matter of course. We must protest that too many theologians today assume that their presuppositions—ontological, epistemological, hermeneutical, etc.—are just fine, unquestionable, drawn from some modern world view or some critique of the modern world view—without ever looking at themselves as political and economic beings. The ease with which the liberal and neoliberal theologians assume to know who we are—secular men!—is difficult to take. All we need to do, it seems, is to adjust God and Christ to secular manhood!

A case in point is the Christology of John A. T. Robinson which is widely accepted among liberals and neoliberals in America as standard truth. From the perspective of our present black/white confrontation in theology, we can see how on Robinson's grounds the theological enterprise is grinding more and more to a halt. On several levels one can be quite sympathetic with the dilemmas Robinson sees. But without taking a good hard look at man's self-image the melancholy over these dilemmas is to no avail.

If we look at contemporary man's view of himself in the light of the biblical story we need to take one particular difficulty into account, one that has not as yet been mentioned. Besides liberalism and neoliberalism there is still a strong current of fundamentalism around in this country. The general reaction of the young college-trained religionist is to reject it as irrelevant. So he turns to religious-language analysis, all the while still assuming, however—unconsciously, that is—the basic fundamentalist posture toward the biblical categories. All that needs to be done, he thinks, is to interpret these categories in terms of the more epistemological framework of religious language. But the real problem is that fundamentalism misunderstood the biblical categories in the first place. They are not at all significant in themselves. The story to which they point must be recaptured. Here lies the theological difficulty. Part of the task of liberation theology is to smash the misconstrued biblical categories of fundamentalism relative to a new image of man, so that God's story can break through.

In principle, the struggle against liberalism/neoliberalism and fundamentalism is the same. What we are up against we can briefly specify in regard to John A. T. Robinson. In a November, 1970, *Christian Century* article he claims that Christ is the one who says that men's attitude to him will determine God's attitude to them. He is "God's representative, called to stand in God's place. He does not assume identity with God, but he desires to represent God: he claims to be sent by God as his representative." This is interpreted to mean: "A representative is one who keeps your place *open*. What Christ the representative does is to hold God's place open, to enable man to believe and hope in the unrealized transcendent possibilities. And the church in turn exists to hold the world open for God." In summing up the new Christology, Robinson is quite plain as to what results on these premises: "The realization is fitfully dawning that 'God' now means, for us, not an invisible Being with whom we can have direct communication on the end of the telephone, but *that by which he is represented*, his surrogate—the power of a love that lives and suffers for others." Robinson's Christology does not want to eliminate God. It wants to say: Christ is the one who holds the world open for God. But man, too, can hold the world open for God. Again, God becomes quite manageable. What does it mean: to keep the world open for God? Is God not able to keep the world open for himself and for us? Is not man here again producing God as the *imago hominis,* the image of man? Here is no otherness, no judgment under which he stands. "God is made dependent on man and man's response." According to Robinson, it seems any man would agree to this Christology, consent to its truth, if only properly explicated. This is a primal mistake. All the enterprise amounts to is some rearranging of the metaphysical "toys" with no horror over man's corruption.

The basic flaw in the neoliberal presupposition is that man's inability to grasp Christ lies in poor Christ's inadequate adjustment to the modern world view. But Jesus did not at all introduce himself in terms of a mythological event that would have to be rearranged. One of the first things Matthew says about him is: "And he went about all Galilee, teaching in their synagogues and preaching the gospel of the kingdom and healing every disease and every infirmity among the people" (Mt. 4:23). The issue of grasping Jesus as the Christ on the primal level is not at all a problem of the modern world view, but of man's persistent corruption of his self. Jesus is the Christ because he brings a new self: he is the liberator of man's every disease and infirmity. This presents the *difficulty* of appreciating the man called Jesus.

John 3:3 must be taken with utter seriousness: "No man can see the kingdom of God unless he becomes black." No naive conversionism is involved, but a radically different perspective of thought: a grasp of the corporate self, *seeing* the wretched of the earth, experiencing the *unblinding of reason.* Robinson bases his Christology on an utterly unexamined self. He takes for granted that so-called modern man is the proper self that can appreciate the Christ.

The turning from the private modern self to the corporate self will not come easy. It will take, for instance, an examination of the history of selfhood in the last three hundred years of Western civilization. Tawney points out that individualism "became the rule of English public life a century

before the philosophy of it was propounded by Adam Smith."
In the older medieval view man had been related to the church
"in a mystical corporation, knit together by mutual obliga-
tions," so that no man could press his private advantage to the
full. This is also the perspective of the Old Testament. Hebrew
faith was a corporate faith in every respect. In Puritan economy things gradually came to be viewed differently. It was
understood as an undeniable maxim "that everyone by the
light of nature and reason will do that which makes for his
greatest advantage. . . . The advancement of private persons
will be the advantage of the public." No longer was the social
character of wealth understood. In fact, according to Tawney
the whole theology of the poor had to be changed: "A society
which reverences the attainment of riches as the supreme fe-
licity will naturally be disposed to regard the poor as damned
in the next world, if only to justify itself for making their life
a hell in this." In the words of Karl Marx, the dissolution of
the medieval bonds between man and man "left remaining
no other bond between man and man than naked self-interest
and callous cash payment." The person determined by naked
self-interest and callous cash payment is a peculiar kind of self:
the private self that cannot understand the Gospel. Not a
wrong world view is the obstacle, but a wrongheaded view of
the self.

This of course can be said only from within the context
of a particular community. The self is not self without being
self-in-community. The real difficulty for the Protestant theologian today—whether he be black or white—is that the Christian church has become disincarnate or Gnostic. For this reason we need to covenant anew, so that talk about the corporate self does not remain private. Here the inevitability of the
liberation church becomes evident. The "anthropological"
premise for the realization of the liberation church is the unblinding of reason.

NOT AS A STRANGER   10:1–42

Recognizing the Free Man   10:1–6

 1 "Believe me, he who does not enter the sheepfold by the gate, but climbs in somewhere else is a thief and a robber. 2 He who enters by the gate is the shepherd of the sheep. 3 The gatekeeper opens the gate for him, and the sheep recognize his voice; he calls his own sheep by name, and leads them out. 4 After he has driven out all his sheep he goes ahead, and the sheep follow him because they know his voice. 5 They will not follow a stranger, but will run away from him, because they do not recognize the voice of strangers." 6 This was a parable Jesus told them, but they did not get the point.

In parabolic language the passage speaks of sheep in a fold and a gate. The shepherd enters by the gate while thieves climb over the fence and steal. The sheep recognize only the shepherd. While all this made immediate sense in the pastoral societies in the time of the Fourth Gospel we at least should have no difficulty getting the message, even though we are far removed from the pastoral mood.

Continuing to be hidden to ourselves, in the man called Jesus we are unblinded and behold the open direction of our manhood. Here we learn who we truly are. The *homo absconditus* is confronted by the *homo liber*, the free man. Those who sense free manhood in Jesus gladly follow him. This is not to say that Jesus is no stranger to us *as a historical figure*. Albert Schweitzer's dictum remains incontrovertible: "Jesus as a concrete historical personality remains a stranger to our time." We cannot grasp the motives of his actions within the framework of Jewish eschatology. But we are invited, in terms of the Fourth Gospel, to grasp God's liberation in him, the voice and the word that lead us to the gate of freedom, in spite of our sheeplike stubbornness. God's liberation of man we can grasp: a process of freedom has begun among men. Jesus does not merely make us ask the question: who is this man? He also compels us to ask: who is God in this man? Confronted with God's liberation in Jesus men can confess that Jesus encounters them not as a stranger, but as the one who gives them true identity: he calls them by name (v. 3)— by their true selfhood.

SHARING FREE MANHOOD   10:7–18

⁷ Again Jesus said, "Believe me, I am the gate to the sheepfold. ⁸ All who preceded me are thieves and robbers, but the sheep would not obey them. ⁹ I am the gate. If a man enters through me he will be freed. He will move about freely and find food. ¹⁰ The thief comes only to steal and kill and destroy. I have come that they may have life, the truly full life. ¹¹ I am the good shepherd. A good shepherd risks his life for the sheep. ¹² The hired man, who is not a shepherd and does not own the sheep, deserts them and runs away when he sees the wolf coming. The wolf seizes and scatters them. ¹³ The man flees because he is a hired man and cares nothing for the sheep.

¹⁴ "I am the good shepherd. I know my own and my own know me, ¹⁵ as the Father knows me and I know the Father. I sacrifice my life for the sheep. ¹⁶ I have other sheep that are not of this fold. I must bring them also, and they will obey my voice. Then there will be one flock, one shepherd. ¹⁷ The Father loves me because I sacrifice my life to receive it back. ¹⁸ No one has taken it from me, but I sacrifice it of my own accord. I have the power to sacrifice it, and I have the power to receive it back. This is the order I have received from my Father."

Free manhood is not privatistic enjoyment of the self, but involvement in corporate selfhood. "Entering" through the free man to humanity we find the black (and the red) as neighbor, and vice versa. Man is not man without the black (and the red). Those who come apart from the free man to liberate man only conceal him all the more from his true selfhood, stealing it, as it were (vv. 7 f.).

Jesus is the entrance to the true self. Entering into true selfhood is what should come most naturally to man. The sheepfold is not a restrictive enclosure, but a public space for freedom and fulfillment in a common life. There is no better "pasture" for man's spirit than sharing in the corporate self (v. 9). The one who walks through this entrance (gate) to others finds as much as he gives. He finds that free manhood has already reached the black and the red, the Mexican-American and the Vietnamese, long before he reaches them. Every man has already been reached by corporate selfhood. What . he still lacks is that his eyes be unblinded, so that he can see it.

The free man is not only the "gate" of freedom, but also the shepherd. Not only does his disciple go through him to the wretched of the earth, but the free man has reached them long before the disciple tries to reach them. Those who try to help others to liberate themselves apart from the free man do not show real concern. They are like the hired man who cares little for what is entrusted to his keeping (vv. 12 f.). The free man risks his life for men. In him God himself risks his life. Since God is no stranger to the free man, the free man is no stranger to the one who trusts. The shepherd is known by his own because he radically risks his life for them. And by the risking of his life they also know God (vv. 14 f.).

The fold of the free man is wider than those who already belong to him. His sheep are all those wretched of the earth who do not claim that they can liberate themselves. Wherever they are, he also gathers them. They are the "poor" and the "poor in spirit" everywhere who hunger and thirst after righteousness. They gladly hear the message of liberation. The free man gathers them more and more into a common grasp of unconcealment (v. 16).

Here the basic character of Christian missions is determined. It is not an attempt to impose strange dogmas upon other men not Christian, but the radical risk of sharing corporate selfhood with the wretched of the earth. As a consequence, Christian missions are as much receiving as giving. Mission is always outreach to the wretched lest we forget who the man called Jesus is. It is not at all conversion of "primitives" to a "civilized" way of life or of heathen to the Christian religion, but the surrender of the private middle-class self.

Jesus does not bring a new religion, but the experience of corporate selfhood. Faith in Jesus over the centuries has of course also been institutionalized as a religion, the Christian religion. But this is not what distinguishes his "sheep." Religions are basically very much alike. They are man's way of making a profit from his sense of transcendence, sanctioning the status quo of exploitation with the divine. In this respect the Christian religion can claim nothing unique over other religions. Unique in Christianity is only Jesus as the free man identifying with the wretched of the earth and compelling his "sheep" to do the same through him.

In liberating men, Jesus offers them a fulfillment of life they cannot find in the organization church, the religious fold. It takes a new covenanting for free manhood to experience the fulfillment. Jesus risking his life for free manhood seals this risk in his death and opens men for a new direction of destiny.

In the risking of his life the free man does not lose himself. In fact, in the very giving of his life lies the empowerment of receiving it back. He gives his life for others in order not to lose it. Thus we see God's very own selfhood. It is the selfhood of unoppressed life (vv. 17 f.).

Ultimate Corporateness   10:19–30

¹⁹ Again the Jews were divided over him because of these words. ²⁰ Many of them said, "A demon got a hold of that man, he is mad! Why listen to him?" ²¹ Others said, "A madman would not talk like that; besides, can a demon open the eyes of the blind?" ²² At that time the Dedication festival was being held in Jerusalem. It was winter, ²³ and Jesus was walking in the temple precincts, in Solomon's cloister. ²⁴ The Jews surrounded him and said, "How long are you going to keep us in suspense? If you are really the Christ, say so!" ²⁵ Jesus replied, "I have told you, but you do not trust. What I do in response to my Father's being proves my claim, ²⁶ but you do not trust me because you do not belong to my sheep. ²⁷ My sheep obey my voice and I know them. They follow me, ²⁸ and I give them prevailing life. They shall never get lost, and no man can snatch them out of my hand. ²⁹ My Father who has entrusted them to me is greater than all, and no one can snatch them out of my Father's hand. ³⁰ I and the Father are one."

For the ecclesiastical establishment Jesus remains an offense. And if he does not offend it, he certainly continues to confound it. To some Jesus seems insane. Others are touched by his words (cf. 7:45–52) and begin to question the insinuation that he is out of his mind. But they also do not really grasp his significance (vv. 19–21). The organization church always has a hunch that the human condition ought to be changed. Some wonder about the Christ who is to transform the human condition (v. 24). But a Christ who waits on man seems irrelevant.

Jesus can only point to his deeds. They are the evidence of what his mission is all about. He asks that *they* be taken seriously, and not some fuzzy ecclesiastical doctrine. His deeds are in keeping with the ultimately real (v. 25). They give expression to the ultimate.

The ecclesiastics, however, presume to possess criteria by which to judge claims of ultimacy. Since they think they "see," they are suspicious of everything that does not fit their mold of truth. Only those who do not claim to see, the wretched of the earth, can appreciate what Jesus has to offer (v. 27). Responding to him they find new life. Participating in him they will never be severed from lasting life (v. 28), since through Jesus they are ingrafted into corporate selfhood (v. 29).

"I and the Father are one" (v. 30). This is the most awesome claim thus far in the Fourth Gospel. But in the light of what has gone on before faith might grasp what it involves. In the man called Jesus we find corporate selfhood. Jesus does whatever God does. So corporate selfhood is not merely a matter of historical or human reality, but of ultimate reality. In the concerted action of Father and Son ultimate reality is unconcealed. For faith it makes sense to act in terms of corporate selfhood identifying with the wretched of the earth because this is the most ultimate to which man can relate. It is the corporate selfhood to which Jesus has appealed all along: "The Father loves the Son and has put him in charge of all things" (3:35). Who man is must always be measured by this ultimate truth. What Jesus is reported as claiming is not a matter for fantasizing in metaphysical speculation, but a challenge to hammer out man's very being in the vicissitudes of his wretchedness. Only in identification with the wretched of the earth will a man understand that the Father and the Son are one.

Doing Theology   10:31–42

³¹ The Jews again picked up stones to stone him. ³² But Jesus told them, "I have shown you many good deeds wrought by the Father. For which of them would you stone me?" ³³ The Jews

retorted, "We are not going to stone you for a good deed, but for blasphemy because you, a mere man, make yourself God." [34] Jesus replied, "Is it not written in your law, 'I said, you are gods'? [35] If those are called gods who shared God's Word (and the Scripture cannot be annulled), [36] why do you say of him whom the Father has ordained and sent into the world, 'You are blaspheming,' because he said, 'I am God's Son'? [37] If I do not act as my Father does do not trust me. [38] But if I do, even if you do not trust me, trust the deeds, so that you may know and understand that the Father is in me and I am in the Father." [39] Again they tried to seize him, but he escaped them [40] and withdrew once more across the Jordan to the place where John first used to baptize. There he stayed. [41] Many people went out to him and said, "John did no sign, but what he said about this man was true." [42] Many of them trusted him there.

In the man called Jesus we see how true manhood functions. Part of true manhood is "doing theology." Unfortunately, theology has time and again become the arcane science of the privileged class of men called theologians, who justify God on paper or declare him dead—also on paper. What God is all about one learns, however, only by what man in Christ is all about. And what man in Christ is all about we discover by *doing* theology.

God, time and again, is thought of as "the wholly other." But Jesus embodied him—doing theology. Thus he also showed who man is: the being created for doing theology. His life calls for a poetic act, for seeing reality from a new and creative perspective and liberating it.

When the organization churchmen want to stone Jesus for his offensive claim, he appeals to his deeds. They were unconcealed deeds. The ecclesiastics say they would not stone him for his deeds, but for the way he interprets them: "You, a mere man, make yourself God" (v. 33). Apparently they can think of a man's deeds only in terms of status-seeking. What is more, God for them seems no more than the barren absolute, so that corporate selfhood as ultimate reality must appear senseless. A man who seeks to free his neighbor from the bondage of oppression is too insignificant to show who God is. The Absolute or the Holy would hardly appear in human form, and certainly not in a man identifying with human wretchedness. A holy man from Qumran might have been more convincing. But, then, ecclesiastics do not expect theology to be done at all. It is to be shelved away in books.

The free man appeals to Psalm 82:6: "I say, you are gods." He affirms that human life, as it were, embodies God whenever it embodies God's Word. Man *can* incarnate God's being if he responds to the Word of ultimate destiny. Should it be so astounding that the man who fully responds to God's Word regards himself as God's Son? (v. 36) Who man is becomes clear whenever he "does God." And how else can he do it than by identifying with the wretched of the earth through Jesus, the free man?

Men sharing in the *sensus communis*, the common sense of truth, should know the free man by his deeds. Here they see the reality at work that also makes them "tick." Jesus as God's true Son is no stranger to man. Men who try to grant each other being by granting each other status are offended when confronted by the free man. But they need not look for ultimate fulfillment beyond him. The ultimate is not beyond man. Its presence among men is witnessed to in the man Jesus (vv. 37 f.).

The Word was embodied in the flesh, so that men would take manhood seriously in the flesh. Jesus appeared in history not for the purpose of proving a supernatural God, but for making man cherish his manhood as constituted by transcendent freedom. God no man sees. "God's unique Son, the

Father's most intimate, has made him concrete" (1:18). Trust knows that it dare grasp the ultimate *in man*, in the incarnation of the Son, in the shape of his deed, as freedom become concrete. "Many trusted him there" (v. 42). Trusting the doing of theology in Jesus, men behold who they are: beings destined to make freedom prevail.

THE INCARNATE RESURRECTION   11:1–57

No Funeral Director   11:1–16

¹ A man named Lazarus was ill. He came from Bethany, the village of Mary and her sister Martha. ² Lazarus was the brother of the same Mary who poured perfume upon the Lord and wiped his feet with her hair. ³ The sisters sent a message to Jesus, "Sir, the one you love is ill." ⁴ When he heard this he said, "This illness is not for death to triumph, but for the glory of God, so that the Son of God may be glorified thereby." ⁵ Jesus loved Martha, her sister, and Lazarus. ⁶ But when he heard that Lazarus was ill he stayed where he was for two days. ⁷ Only then did he say to his disciples, "Let us go back to Judea." ⁸ The disciples said, "Rabbi, just recently the Jews wanted to stone you, and you go there again?" ⁹ Jesus answered, "Are there not twelve hours daylight every day? As long as a man walks in daylight he does not stumble, for he has the light of this world to go by. ¹⁰ But if he walks at night he stumbles, because he lacks light."

¹¹ After these words he added, "Our friend Lazarus has fallen asleep, but I shall go there to wake him." ¹² The disciples said, "Lord, if he has fallen asleep he will recover." ¹³ Jesus had spoken of his death, but they thought he meant natural sleep. ¹⁴ Then Jesus made it quite plain to them, "Lazarus is dead. ¹⁵ For your sake I am glad I was not there, so that you may trust. Now let us go to him." ¹⁶ Thomas, called the Twin, told his fellow disciples, "Let us also go and die with him."

To be a man is not only "to do God," but also "to do the resurrection." Manhood is not to cast itself upon the absolute outside itself, but to acknowledge in itself every dimension of transcendence and future that religion otherwise objectifies as being outside of man. The liberation of man for free manhood involves man's seeing himself as the focus of life and new life here and now.

The way the story is told it does not appear strange that Jesus does not rush to his friend to save him or, at least, to be present at his funeral (v. 6). Also this incident shows who God and his Son really are (v. 4). Jesus' function is not to worship death, but to celebrate life. He is not sentimental about the fact of death. In Matthew and Luke he is reported to have said: "Leave the dead to bury their own dead" (Mt. 8:22; Lk. 9:60). Death, in Jesus' sphere of influence, is not an occasion for pomp and circumstance. If the Christian religion approves the death business, lavish funerals with ministers in the supportive role, it certainly does not find any sanction in Jesus.

"Our friend Lazarus has fallen asleep, but I shall go there to wake him" (v. 11). No one will benefit from believing in the raising of Lazarus just because he likes to believe in miracles. Lazarus' resurrection is not told for feeding credulity. It summons to a new freedom, a new lifestyle. It does not answer all questions about life after death. In fact, it raises several unanswerable questions.

Lazarus' resurrection occurs within the context of Jesus' way to the cross (v. 16). Its meaning cannot be grasped apart from Jesus' death. It shows what Jesus attained by his freedom of waiting on man even in his death. Lazarus' resurrection is one more occasion to show the purpose of God's embodiment in Jesus (v. 4).

This chapter is not only formally the center of the Fourth

Gospel in its present form, with ten chapters preceding and ten following it. It also holds materially the key to the whole story. One man speaks of himself as the resurrection and the life, and calls another man back to life.

Neither Dust nor Superman   11:17–31

17 When Jesus arrived he found that Lazarus had already been four days in the grave. 18 Bethany was not even two miles from Jerusalem. 19 Many of the Jews had come to condole with Martha and Mary over their brother's death. 20 Martha, having heard that Jesus was coming, went to meet him, but Mary stayed home. 21 Martha said to Jesus, "Sir, had you been here, my brother would not have died. 22 Even now I know that God will grant you whatever you ask of him." 23 Jesus said to her, "Your brother will rise again." 24 Martha replied, "I know he will rise again at the resurrection on the last day." 25 Jesus said to her, "I am the resurrection and the life. He who trusts me will live, even if he die, 26 and everyone who is alive and trusts me will never die. Do you believe this?" 27 Martha answered, "Yes, Lord, I have come to trust that you are the Christ, the Son of God, who is coming into the world." 28 Having said this she left and called her sister Mary. Taking her aside she told her, "The Teacher is here. He wants to see you." 29 When Mary heard this she quickly got up and went to him. 30 Jesus had not yet entered the village, but was still at the place where Martha had met him. 31When the Jews who were in the house condoling with her noticed Mary rise quickly and leave, they followed her, supposing she was going to the grave to weep.

All men conjecture what will be after death. How man sees himself after death is probably the best criterion of how he regards himself before death. Reflection on death and resurrection most dramatically reveals what man thinks of himself. If he does not envision personal immortality, he might think of persistence in matter, a mixing "forever with the elements" (William Cullen Bryant). While a number of modern men feel they must accept death as absolute termination, some persist in the thought that somehow after death they will prevail.

In Western culture, many men do not like to think of surrendering their individuality. Might it be possible that human life could be made to persist indefinitely *on earth*—if there is no life after death? Corliss Lamont has written a book about the illusion of immortality while simultaneously promoting a life that could continue on earth. Science might advance enough, so that man's earthly life could be prolonged indefinitely: "It is conceivable that man might ultimately learn how not to die."

Lamont, trying to free man from the illusion of immortality, succumbs to another, the illusion of Superman. Some day man might discover "how to bring about the mutation which would result in a new species, Superman. It is conceivable that either man or Superman might, through science and particularly through atomic power . . . gain such control over the mechanisms of the whirling planet, the solar system and the sources of energy and heat that extinction of life on this earth would be postponed indefinitely." If immortality is not sought after death, some men seem to talk themselves into trying to create it on the hither side of death.

So man's wish to persist cannot be suppressed. It may express itself in a simple faith: "Sir, had you been here, my brother would not have died" (v. 21). It may take on the form of a lofty dogmatic claim: "I know he will rise again at the resurrection on the last day" (v. 24). From the perspective of the Fourth Gospel, simple faith as well as dogmatic claims stand in need of correction. Man is destined neither to be dust nor Superman. He is called to do battle for unoppressed life.

Jesus liberates man from the question of the after-life and
future resurrection, to the concern for unoppressed life. The
free man is already the resurrection and the life to come (v.
25). He embodies it because in waiting on man he has been
empowered to free man from bondage. In his freedom we are
confronted with the direction of our destiny. Resurrection
takes place *now* as freedom from oppression or it will never
take place. The one who trusts the free man who embodies
the resurrection in his freedom already shares in ultimate destiny (v. 26). Death has no power over the life that brings
liberation in embodying costly love. Jesus asks the woman:
"Do you believe this?" (v. 26). She answers: "Yes, Lord, I
have come to trust that you are the Christ, the Son of God,
who is coming into the world" (v. 27). She trusts that death
has no power because she experiences freedom over death in
the free man. Resurrection is already real in what the free man
does. Man need not perish. He also need not transcend himself in Superman. Transcendence has transcended into human life in the free man. That is sufficient. Man is asked to
become man in trusting the free man and in working together
with him to discover unoppressed life.

Unoppressed Manhood   11:32–44

32 When Mary arrived where Jesus was she looked at him
and fell at his feet and said, "Sir, had you been here, my brother
would not have died." 33 When Jesus saw her weeping and also
the Jews who accompanied her, he sighed indignantly and was
deeply disturbed. 34 "Where have you buried him?" he asked.
They replied, "Sir, come and see." 35 Jesus wept. 36 The Jews said,
"Look, how he loved him!" 37 But some of them remarked, "Could
not this man, who opened the blind man's eyes, have kept Lazarus
from dying?" 38 Again sighing indignantly Jesus went to the grave.
It was a cave, with a stone laid against it. 39 Jesus said, "Take away

the stone." Martha, the dead man's sister, said to him, "Sir, he has been dead four days, by now there must be an odor." ⁴⁰ Jesus said, "Did I not tell you, if you would trust, you would see the glory of God?" ⁴¹ They took away the stone, and Jesus looked upward and said, "Father, I thank you for hearing me. ⁴² I know that you always hear me, but I mentioned this for the sake of the crowd standing around, so that they may trust that you commissioned me." ⁴³ Then he called out in a loud voice, "Lazarus, come out!" ⁴⁴ The dead man came out, his feet and hands wrapped in bandages and his face covered with a cloth. Jesus said, "Take off the wrappings and let him go."

Not all Jews in Jesus' day looked forward to a resurrection. Those who did saw it as part of the eschaton, the end of history. Now Jesus points to himself as the end of history by speaking of himself as the resurrection and the life. Lazarus raised from the dead verifies his claim. A man raised from the dead is together with the free man. The following chapter, Chapter 12, records that Lazarus, together with others, eats with Jesus while visiting at Bethany. Nothing more is told of what the man raised from the dead did with his resurrected life. He had fellowship with the free man. And he was still Lazarus. All he did was to share in corporate selfhood.

Jesus promised Martha she would see God glorified (v. 40). This is his glorification: the Word incarnate communing with man beyond death. In the corporate selfhood of Jesus and Lazarus at table God's reality is embodied. It is man's destiny to show who God is by prevailing over death in corporate selfhood. What man does on earth in response to God as embodied in Jesus, he will be doing for all eternity. This is not an easy thing like a walk in the woods in springtime, but the hard battle with the recalcitrant structures of oppression —bringing true joy and fulfillment.

Some might hope for a moment when they will behold the glory of God directly, apart from any embodiment of God. But this is a hope for an abstract God. The story of Lazarus' resurrection claims that man will commune with God *through Jesus*, "something concrete and human; it is the vision of the living God, not of the idea of God" (Unamuno). Jesus is not sacrificed to the Christ. Jesus does not vanish. The Christ is Jesus. Beholding the man Jesus, Lazarus sees Christ, the Son of God, and through him, God.

It is exactly here that we learn who man is. Death is not the ultimate oppression that keeps man from grasping his freedom. Jesus says: "Take off the wrappings and let him go" (v. 44). He sets man free from the powers that keep him in ultimate bondage. When we grasp that God does not let man perish in the shackles of death we note the radical summons for all oppression to be shaken off.

The point of the resurrection of Lazarus lies in its summons to decision. We always decide in the light of who we believe we are. The free man is willing to live together with his neighbor beyond death, to face him forever. Only in being willing to live together with a definite neighbor forever does a man learn why Jesus is the resurrection: "We know that we have passed out of death into life, because we love the brethren" (I Jn. 3:14). Says Erich Fromm: "We shall never 'grasp' the secret of man and of the universe, but . . . we can know, nevertheless, in the act of love." Lazarus' resurrection invites man to be willing to live with the neighbor. Only in being willing to live with the black and to face him forever will the WASP understand the resurrection.

For the scientifically trained mind a resurrection from the dead is absurd. Its point, however, is not to promote credulity, but to increase liberation, to free man from the fear of living with his neighbor. "Hell, that's other people," says Sartre.

Eternity, that's life together, says the Fourth Gospel. Resurrection is a summons: be ready to do battle together with your neighbor for unoppressed life.

What we encounter in the raising of Lazarus is not *realized* eschatology. The end is not as yet here. But we do meet an *embodied* eschatology. In the flesh of Jesus the end is incarnated. Taking on present concrete form, it is no longer an idea. In the process of incarnating decisions that free oppressed men the resurrection begins to make sense for the ghetto, the reservation, and the prison. Thus Resurrection City! And it also makes sense for the struggle of the Vietnamese. The eschatological becomes concrete. If the eschatological is not felt in concrete persons any future fulfillment is pointless. The removal of the eschatological into the future perpetuates concealment of men from themselves and leads to new self-alienation.

Liberation is the possibility to experience resurrection now. That is, liberation is the unoppressed relationship between men on the model of Lazarus' relationship to Jesus. Freedom is the ability to grasp the *novum*, the new, in the public space between persons. More cannot be attained.

The Incarnate Resurrection in a
Vicarious Death   11:45-57

⁴⁵ *Many of the Jews who visited with Mary and saw what Jesus had done trusted him.* ⁴⁶ *But some of them went to the Pharisees informing them of what he had done.* ⁴⁷ *Then the chief priests and the Pharisees summoned the Council and said, "What shall we do? This man is performing many signs.* ⁴⁸ *If we let him carry on this way, everybody will trust him. Then the Romans will come and take away both our Holy Place and our nation."* ⁴⁹ *But one of them, Caiaphas, who was High Priest that year, said, "You are ignorant.* ⁵⁰ *You do not understand that it is in your best in-*

terest that one man should die for the people instead of the whole nation being wiped out." [51] He did not say this of his own accord. But as High Priest that year he prophesied that Jesus would die for the nation, [52] and not for the nation only, but also to unite the scattered children of God. [53] From that day on they plotted to kill him.

[54] Jesus no longer appeared publicly among the Jews, but went into the area near the desert to a town called Ephraim. There he stayed with his disciples. [55] The Jewish Passover was approaching, and many people from the country went to Jerusalem for religious cleansing ceremonies. [56] They kept looking for Jesus and asked each other as they stood in the temple, "What do you think? He will not show up at the festival, will he?" [57] Now the chief priests and the Pharisees had given orders that, if anyone knew where he was, he should inform them, so that they might arrest him.

Lazarus' resurrection is accompanied by references to Jesus' death. The same Jesus who speaks of himself as the resurrection will also die. The high priest's remark on the expediency of Jesus' death is interpreted by the author of the Fourth Gospel as an unintentional prophecy of its vicarious character (v. 50). After Jesus' death it would be unnecessary for any man to die for the same reason. By his free decision Jesus drew death into his liberating work, taking it upon himself, so that others could go scot-free. No man would have to die again in order for man to be truly liberated.

The liberation Jesus embodied stands out in a stark contrast to the bystanders in the story, the Pharisees, the priests, and the people. The organization churchmen were unwilling to tolerate Jesus as a man; life for them was meaningful only in terms of political and social security. The people by and large showed little more than passing interest in a somewhat odd countryman. So the free man walks a lonely road among

the fearful and the curious. He shows that to become a man
is to acknowledge the prevailing justice of an unoppressed life.
Lazarus' resurrection is the core of this acknowledgment.

DEATH AS OCCASION FOR
FREE MANHOOD   12:1–50

THE FREE MAN FACING DEATH   12:1–11

¹ Six days before the Passover, Jesus came to Bethany where
Lazarus lived whom he had raised from the dead. ² They gave him
a dinner there. Martha served, and Lazarus was among those eating with him. ³ Mary took a pound of very expensive, genuine
perfume and anointed Jesus' feet. She wiped his feet with her hair,
and the whole house was scented with perfume. ⁴ Judas Iscariot,
one of his disciples, the one who was going to betray him, said,
⁵ "Why was not this perfume sold for thirty dollars and the money
given to the poor?" ⁶ He said this, not out of concern for the poor,
but because he was a thief. He carried the purse and used to keep
for himself what was put in. ⁷ Jesus replied, "Leave her alone, let
her do this for the day of my burial. ⁸ The poor are always with
you, but not I."

⁹ A large crowd of the Jews learned that he was at Bethany.
They went there not merely to see Jesus, but also Lazarus whom
he raised from the dead. ¹⁰ So the chief priests planned to kill
Lazarus also, ¹¹ since on his account many of the Jews were going
over to Jesus and trusted him.

Trust in the free man is no escape mechanism that makes
men evade death. Lazarus' resurrection stresses that the free
man who will also die does not retreat in the face of death,
but protests its oppression. Chapter 12 continues the note
struck in Chapters 10 and 11. To be a man not only means "to
do God" and "to do the resurrection," but also "to do death."

The doing of death, however, is prefaced and encompassed by the doing of the resurrection. Lazarus is at table with the man who will also meet death.

At the table a woman pours perfume over Jesus' feet and wipes them with her hair. A foolish thing to do! Apparently no respectable woman in Palestine would have loosed her hair in public. But in regard to the free man her deed makes sense. Her self-abandonment witnesses to who Jesus is, symbolizing his waiting on man. Her witness points radically to his death. He faces death freely in radical self-giving.

By contrast, Judas' faked concern for the poor illumines man's absentminded facing of the human predicament. Money for the poor is important, but only a partial solution. Life needs to be freed in its entirety. For that reason Jesus faces death in a new way. Social ills can best be attacked by that power of corporate selfhood that will seek to liberate man in his wholeness, soul and body.

Besides Judas, the curious appear again (v. 9), and behind the scenes the plotters who want to do away with Lazarus as well as with Jesus (v. 10). In contrast to those who waste their time in curiosity-seeking and those who want to waste their neighbor's life, Jesus' attitude makes a difference as to who man can become. He battles for life as he faces death. He seeks to bring life to others as others try to deprive him of it. This is not a stoic facing of death, but a life-generating, existence-empowering resistance to death.

Our society worships death and killing as "necessities." But in Jesus the facing of death is for the celebration of life. "You know how many ways there are to die. I do too. So do the Vietnamese. So do black people. Indeed, one of the perverse triumphs of technology is to reverse the biblical promise in favor of death: 'Where life aboundeth, death did more abound.' The improved families of antipersonnel weapons, the

improved napalm, the germicides and herbicides and defoli-
ants press upon victim peoples at home and abroad the presence of death as the prime ingredient of American consciousness" (Daniel Berrigan). Jesus' facing of death is a world
apart from "the presence of death as the prime ingredient of
American consciousness." We have no appreciation of Jesus'
death because the constant presence of death in our consciousness makes life worthless. Our brutalized sensibility cannot
grasp why a man should be greatly concerned about life in the
face of death.

Some, however, do trust the man called Jesus (v. 11).
Several times in the Fourth Gospel this ray of hope breaks
through. Man's darkness is not absolute. There is hope that
also today men will celebrate life in the face of death.

The Free Man Entering Jerusalem   12:12–19

¹² *The next day the large crowd that had come for the festival
heard that Jesus was coming to Jerusalem* ¹³ *and went out to meet
him with palm branches shouting, "Hosanna! Blessed is he who
comes in the name of the Lord, the King of Israel."* ¹⁴ *Jesus found
a young ass and sat on it, according to the Scriptures:* ¹⁵ *"Fear not,
daughter of Zion, see, your king is coming, sitting on an ass's colt!"*
¹⁶ *At the time the disciples did not understand this. But after Jesus
had been glorified they remembered that this had been written of
him and done to him.* ¹⁷ *The people that were present when he
called Lazarus out of the grave and raised him from the dead continued to talk about it.* ¹⁸ *That is why the crowd went to meet him;
they had heard that he had done this sign.* ¹⁹ *The Pharisees then
said to one another, "See, you cannot do a thing! The whole world
has run after him!"*

It has been said that Jerusalem is not just a city, but an
affair of the heart. The first Soviet Jews entering Israel in 1971

knew this meaning very well; and Naomi Shemer-Sapir elo-
quently testified to it in her song, "Jerusalem the Golden."
To enter Jerusalem is to enter the city of God. It is a sacred
moment for every Jew. The man called Jesus found little understanding of his view of entering the city. The crowds hailed
him as Jesus Christ—Superstar. Whatever fulfillment of the
Messianic dogmatics they saw in him (v. 13), it did not agree
with his self-understanding. He fulfills the Old Testament
prophecies (v. 15; cf. Zech. 9:9) in ways that contradict the
shouting crowd. Even his disciples did not understand the
point of his entrance into Jerusalem. Only *after* Jesus had consummated liberation on the cross did they come to understand in what sense the "Messianic entry" into Jerusalem fulfilled the Messiahship (v. 16).

The truly free man fulfilled Zechariah 9:9: "Rejoice
greatly, O daughter of Zion! Shout aloud, O daughter of Jerusalem! Lo, your king comes to you; triumphant and victorious
is he, humble and riding on an ass, on a colt the foal of an
ass." Jesus embodied the expected Messianic entry into God's
city not by making himself the Messianic king, but by being
the free man in freely facing death. The image of the Messianic king was smashed by the free manhood of him who
sought life in the face of death. The loud acclaim (v. 13) is
not the real point of the story. The real point is that there
will never be any other Messianic entry into Jerusalem than
that of the free man who seeks life in the face of death. The
memory of Lazarus' resurrection is central in grasping the
point: "The people that were present when he called Lazarus
out of the grave and raised him from the dead continued to
talk about it" (v. 17). The mythological images of a future
Messianic age have now been embodied by the free man in
the city where men are promised to be free. An "imperious

ruler" has forced the future into the present and has made life more real. Only where future and present coinhere is unreality overcome and death radically resisted by life.

Beholding the Free Man in Death   12:20–33

20 There were some Greeks among those who had gone to worship at the festival. 21 They went to Philip who was from Bethsaida in Galilee, and said to him, "Sir, we would like to see Jesus." 22 Philip went and told Andrew, and both went to tell Jesus. 23 Jesus answered them, "The hour has come for the Son of Man to be glorified. 24 Believe me, a grain of wheat remains by itself unless it falls into the ground and dies, but if it dies it multiplies much. 25 Whoever loves himself loses his self, but whoever hates himself in this world will be kept for prevailing life. 26 If anyone wants to be my servant he must follow me; where I am, my servant will be also. My Father will recognize the man who waits on me. 27 Now I am distressed, but what can I say? Father, save me from this hour. But for this purpose I got into this hour. 28 Now, Father, glorify who you are." Then a voice came from heaven, "I have glorified myself, and I will glorify myself again." 29 The crowd of bystanders, on hearing the voice, said it had thundered. Others remarked, "An angel spoke to him." 30 Jesus replied, "This voice came not for my sake, but for yours. 31 Now the judgment of the world is taking place; now the ruler of the world will be thrown out. 32 And I, when I am lifted up from the earth, will draw all men to myself." 33 He said this to indicate the kind of death he was to die.

We are not told whether or not the Greeks who want to see Jesus (v. 21) get to see him. But Jesus addresses the issue of what it means to see him. The hour has come in Jesus' life when God's freedom will be fully embodied in the Son

of Man. Only in facing death for the sake of life does Jesus
plumb the depth of human destiny.

Unless planted in the ground, a grain of wheat does not
yield fruit. The same is true of a man in his sphere. As long
as a man hangs on to his private self, he is concealed even to
himself, without real identity. Freedom is not found in isolation, but in participation in the corporate self. It involves full
awareness of the neighbor as neighbor. "Your life and death
are with your neighbor" (St. Anthony). Only in costly love
can a man fully reach the neighbor. And costly love is crucified
eros, crucified self-love. The man who can say, "My eros is
crucified" (Ignatius) will live and be free. Sin is to cling to
the private self, to love isolation. In order for the new self to
appear the old self has to die. Eros as self-love represents a
distorted selfhood. Seeing the free man in death is to see the
liberation of man to true selfhood. Jesus as the free man is
the one who began to crucify eros and who thus can offer
prevailing life to all (*cf.* v. 25).

But how can a man behold Jesus? How can he encounter
his death? Does not Jesus remain hidden in the mist of the
historical past? "If anyone wants to be my servant he must
follow me; where I am, my servant will be also" (v. 26). Whoever looks for Jesus in the historical past looks in vain. To
follow Jesus is to share in the crucifixion of the self and to
discover life in the neighbor. The man who waits on the neighbor in crucifying his eros knows Jesus and thus also God—
who gives him the recognition that brings self-certainty, something we seek in vain even in the fellowman. But only through
the encounter with the neighbor initiated by Jesus do we encounter God. The crucifixion of the private self breaks open
the real inside of the *sensus communis* to which in sin we are
blind. In fact, crucifying the WASP self is the unblinding of
reason.

Ultimately, in his death, the man called Jesus shows not only who man is, but also who God is. In Jesus' death God shares in man's misery. That is, God identifies with the crucifixion of man's self, takes the crucifixion upon himself—the "wages" of sin—and defeats death. For the American today, death is an end in itself, an end toward which to gear the economy and the government. God's sharing in death is the death of death. So we must resist the worship of death that supports the merchants of death.

The crowd standing around Jesus does not understand. The crowd never understands—voices from heaven. With fixation on the course of nature (thunder) or supernatural beings (angels) we too will not understand voices from heaven. But in the readiness to crucify the private self, heaven is open. In fact, Jesus' death points up full unconcealment.

"Now the ruler of the world will be thrown out" (v. 31). Now man's self-distortion is exposed: obscenity and blasphemy, and the denial of life in the worship of death. In the encounter with the neighbor their power proves to be phony. "The ruler of the world" only apparently rules. Mars is not God. He is expelled from reality as a lie, unmasked as having no created being. He only pretends to exist.

What truly rules human life is Jesus' crucifixion of eros. His death unites all men in the corporate self (vv. 32 f.) bringing forth life. All men are drawn into this death, since it is here that costly love emerges as universal bond uniting all men in freedom. In this liberation human life prevails.

God as man's origin and destiny is embodied in the man who waits on man on the cross (v. 28). The lofty God of man's imagination turns out to be the lowly God who resists evil in bearing man's lot. Jesus does not point to himself. He points away from man to God. What God is in unconcealment is incarnate in his life.

Death Instead of Glory   12:34–36

³⁴ The crowd replied, "We have learned from the law that
the Christ lives forever. Why do you claim the Son of Man must
be lifted up? What Son of Man is this?" ³⁵ Jesus answered, "The
light will be with you only a little while yet. Walk while you have
light before darkness takes you by surprise. He who wanders about
in the dark does not know where he is going. ³⁶ Trust the light
that you may become sons of light." With these words Jesus left
and hid himself from them.

The crowd remains uncomprehending, as crowds do. Un-
thinking men persist in measuring Jesus by their utopistic image of the Christ. Is he not to be Superstar, one who will be
"around" forever? What's the point of Jesus' strange talk of
being "lifted up"? (v. 34)

The man called Jesus defines manhood as simply waiting
on man. True manhood is not tied to an impressive religious
show. Man is summoned to find his manhood—his being a
person—in response to the shape of Jesus' crucifixion. The
direction of his destiny is now illumined—he can walk in the
light that the shape of Jesus' cross sheds on human life (v. 35).
In the encounter with the shape of this cross, man is summoned to discover the shape of his selfhood. The light that
illumines every man is already there. The *sensus communis* is
bestowed upon every man. All a man needs to do is to walk
by the light of the *sensus communis* reflected in the cross of
Christ.

There is no external evidence which could prove this to
be true. Man must find the evidence in himself, in the *sensus
communis*. The cross calls him to open his eyes to his true
selfhood. It is exactly in the cross that man can see his true
self and that of his neighbor—in view of God's unconceal-

ment. Here a man can become a son of light (v. 36), a child of openness.

While the light of God's openness is always present to man in the Word as the *sensus communis*, it was present in the concrete embodiment of one man only for a short while. But the memory of this embodiment is still with us. The cross opens our eyes to see the light everywhere. What we need to see is the reality of crucified eros—as a possibility in every man. But as soon as we take our eyes away from Jesus' cross all this will become blurred, and darkness will envelop us again as by surprise (v. 35).

DISTRUST OF THE MAN SQUARELY FACING DEATH 12:37–43

[37] *Even though he had done many signs in their sight, they did not trust him,* [38] *so that the word of the prophet Isaiah fits the event, "Lord, who trusted our witness, and to whom has God's authority been disclosed?"* [39] *They could not trust because, as again Isaiah puts it,* [40] *"He has blinded their eyes and made their hearts insensible, lest they should see with their eyes or understand with their heart and turn to me, that I should heal them."* [41] *Isaiah said this because he foresaw his glory and spoke of him.* [42] *Nevertheless, many of the leaders trusted him, but because of the Pharisees they would not confess it for fear of excommunication.* [43] *They loved their status before men more than their status before God.*

Jesus had witnessed to true personhood in many signs. And yet the crowd was unconvinced (v. 37). The shape of his cross was too offensive or irrelevant. But it is nothing foreign to man, utterly pointless or incomprehensible.

The opportunity for recognizing free manhood had always been there. Isaiah already had been puzzled by the rejection of his witness to the real. Men always seem to have difficulty acknowledging the real. "To tell it like it is" seems a commonplace. But who really tells it like it is? And if someone does, will men hear? Did not Lyndon Johnson have beans in his ears? Is it different with Richard Nixon? Who found in Isaiah's witness a hint of God's unconcealment? Who "plugged in" to the *sensus communis?* Isaiah sensed the Word of ultimate meaning, the light that illumines every man (v. 41). Only he did not see it embodied. Usually, however, men's hearts are as little sensitive to God's unconcealment in the *sensus communis* as they are to its embodiment in Jesus.

Why the majority of men will not acknowledge God's unconcealment is ultimately incomprehensible. It would seem that unconcealment itself would make some men affirm their ultimate destiny by denying it, rejecting themselves forever, in the sense that God even makes the wrath (and blindness!) of men to praise him (v. 40). But it is not for us to grasp this "logic" now. What we *can* grasp is that in the Word all men have been nailed down on their *sensus communis.* Man's accountability—something from which no one is exempt—means that in response to Jesus' cross a man can discover who he is. He may not discover it immediately. He may have to struggle with it for years. What counts is persistence in the struggle, not immediate success.

The miracle of trust in Jesus can occur. In this particular instance, however, those who trust fear rejection by the organization church (v. 42). As long as man externalizes his imaginary private self in the minds of others, he distorts his selfhood. The result is fear—fear of losing one's status (v. 43). Only in the corporate selfhood of freedom which inheres in man and which man himself does not have to create (v. 32) is man truly at home with himself.

Trust in Jesus as Trust in God   12:44–50

[44] Then Jesus proclaimed with a loud voice, "He who trusts me does not trust me, but him who commissioned me, [45] and he who sees me, sees him who commissioned me. [46] I have come into the world as light, so that he who trusts me should not be left in the dark. [47] If a man hears my words and fails to obey them, it is not I who dooms him; for I have not come to doom the world, but to liberate it. [48] He who ignores me and does not accept my words has one who dooms him. The word I shared will doom him on the last day. [49] I have not been promoting myself, but the Father who commissioned me has ordered what I must communicate and share. [50] I know his order is prevailing life. Whatever I share, I share as the Father communicated it to me."

Seeing and trusting the free man in death we trust God. It is in the crucifixion of the private self that God is most fully concrete. There is no other way to acknowledge unconcealment than trust in him who in crucifixion seeks to turn death into life. But the free man is not the ultimate himself. It is pointless to say that Jesus is God or that God is Jesus! Only to the extent that Jesus points to God's freedom, only as he witnesses to God, is he relevant.

The free man does not doom man. His mission is to liberate him from his concealment. Men *doom themselves* if they do not come to terms with Jesus' words. To trust these words means to struggle with them in the hope that they will mediate liberation. The person who ignores the words dooms himself to continued bondage. "Hell" is man's choice to live in isolation: in perpetual concealment from the Word. The man called Jesus we do not see. But as we struggle with his words that seek to give shape to his activity we find the new direction of our destiny, not doom, but liberation (v. 47).

If a man wills to be free in acknowledging unconcealment, he acknowledges what is truly human. He himself thus
walks in openness and is not left in the dark (v. 46). To ignore
the openness of life is to ignore history in its core and thus to
destroy oneself.

We raise too much fuss about the difficulty of encountering the man called Jesus. He meets us as *the* question. He
throws us into a radical struggle with *our* selfhood, not with
the idiosyncracies of his first-century psyche. He makes us ask
whether or not we will want to take a dimension of our life
seriously which we usually ignore. As soon as we realize this
much, manhood becomes a quest. The battle for survival goes
on. The struggle continues. In fact, Jesus intensifies it. We
come to understand that becoming a person is an endless
process. We are not the *imago dei*, not yet. At best we are an
imago futuri. We do not as yet know what we will be. In the
constant struggle with becoming the "sharing" self (vv. 49 f.)
of which Jesus was the firstfruits we begin to sense what it
means to be a man—a person.

It is clear that these reflections on man are far from being
definitive. What Chapters 8–12 do is to break open the hard
forms in which we have become accustomed to think of man.
The author of the Fourth Gospel is like a farmer plowing open
the ground after a long, hard winter. We are not offered a
definite yield of fruit as to how to think about man, but a
new possibility for starting over again. We need to think out
for our day what "doing God," "doing resurrection," and "doing death" mean. The issue is how we can build these words,
God, resurrection, and death, into our existence. The word
"God" is an energy agent. It leads to action. With the word
"resurrection" it is similar. And the word "death," as used
by the man called Jesus, challenges us not to succumb to its
fate. Man can have power over death, resisting it in a resur-

rected life, in the words of I John 3:14: "We know that we have passed out of death into life, because we love the brethren."

Human life thus becomes more of an experiment: what will happen when we put the words "God," "resurrection," and "death" into new action? We are not saying that God, resurrection, and death can be understood *only* in action. But who man is becoming, cannot be understood without action in which these words are operative. It is often said that words are cheap. But actions can be cheap too. It takes the constant involution of words and action to bring about new personhood. So for the time being we venture to claim—in words—that man is the being that *does* God, that *does* resurrection, and that *does* death.

It goes without saying that we cannot fully grasp what this doing of God, resurrection, and death, meant for Jesus. And we are not asked to imitate him. An *imitatio Christi* is not called for when we speak of who man is becoming. Jesus was the Son of God—something we cannot say of ourselves. But the stories about him in Chapters 8–12 invite us to think through for ourselves how we could possibly experience new manhood, if we would but do these words. There is the invitation to the *innovatio Christi:* finding Jesus relevant for us in new ways heretofore untried, in thinking black, in becoming one with the oppressed.

PART IV

THE
LIBERATION CHURCH,
THE COUNTERCHURCH

THE COUNTERCHURCH   13:1–38

What happens in all this doing of theology? As men see
themselves becoming new men, they find themselves in a community of mutual support. Jesus had already found himself in
such a community with his disciples. Now the dynamics of
this community are made a specific topic of reflection. The
counterself as embodied in Jesus entails a countercommunity.
The theme of Chapters 13–17 is the sharp antithesis between
this community and the secular world.

The Fourth Gospel shows no special interest in an elaborate ecclesiology. The New Testament term for church, *ecclesia,* nowhere appears on its pages. There are merely the
"disciples" (*cf.* 13:35 and 15:8), the "friends" (15:13), or
"his own" (13:1). But they appear, as a group by itself, within
the framework of the Jewish organization church, the leaders
and the Pharisees. A new church dynamic is introduced. The
liberation Jesus brings is the opposite of the traditional religious institution. In this polarization the old church stands
in the way of the coming new manhood.

The mandate of the liberation Jesus embodies supersedes all previous values of religious community. Man's attempts to create church are controlled by desire for security and status, and often by an expectation of political or economic success. Jesus' appearance challenges men to start all over again in their life together by opposing "the secular kick." It compels men to join forces in a freedom covenant that makes liberation real.

Discipleship is nothing unusual. Many teachers in Jesus' day had disciples. Today it is not different. Philosophers, theologians, politicians, and even hippies have disciples. Men enjoy imitating each other. Jesus creates discipleship with a difference, a corporate manhood that risks life for freedom.

Community was no longer understood in the institutional church. So the free man created a new public space for freedom, a space where liberation would not be an abstract idea, but a concrete reality. Thus far we have largely seen Jesus countering the organization church as an individual. Now we see him opposing the secular church in company with his disciples. In order to understand what is going on in Chapters 13–17 we must constantly keep in mind the radical distance, in terms of "inner space," between the secular church and Jesus' new covenant.

THE BASIC MANDATE OF THE COUNTERCHURCH   13:1

¹ *Before the Passover festival, Jesus knowing that his hour had come to leave the world and to go to the Father, having loved his own who were in the world, he loved them to the end.*

God called a people, the people of Israel, to live in a freedom covenant. Beginning with the Exodus, Israel had a special mission: embodying liberation from bondage in a new community. Time and again, however, the Exodus church was corrupted by prideful institutionalization. The prophets already spoke out against the perversion of the covenant in mere ritual that slighted justice, mercy, and love. It is in the prophetic tradition that Jesus performs his signs. They are concrete actions battling the corruption of the freedom covenant.

In this battle we occasionally hear of some who trust the man who stands up for God's freedom covenant. It is not said that Jesus groups them especially into a separate church. They suddenly find themselves standing apart in the mammoth church. This is nothing contrived or planned on their part. They have been elected to stand in company with the free man against the secular church—as "Jesus freaks." They suddenly discover themselves as "his own."

"Having loved his own who were in the world, he loved them to the end" (v. 1). *Because of his love*, Jesus finds men who stand with him against the organization church. But what is this love? The Greek word for it is *agape*, for which no exact English equivalent exists. Anders Nygren claimed that it is unmotivated or unmerited love, while love as *eros* is motivated by the desirability of its object. We have referred to *agape* thus far as costly love, waiting on man, concretized in signs and specific events. Its mystery is that for the first time we are radically *being loved*. Descartes defined himself as *cogito, ergo sum* (I think, therefore I am). We said earlier, it would be better to say, *compatior, ergo sum*. Now we can state the reason behind our claim: we can love, because we have been loved. Because of this love, *we are*. The Cartesian formula thus reconstructed would read, *amor, ergo sum* (I am being loved, therefore I am). Even better: I am being loved, therefore *we are, amor, ergo sumus*.

Before we turn to the event that dramatizes the *amor, ergo sum*, we ought to articulate what principle is at stake in the appearance of the counterchurch. If liberal theology today is not geared to some search for God in the depths of the self, it at least seeks to tie itself to the so-called secularity of our age. Liberal (or neoliberal) theology in all shades wants to be secular theology. Langdon Gilkey, in *Naming the Whirlwind*, almost immediately demands paying respects to secularity: "Any current theology, Continental, English, or American, that does not recognize and seek reflectively to deal with this presence of secularity . . . inside the Church as well as outside, and so inside the theologian and believer, is so far irrelevant to our present situation." Obviously we are secularized. But this does not justify our turning away from the Word within the church to secularity in order to take our cue from secularity. Secularity indeed needs to be dealt with. Not, however, in joining it, but in resisting it. Had an alliance with secularity been demanded of Jesus and his disciples they would have had to take their cue from the leaders, the Pharisees and the people. The beautiful thing that happened was that the man called Jesus took the church more seriously than it took itself—appealing to her freedom covenant. He took what was present in the church as Word and embodied it, thereby beginning a new community countering the secularization of the church.

Today we need to cue in on the same rationale. After its complete secularization our task is the christianization of the church (in the spirit of Kierkegaard!). What we need to work on are not the various novelties of secularity, but the *novum* brought into the world by Christ as the power of liberation. Jesus Christ had to begin with the presupposition of the presence of the Word in the church—against the faithlessness of those who were obligated to acknowledge this presence. In trust in the continuing presence of this Word, he fulfilled his work. Secularity as Christian secularity is simply unwillingness to acknowledge the presence of the Word in the covenant community and to live by it. It was by the power of the present Word that Jesus sought to follow its claim in healing the king's officer's son, the man thirty-eight-years sick, and the boy born blind. What makes a man risk his life for the liberation of the neighbor is not sheer fancy, but the compelling presence of the Word in the freedom covenant.

LOWER THAN A SHOESHINE BOY   13:2–11

2 *At the supper when the devil had already put the thought of betraying Jesus into the heart of Judas Iscariot, Simon's son,* 3 *Jesus, certain that the Father had put him in charge of all things and that he had come from God and was going to God,* 4 *got up from the meal, put aside his robe, took a towel, and tied it around his waist.* 5 *Then he poured water into a basin, began to wash the disciples' feet and to wipe them dry with the towel that was around his waist.* 6 *When it was Simon Peter's turn he said, "Lord, you want to wash my feet?"* 7 *Jesus replied, "Right now you do not grasp what I am doing, but afterward you will understand."* 8 *Then Peter said to him, "You are not going to wash my feet, never!" Jesus told him, "Unless I wash you, you will not share in me."* 9 *"Lord," Simon Peter said, "in that case not just my feet, but also my hands and my face!"* 10 *"A man who just had a bath," Jesus replied, "has no need of washing but is altogether clean. You are already clean, but not all of you."* 11 *He said, "But not all of you are clean," because he knew the one who was going to betray him.*

Earlier, in 12:20–33, we heard of the crucifixion of eros. Now a symbolic action, a sign, dramatizes it. Jesus has supper with his disciples. At the meal he does something puzzling, at least puzzling to Peter. He cannot understand the master doing the work of a slave. The clash between the secular and the Christian lifestyle becomes clear. What the man Jesus is about does not fit into the neat secular patterns we are familiar with. In secularity one is concerned with doing one's thing, getting along, thinking straight. Doing God's thing is not part of the picture.

In Jesus' day people walking even great distances wore only sandals. Feet needed washing after travel on dusty roads. When company gathered for a feast, a slave did the washing.

Jesus viewed the social custom as an opportunity to dramatize costly love. It is as though he had used the American institution of the shoeshine boy who, by the way, only takes dirt off shoes. Jesus washed feet. He stooped down "lower" than a shoeshine boy. Stooping down, he bore witness to the fact "that he had come from God and was going to God" (v. 3). One cannot understand the footwashing unless one sees the background of Jesus' action. He was not involved in clever playacting to sell himself, but in a radical effort to make God known within a church that did not make him known. What Jesus here does to twelve people creates a counterchurch. He had already gathered them as "his own," as witnesses of his unique action. Now he stresses emphatically in a symbolic act the purpose of their existence as disciples.

The entire passage stands in the context of the approaching crucifixion. In verse 31 we read: "Now the Son of Man is glorified, and in him God is glorified." In Jesus' cross God's reality is incarnate—as *agape*, costly love. This is God's glorification. The footwashing draws together the substance of Jesus' signs and prefigures the cross as a corporate event. Here Jesus draws all men to himself to form a corporate self. Jesus' waiting on man relates man to God's reality. This does not happen as a plunge into mere secularity, but as an identification with God's ongoing work of liberating the oppressed. What we witness here is not the formation of a cozy little group that withdraws from the world, but the unmistakable

sealing of the covenant of those who risk their life for the lost.
It takes Jesus and "Jesus freaks" to make clear what God is all
about at the rugged edges of life.

God's waiting on man is twofold. It is service meeting
human need in its most dire form, and service that lets man
be, waiting for man to find his selfhood. That God should wait
on man seems innocuous. But this is exactly what the footwashing underscores. God does not do the stupendous to make
himself known. In the humor of playing a fool he comes
through as the creative poet he is. Who has eyes to see let
him see—God's humor.

Jesus gives Peter what he needs. He needs to have his feet
washed! First Peter does not understand. After Jesus clarifies
what is at stake Peter gets excited: "Lord . . . in that case
not just my feet, but also my hands and my face!" (v. 9). He
seems to take things too literally—without humor. Jesus has
to tell Peter that he wants too much. He lets Peter be, inviting him to choose freely to be himself. He did not have to do
more to Peter than to symbolize his public activity. There
was no point in repeating what had already happened to Peter
(v. 10).

We would misunderstand Jesus' deed if we would regard
it only as the deed of a good man. Service is not distinctively
Christian. It is a universal human trait expressing the intensity
of one's commitment to the family of man. Jesus' service is
distinct as embodiment of corporate selfhood intending to
reflect the *agape* of God, the waiting on man in servanthood
—waiting for man's response.

SERVANTHOOD VERSUS SECULARITY   13:12–20

¹² After washing their feet and putting on his robe he took
his place at the table again and said to them: "Do you realize what
I have done for you? ¹³ You call me 'Teacher' and 'Lord,' which
is all right, for this is what I am. ¹⁴ But if I, your Lord and

Teacher, have washed your feet, you also should wash one another's feet. [15] I have set you an example to practice what I have
done for you. [16] Believe me, a servant is not above his master, nor
a messenger greater than the one who sends him. [17] If you understand this you will be happy if you practice it. [18] I am not speaking
about all of you. I know whom I have chosen; but the events must
agree with the Scripture, 'He who is eating my bread has lifted
his heel against me.' [19] I tell you this now before it happens, that
when it happens you may trust that I am who I am. [20] Believe me,
the one who associates with anyone I send associates with me, and
he who associates with me associates with him who sent me."

"I have set you an example to practice what I have done
for you" (v. 15). A challenge to service is bound to find approval among an activist people that abounds in service clubs
and service projects. But Jesus is not interested in service in
general. He calls for service with a difference: "If I, your Lord
and Teacher, have washed your feet, you should wash one
another's feet" (v. 14). Here we must pause for careful
thought, because a crucial decision is called for. By washing
the disciples' feet no leper was healed, no hunger stilled, no
thirst quenched. Here Jesus does not say as to the rich young
ruler: "Sell what you possess and give to the poor. . . ." He
almost seems to say: do the absurd. But upon closer examination we realize that he is offering a dramatic sign by which
we can remember the point of his work. It is all about *servanthood at the boundary of life* where no one else cares. "The
Son of man is come to save that which was lost" (Mt. 18:11).
There is a distinct difference between the Christian and the
secular. Secularity does not relate man to man in terms of
crucified eros.

What happened in Jesus was not primarily the shaping
of new community. The primal thing was Jesus' servanthood
at the boundary of life. It was the miracle and mystery of this
event that created community. In fact, the appearance of this

community was a miracle and mystery itself. A few men were gripped by servanthood. Now these few are reminded of how it all happened and why they are never to forget it. The counterchurch is the event of not forgetting what Jesus did at the boundary of life.

Those who do not forget will appear to be freaks. It does not make much obvious sense to wash one another's feet. The humor of the footwashing is that the benefit of the deed first of all accrues to the doer. It reminds him of people at the boundary of life, the *marginales*, the wretched of the earth. And of one who radically identified with them.

In identifying with the struggle for survival at the boundary of life, a "Jesus freak" takes the risk of servanthood. It is nothing other than becoming black. But this does not create community as a matter of course. It is a miracle if there is one other person who feels the same.

THE REJECTION OF SERVANTHOOD   13:21–30

²¹ After saying this Jesus was deeply disturbed and exclaimed, "Believe me, one of you will betray me." ²² The disciples looked at one another at a loss to know of whom he spoke. ²³ One of them, the disciple he loved, was leaning toward Jesus. ²⁴ Simon Peter nodded to him and said, "Tell us of whom he is speaking." ²⁵ That disciple leaning over still more toward Jesus said, "Lord, who is it?" ²⁶ Jesus answered, "It is the one for whom I shall dip this piece of bread in the dish and to whom I shall give it." When he had dipped it he took it and gave it to Judas, Simon Iscariot's son. ²⁷ As soon as Judas had taken the piece of bread, Satan gripped him. Jesus said to him, "Do quickly what you want to do." ²⁸ No one at the table knew what he meant. ²⁹ Some thought, since Judas was the one who carried the money, that Jesus had told him to buy what they needed for the festival, or that he should give something to the poor. ³⁰ As soon as Judas had taken the piece of bread he left. It was night.

We have learned before, not everyone will wish to be part of the new corporate self. Judas is the most devastating case in point. But what can the one who embodies costly love do about it? The one who rejects costly love can only be left to dooming himself: "Do quickly what you want to do" (v. 27). He prefers isolation to community, darkness to light: "As soon as Judas had taken the piece of bread he left. It was night" (v. 30). Words cannot interpret the rejection of the light. Concealment self-destructs. And so does privatism.

The New Embodiment of Servanthood   13:31–35

³¹ When he had gone Jesus said, "Now the Son of Man is glorified and in him God is glorified. ³² If God is glorified in him, God will also glorify him in himself, and that at once. ³³ Little children, yet a little while I am with you. You will be searching for me, but I tell you as I told the Jews, you cannot enter where I am going. ³⁴ I am giving you a new order: Love one another. Love one another as I have loved you. ³⁵ By this all men will know you as my disciples, by your love for one another."

Of himself a man is not able to identify with those who struggle for survival at the boundary of life. Only by the power of its Lord is the counterchurch able to act differently: "Love one another *as I have loved you*" (v. 34). The emphasis lies on the *as I have loved you*. In 15:5 Jesus will say: "I am the vine, you are the branches. He who shares in me as I share in him bears much fruit; for apart from me you cannot do a thing." As one searches in the Fourth Gospel for specific events in which Jesus directly expresses his love for his disciples one looks in vain. Only indirectly does it become clear what his love was: he loved his disciples in letting them share in his identification with the lost. He loved them in making them participants of the embodiment of corporate selfhood.

By the power of this love the disciple is to act. In this love Jesus continues to be present and known.

At this point we must try to eliminate a misunderstanding. Charles Williams, in *The Descent of the Dove*, quotes an early Christian: "It is right for a man to take up the burden for them who are near to him, whatever it may be, and, so to speak, to put his own soul in the place of that of his neighbor, and to become, if it were possible, a double man, and he must suffer, and weep, and mourn with him, and finally the matter must be accounted by him as if he himself had put on the actual body of his neighbor, and as if he had acquired his countenance and soul, and he must suffer for him as he would for himself. For thus it is written *We are all one body. . . .*" It is right to put oneself in the place of the neighbor. This is what identification with the wretched of the earth is all about. But it makes sense only if a person becomes free and finds his true identity, and his neighbor finds it too. It is not a sign of crucifying eros if one lets the other walk all over oneself. Love waits on the other, liberates him, so that he can find his own selfhood. It does not make us one another's "doormats." There is a world of difference between a "footwasher" and a "doormat." No man can actually be a "double man." Love as *agape* is *being with the other* in his struggle for survival. There are those who lose themselves in service without ever finding themselves. Jesus did not want perverse love. Costly love is always a matter of being present where life is most threatened and of battling the threat. Its first move is *to get off the other's back.*

This does not mean that we are invited to become *like* Jesus. We noted before, *imitatio Christi* is not what is called for, an imitation of the detail of Jesus' life. Jesus did not want "Jesus copies." He expected each man to become free in his very own freedom. Instead of the *imitatio Christi* the *innovatio*

Christi will demand an innovation of freedom *on grounds of his liberating act.* So each disciple must find out for himself what his particular waiting on man can be. He must radically be himself. What we receive from Jesus is the new motive for freedom.

This is most fully expressed on the cross. The glorification of the Son of Man and of God (vv. 31 f.) is the full embodiment of this motivation. Suffering love is nothing new. What is new about the love of the cross is that God embodies himself as crucified eros. *Truth forever on a scaffold*—this is the reality of God. It does not depend on an appreciative response to be real. But it does invite a response.

THE COUNTERCHURCH AS RADICAL DISCIPLESHIP   13:36–38

[36] *Simon Peter said to him, "Lord, where are you going?" Jesus answered, "Where I am going you cannot follow now, but you will follow later."* [37] *Peter replied, "Lord, why can I not follow you now? I would give my life for you!"* [38] *Jesus replied, "You would give your life for me? Believe me, you will disown me three times before the cock crows."*

The disciples pay a high price for their discipleship. It implies, as Peter realizes, the risk of life. But Jesus alone had to take upon himself the cross to become the liberator. Discipleship is thus not doing over again what Jesus did. It is freely living *by what he did.* Peter cannot liberate the world. Every man, even in his best deed of freedom, distorts his humanity. "There is no health in us," no ultimately liberating power to free others from oppression. Only in Jesus does the disciple find this power.

Radical discipleship hinges on the word "later" (v. 36). The counterchurch depends on the embodiment of costly love on the cross. Jesus did not take Peter along to be crucified with him. "Later" he would follow—after liberation had been accomplished. Costly love might occasionally compel a disciple to sacrifice his life. But the less one boasts about one's readiness to sacrifice oneself the better! "You would give your life for me? Believe me, you will disown me three times before the cock crows" (v. 38). Martyrdom is a possibility for the disciple, but an extreme one. It is not a mandate of discipleship. The disciple should not "maneuver" himself into it. He cannot "make" himself a martyr. Should martyrdom be his vocation—he probably would not realize it before death were upon him. True martyrdom is always unpremeditated. What we need to be ready for is to risk our lives in joining men who struggle for survival.

What the disciples can premeditate is their love "for one another" (v. 35), which comes as a gift as they meet the lost at the boundary of life. The counterchurch is born as people meet the oppressed. Its birth is not without birth pangs: an agonizing process that reflects the unceasing struggle for life. Anyone who expects easy answers or straight-line logic will be disappointed.

THE COUNTERETHOS   14:1–31

The Christian Way of Life   14:1–7

[1] "Do not lose heart. Trust God, and trust me. [2] In my Father's house are many rooms. If it were not so, I would have told you, for I am leaving to prepare a place for you. [3] And though I go to prepare it, I am coming to you to receive you into full communion, so that you may be where I am. [4] You know the way where I am going." [5] Thomas said, "Lord, we have no idea where you are going, how can we know the way?" [6] Jesus answered, "I am the way, the truth, and the life. No one comes to the Father but by me. [7] If you really knew me, you would know my Father also. From now on you know him; you have seen him."

By now many might be looking for concrete ethical advice as to how to shape the Christian life. We find, however, that Jesus draws us to a different concern. He first of all articulates the ethos of the Christian life. The sharp distinction between the world and the disciple is accented more sharply. The context of Jesus' stress on the character of the Christian life seems to be a trial between world and church. The world —society organized without God—is viewed as attacking the disciple and bringing charges against him. For this reason it is said that the disciple needs another advocate or defense attorney (v. 16) who stands up for him in behalf of his Lord.

We often argue the case for the Christian life on a mistaken premise. We assume that we already know what it is all about. And we conclude that what we need to do is to make a dent in the world. But the world is not waiting for us to make a dent in it. The fact is that it is trying to make us buy into its system. It is a totalitarian type of thing. We are expected to bow, to worship, and to surrender. Here lies the real issue. Secularity wants control. Hollywood, Wall Street, Madison Avenue, and the Pentagon cannot tolerate less than total allegiance. They want to be worshipped as the ultimate in view of which decisions must be made. Their ethos is self-advancement, self-enhancement, and self-enjoyment.

Jesus invites us to consider another ultimate in view of which we may make our decisions: transcendent freedom. It is not a gray Nirvana or a blank nothing. There are "rooms" (v. 2), which point to a space for freedom in the ultimate. We all live in some space. Jesus points to a new space in which he wants us to live. Men are to experience liberation living together with the free man forever. Also the neighbor will be there. And we will have room to glorify God forever.

We have to be reminded time and again in what sense becoming a Christian is developing a different lifestyle, a new ethos. Rules are not the primary concern. Even the disciples had a hard time understanding it immediately: "We have no idea where you are going, how can we know the way?" (v. 5). So the free man has to call us time and again back to himself as the new ethos: "I am the way, the truth, and the life" (v. 6). He is the way, the truth, and the life—as the one who identifies with the wretched of the earth. Herein he also embodies God (v. 7). One easily forgets identification with the oppressed as one thinks about the church. Religious pursuits seem to be central here. So we need to be reminded of Jesus' different lifestyle, the new ethos he introduced. *Truth* is found only in corporateness unconcealed through Jesus. *Life* is found in identification with the corporate self. Clinging to the private self is death. Thus the Christian way of life is to will one thing: to resist the world of private gain in the search for the corporate self.

The Core of the Christian Ethos   14:8–14

⁸ *Philip said to him, "Lord, show us the Father, and we shall be content." * ⁹ *"Have I been with you so long," Jesus answered, "and you do not know who I am, Philip? Anyone who has seen me has seen the Father. How can you say, 'Show us the Father'?* ¹⁰ *Do you not trust that I am in the Father and the Father is in me? The words I share with you are not my own, but the Father is in me and works through me.* ¹¹ *Trust me that I am in the Father and the Father in me, or, at least, trust because of my deeds.* ¹² *Believe me, he who trusts me will do what I am doing. In fact, he will do greater things because I am going to the Father.* ¹³ *Anything you ask in response to what I am I shall do, so that the Father be glorified in the Son.* ¹⁴ *Anything you ask in response to what I am I shall do."*

The Christian ethos is not concerned with God as ground of the religious trip, but as ground of corporate selfhood.

There is interaction between Jesus, the Father, and the disciple. This is the core of the Christian ethos. It is not a moral principle, but a dynamic power. Men find it difficult to believe that this power is the ultimate. Thus the last resort for trust in corporate selfhood are Jesus' deeds (v. 12). Anyone who has seen the deeds has seen the Father himself (vv. 9 f.). And the disciple must also engage in deeds. This does not mean that these deeds should be imitations of Jesus' deeds. They will always be *new* deeds of freedom. But they will be deeds of *freedom*. They will be acts of participation in corporate selfhood. The disciple is even promised that he will do greater deeds because of Jesus' going to the Father (v. 12). Jesus' deeds are now present as the *power* of the new community working for the liberation of mankind far beyond the limits in which Jesus had to work.

Prayer is the center of the disciple's work of liberation (vv. 13 f.). Every moment of his life must be a response to the reality of corporate selfhood that undergirds all truly corporate action. In fact, every action of the disciple must be prayer, an asking for corporate selfhood to increase through him, so that his action can reflect who Jesus is. Only thus will God become more fully known.

THE RESISTANCE SPIRIT   14:15–24

[15] "If you love me, keep my commandments. [16] I will ask the Father to give you another resistance counselor, to be with you forever— [17] the Spirit of truth. The world cannot share in him because it neither sees nor knows him. But you know him because he remains with you and is in you. [18] I will not leave you orphaned. I am coming to you. [19] In a little while the world will see me no more, but you will see me because I live and you will live also. [20] Then you will know that I am in my Father, and you in me and I in you. [21] He who has accepted my order and obeys it is the

one who loves me. My Father will love him who loves me, and I shall love him and be unconcealed for him." ²² Judas (not Judas Iscariot) said to him, "Lord, why is it that you are going to be unconcealed only for us, but not for the world?" ²³ Jesus answered, "If a man loves me he will respond to my word. My Father will love him and we shall visit him and make our home with him. ²⁴ He who does not love me does not respond to my words. The word you hear is not my own, but the Father's who sent me."

If one wants to understand growth in corporate selfhood one has to take into account that the man called Jesus is no longer with us. He has already pointed away from himself and made it clear that as separate individual he is insignificant. What is significant is the transcendent relationship he represents. Now he points once more away from himself. His place will be taken by another: the Spirit of truth.

It is difficult to imagine what the Paraclete image (v. 16) conveyed to the disciples. It is clear that he also was an advocate, a kind of lawyer who helped the individual resist the charges lodged against him. Today it is especially this connotation that needs to be drawn out dramatically: the Spirit is the resistance counselor who helps the disciple resist the claims of secularity. The disciple is not completely on his own (v. 18). He will be informed by a power that principally wants man to resist. This is the least understood aspect of the Christian ethos. It does not only imply becoming draft resisters or helping them, but principally resisting the world of which the draft is but a symptom.

"To resist is to become alive, truly alive for the first time. It is to say not only will I not accept what you are doing, I will stop you from doing it. No one shall sleep peacefully again until you cease, desist, and abdicate.

To resist is to say if the parents of Vietnam weep for

their children then the parents of America shall weep for theirs.

If the people of Vietnam are unable to harvest the crop without fear, to live their lives without being shrouded by the shadow of death, then no American shall harvest his crop without fear, no American shall live outside the shadow of death.

To protest is to dislike the inhumanity of another.

To resist is to stop inhumanity and affirm your own humanity.

One does not protest murder.

One apprehends the murderer and deals with him accordingly."

—*Julius Lester*

The Spirit is the spirit of truth, of unconcealment. So the crux of resistance lies in the rejection of the world's expectation of concealment. Since mankind does not acknowledge unconcealment, it can neither see nor know the Spirit (v. 17). The Spirit is not something newfangled and odd. It is the continuing presence of the free man in the love the disciples share (v. 23). God and the Son come to the disciple in *this* life through the Spirit. It is in this sense that they make their home with the disciple. In the beginning of this chapter Jesus said that he was making room for the disciple in the many rooms of the Father. In this life the disciple himself is the room where Father and Son dwell.

In the Spirit of resistance there cannot but emerge a counterchurch. But the grasping of this Spirit is an awesome task. No one really seems to realize how difficult it is. Church reforms offered in scores of books today intimate that everything depends on the right technique, the proper organization, and the effective program. But without recouping the awesome

No that is part of the Christian way of life, the absent-minded will go to work on doing what cannot be done: organizing the church as though it were a Kiwanis club.

Perhaps in our barren age all we can learn in trying to become Christians is the spirit of resistance—fundamentally resistance against self-liberation. We need not try to do what we cannot do. We need not free ourselves. God has already liberated us. This does not mean that we can now sit back and relax. It means now to have the power to stop inhumanity and to affirm our own humanity.

THE SPIRIT AS STAND-IN   14:25-31

[25] "I have told you this while I am still with you. [26] However, the resistance counselor, the Holy Spirit, whom the Father will send in accord with what I am, will teach you all things and remind you of everything I have told you. [27] Peace I leave with you. My kind of peace I give you. I do not give it the way the world gives peace. Do not lose heart. Do not be afraid. [28] You heard me say, 'I am leaving and yet I am coming to you.' If you loved me, you would have been glad because I am going to the Father, for the Father is greater than I. [29] I have shared this with you before it happens, so that when it does happen you will trust. [30] I shall no longer talk much with you, for the ruler of the world is coming. He has no power over me. [31] I obey my Father's order, so that the world may know that I love the Father.—Let us rise and go."

Jesus confronts the disciples with the new life of freedom. The Spirit uncovers more and more the liberation he brought. In 1:18 it was said that while no one has seen the Father the Son has made him concrete. Now it is clear that the Spirit is the Stand-In of the Son who bails us out if need be (v. 26). In grappling with the Spirit the disciples discover more and more the significance of the man called Jesus. The Spirit is ultimately not the spirit of many words, but of one word. He stands for peace (v. 27). It is not the kind of peace the world expects. It is not peace of mind. There is no resolution, but intensification of struggle. It is not opium, but salt for our wounds. With Jesus things become more taxing, more puzzling. Sitting "on a balcony of one of the most beautiful hotels in the world, the Royal Hawaiian on the famed and romantic Waikiki Beach" (Norman Vincent Peale) is one thing. Finding peace in battling for survival together with the lost is another thing. It answers few questions. But it raises a lot of questions that are unanswerable. The difficulty of becoming a Christian is very real at this point.

Historical immediacy to Jesus is a thing of the past. There are no external props to verify the historical reality of Jesus. But in the peace resisting the world's peace of mind the disciple experiences Jesus' presence. In the struggle for survival Jesus is near: "I am leaving and yet I am coming to you" (v. 28). In the resistance spirit the liberation Jesus brought continues. So the Christian way of life begins with the No as well as with the Yes. In saying No to secularity it begins to affirm itself. What counts in becoming a Christian is not winning and certainly not losing, but—resisting.

THE LIBERATION CHURCH   15:1–27

THE BASIC STRUCTURE OF THE
LIBERATION CHURCH   15:1–10

[1] *"I am the real vine, and my Father is the gardener.* [2] *Any of my branches that bear no fruit he cuts away, and he prunes every branch that bears fruit, so that it can bear more.* [3] *You have already been pruned by the word I spoke to you.* [4] *Share my life, as I share yours. As the branch cannot bear fruit by itself, unless it shares in the vine, neither can you, unless you share in me.* [5] *I am the vine, you are the branches. He who shares in me as I share in him*

bears much fruit; for apart from me you cannot do a thing. ⁶ If a man does not persevere in me, he is like a branch that is thrown away and dries up. The withered branches are collected, thrown into the fire and burned. ⁷ If you persevere in me and my words persevere in you, ask what you will, and you shall have it. ⁸ As you bear much fruit and so prove to be my disciples, my Father is glorified. ⁹ I have loved you as the Father has loved me. Persevere in my love. ¹⁰ If you obey my order you will persevere in my love, as I obeyed my Father's order and persevere."

We no longer know what church is. It begins with the dynamic of negation and affirmation, of resistance and liberation: an ethos, a lifestyle, a basic stance toward life. And the "counterpoint" of the church as counterchurch comes before the "point" of the church as liberation church. The person who does not "catch" this dynamic will continue to slight the true essence of the church. Obviously the Fourth Gospel does not present us with an ecclesiology. But it does inform us of the core dynamic without which no doctrine of the church can be developed.

It has become clear enough that Jesus' new covenant stands in sharp contrast to the secular. "The world cannot share" in the Spirit (14:17). The peace Jesus gives is different from what the world gives: "My kind of peace I give you. I do not give it the way the world gives peace" (14:27). Besides the negation, however, there is also the affirmation. Its character is more fully outlined in Chapters 15–17.

The present debate about the nature of the church in America moves between two emphases of the renewal movement. On the one hand, there is the conviction that there are churches already liberated: "At the right time of history, a liberated Church in America has been born out of the Movement for peace and justice" (John Pairman Brown). In terms of this perspective there is at least a liberated zone where the true church can be experienced. On the other hand, there is the question: can there be a *liberating* church? Both views grow out of the radical stance, a negation of established structures. Both apparently also agree with Daniel Berrigan that the time of the underground church is past: "I don't like secrecy. Everything aboveboard, out in the open. Free, independent, adult Christians. Let's do what we have to do, but don't hide it."

It appears that the various pronouncements of the liberated and the liberating church are premature. While the time of the underground church is past, the new thing does not as yet exist. The *liberated* church is actually an eschatological reality, a fait accompli of the *futurum aeternum*. Even at our best where freedom is strong we are still struggling for liberation—seeing that the weight of sin fells the most beautiful of our achievements of freedom. As to the church being *liberating*, it remains a question of who really does the liberating. As long as Jesus Christ is not seen as the liberator, it is pointless to speak of the liberating church.

If there is church of Jesus Christ it is a miracle. What we usually talk about as church is what we have in our power to build. "Did we not build this church? Don't we own the church?" "This is our church," we say, and turn the nigger or the hippie away. We do not realize the impossibility of it all. Church as church of Jesus Christ is always created from beyond ourselves, from outside of us. God is always involved in Jesus' creation of the corporate self. What is important is what is being done to us: that God liberates us. We cannot do it. God is always at work destroying our playing church (v. 2). The liberation church is always a human impossibility. Only where the word of the free man takes hold does corporate selfhood break through (v. 3). This depends on the

Word leading us to seek out the oppressed.

Here lies the basic structure of the liberation church. Jesus never acted in the abstract, but always in regard to the lost battling for survival. So being church is never a matter of "baking a religious cake," putting on a bazaar, or raising sanctuary walls, but of getting with the one who stands by the lost. Apart from sharing in Jesus' activity, the church remains a human impossibility. We will always think of something else when we begin to build a church than—standing by the wretched of the earth. "As the branch cannot bear fruit by itself, unless it shares in the vine, neither can you, unless you share in me" (v. 4).

"I am the vine, you are the branches" (v. 5). Important in Jesus' metaphor is its corporate implication. In Israel the vine was a symbol for the nation as a whole. "I had planted thee a noble vine" (Jer. 2:21; cf. Ez. 19:10; Hosea 10:1; Is. 5:7; Ps. 80:8). As one of the main plants of the country, the vine offered itself readily as symbol of the corporateness of the people. Jesus in standing by the lost and joining their struggle replaced the organization church of the Old Covenant. Thus he was the true Israel, the true church. In claiming "I am the vine" he is saying "I am the church"—which is as radically new as saying "I am the resurrection." He embodies the church inasmuch as he embodies freedom.

The one who follows Jesus thus does not find the church in the religious establishment, but also not in the *liberated* church or the *liberating* church, but in liberation, in the fact that God liberates man. Where this liberation takes place should not be difficult to see: in the struggle for freedom among the oppressed. The trouble is, we do not look for the church there. But we need to find the outcast and join God there. Otherwise we won't find the church. "Apart from me you cannot do a thing" (v. 5). We must take this point with utter seriousness. Apart from God's liberation there is just plain nothing we can do about finding the church.

Malcolm X tells of a blonde co-ed who followed him to New York after he had spoken at her New England college. There he had described how the white Southern woman had been abused by the Southern male who had often sired, with or without her knowledge, mongrel-complexioned offspring. The girl followed Malcolm X to New York, where she found him in a Harlem restaurant. He briefly describes the encounter: "Her clothes, her carriage, her accent, all showed Deep South breeding and money. . . . I said at that college that the guilt of American whites included their knowledge that in hating Negroes, they were hating, they were rejecting, they were denying their own blood. . . . I'd never seen anyone I ever spoke before more affected than this little white college girl. She demanded, right up in my face, 'Don't you believe there are any *good* white people?' I did not want to hurt her feelings. I told her, 'People's *deeds* I believe in, Miss—not their words.' 'What can I *do*?' she exclaimed. I told her, 'Nothing.' "

We need to come to the point where we realize that we can do *nothing* about the church—unless we join the free man in his work of liberation. Jesus acts in terms of costly love—which we do not have. Doing God, doing the resurrection, doing death—this is not our thing. We have to be gifted the ability to act in these new ways: we have to receive strength from "the vine." The disciple is compelled to persevere in the love with which Jesus loved him long before the disciple knew him (v. 10). *Amor, ergo sum!* Jesus is "the church" because of his costly love. He lives in prevailing life with the Father, which means that everywhere in history his liberating activity continues. Liberation is the dynamic of history that goes on beyond our theological games. The question is whether we want to get "with it."

If we speak of a liberated church we are probably playing God. If we claim the church is liberating we are close to self-liberation. The point is to keep in touch with God's liberation. Only then might we catch a glimpse of the liberation church.

THE MARKS OF THE LIBERATION CHURCH   15:11–17

How can we recognize the great mystery called the church? According to the *Reformation*, the church is where the Word is rightly preached and the sacraments are rightly administered. This view has still much to commend itself. But it can also make the church subject to neat orthodox measuring sticks where rhetoric and rite hide the dead heart, the cold love, and the failure of nerve. For the *Liberation*, the corporateness Jesus creates will be discerned by vital responses of heart and mind: joy and friendship—and by election. These are the marks of the liberation church.

JOY   15:11–12

11 "I have said this to you, so that you may share my joy and that your joy may be complete. 12 This is my order: Love one another as I have loved you."

Man longs for fulfillment. Jesus offers it as joy—not as fun that often quickly fades, but as joy of the whole man. In the communion of the Father with the Son there is complete joy because it is the communion of waiting on man. Making man free is joy. Those who share in this communion know it as the joy of liberation.

How may we share in it? "Love one another as I have loved you" (v. 12). In love that waits on the lost, joy is com-

plete. It is found in the ongoing struggle for survival. At its
deepest it is black joy, warm and persuasive as vital response
even when it is not named:

> I return the bitterness
> Which you gave to me;
> When I wanted loveliness
> Tantalant and free.
>
> I return the bitterness.
> It is washed by tears;
> Now it is a loveliness
> Garnished through the years.
>
> I return it loveliness
> Having made it so;
> For I wore the bitterness
> From it long ago.
>
> —Lewis Alexander

Joy is a matter of soul.

FRIENDSHIP   15:13–15

   [13] "No man has greater love than he who sacrifices his life for
his friends. [14] You are my friends if you obey my order. [15] No
longer do I call you servants, for the servant does not know his
master's mind. I have called you friends because I shared with you
everything I learned from my Father."

   "You are my friends if you obey my order" (v. 14). This
almost sounds as though Jesus were demanding friendship.
But obeying his order is simply being human where it hurts:
risking one's life at the boundary of life with the lost (v. 13).
God's liberation is at work where people in risking their life
for each other discover each other as friends. Today, however,

American Christians are moving more and more apart from each other. And the church is split wide open. A new style of paranoia is developing. "This seems to be both the Age of Touchiness and the Age of the Beleaguered Minority. . . . Feeling oppressed, in fact, has become something of a national sport with its own succinct rules" (Melvin Maddocks). Everyone seems to feel he is under someone's heel. We are all at each other's throats while we should be risking our lives for the truly oppressed, which is the mandate of the Christian way.

It is among the truly oppressed that the free man makes friends. Friendship makes most sense where life is tough. Those who experience the risking of life for others are not left in the dark as regards what life is all about (v. 15). Friendship may have a thousand names. But it is real friendship only where a man risks his life for others:

When it is finally ours, this freedom, this liberty, this
    beautiful
and terrible thing, needful to man as air,
usable as earth; when it belongs at last to all,
when it is truly instinct, brain matter, diastole, systole,
reflex action; when it is finally won; when it is more
than the gaudy mumbo jumbo of politicians:
this man, this Douglass, this former slave, this Negro
beaten to his knees, exiled, visioning a world
where none is lonely, none hunted, alien,
this man, superb in love and logic, this man
shall be remembered. O, not with statues' rhetoric,
not with legends and poems and wreaths of bronze alone,
but with the lives grown out of his life, the lives
fleshing his dream of the beautiful, needful thing.

—Robert Hayden

Friendship is a matter of becoming soul brothers and soul sisters.

ELECTION   15:16–17

¹⁶ *"You did not choose me, but I chose you. I appointed you to go and bear fruit, fruit that will last, so that the Father will grant you whatever you ask of him in accord with my selfhood. ¹⁷ This is my order for you: Love one another."*

Long before the disciple loves as a friend he has *been loved* as a friend. *Amor, ergo sum.* I am being loved, therefore I am. When the disciple begins to love as a branch of the vine he draws upon the love that is already real in the free man. "You did not choose me, but I chose you" (v. 16). The idea of election has been much abused by the church. It does not mean that God has favorites, but that he is free—free to prevail among those whom man rejects. We cannot control his election of men to be witnesses of his liberation. In Jesus he chose human instruments, so that his work of liberation would increase (v. 16). Those who were oppressed, but were liberated by him, become liberators with him.

Where are the elect today? We cannot claim election for us who profess the Christian faith in the secular church—as though our faith, our Christianity, were proof of our election. Can we then not know God's choice? We have pointed to the black, the man where God struggles for survival. Is this the place where the liberation church emerges? We should be leary of any white pontification—including our own. Our pointing to the black might be nothing but theological exploitation. The black is already being exploited by the white wordmongers. Why should a white theologian be exempt from it? "Aesthetically the Negro is invaluable to the Southern novelist. If he is central to the action, he can be lynched or threatened with lynching to serve in the climactic scene. If he is a friend of the key white character, he can precipitate the moment of truth when the white man must face up to the lynch mob or the illegitimate mulatto child or whatever, and act out the role of hero or villain. . . . His isolation can stand for every man's isolation. His misery is the microcosm of human suffering; and his endurance is everyman's hope for the strength to endure and prevail. In short, he is one of the most valuable components of Southern fiction and one of the reasons for the superior quality of modern Southern literature. The nineteenth-century South exploited the Negro economically; the twentieth-century South is learning to exploit him aesthetically" (Nancy M. Tischler). Is it so unlikely that the twentieth-century South could also learn to exploit the black theologically? So we need to be careful in our theological use of black language. Blacks have to speak for themselves. Our appeal to black experience can only be indirect. There is also the temptation of trying to outblack the black, or of ingratiating ourselves with him. Thus we are in double jeopardy. We are damned—if we don't identify with the oppressed. But we may also be damned—if we do. The oppressed may not want us. They may in fact reject us. It is exactly at this point that we experience the difficulty of becoming a Christian.

Election as a mark of the church is the logical stop card of theology. It is so beautiful because it compels us to realize that ultimately it is not in our power to say where the liberation church is. And yet we know that it always exists as truly as God struggles with those who battle for survival. "Love one another" (v. 17). The miracle may happen that in the act of love—struggling with the lost—you discover your election and —the liberation church.

THE DISCIPLE AND THE SECULAR   15:18–27

[18] "If the world hates you, you know that it hated me first.
[19] If you belonged to the world, the world would love its own.
But because you do not belong to the world, since I have chosen
you out of the world, it hates you. [20] Remember what I said: "A
servant is not greater than his master." If they persecuted me they
will also persecute you. They will obey your word as little as they
obeyed mine. [21] They will treat you this way because of what I
am, since they do not know him who sent me. [22] Had I not come
and spoken to them, they would have no sin, but now they have
no excuse for it. [23] He who hates me, hates my Father. [24] Had I
not worked among them and done what no man ever did, they
would have had no sin; but now they have seen and hated both me
and my Father. [25] Now the fact accords with the word in their law,
"They hated me without a cause." [26] When the resistance counselor comes, whom I shall send from the Father, he will bear witness to me. [27] You are my witnesses, for you have been with me
from the beginning."

Those who try to identify with the lost should not be
surprised if they are rejected. Secularity measures by Who's
Who, Ford Foundation grants, and the right address. Even
the oppressed have been brainwashed into this system. The
one who is the church also was rejected; he died on a cross.
Secular men hated him first (vv. 18 f.).

The test of discipleship is rejection by secularity. Let the
disciple be especially wary of the secular theologian! The secularity that rejected Jesus was first of all the secularity of the
church. "A servant is not greater than his master" (v. 20).
God's liberation is a thorn in the flesh of the system. The
world does not really care about the lost. Men usually do not
acknowledge the one who risks his life for those battling for
survival (v. 21). Secular man cannot break through the layers

of concealment in his consciousness to real freedom. What he wants is secular recognition, status, the power to exploit his fellows.

Where the corporateness of freedom is rejected sin prevails. Only in the truly free man is corporate freedom real (v. 24). In confrontation with him, sin becomes glaring. But there is no good reason for rejecting corporate freedom (v. 25). Man's love of illusion is no good reason. It is incomprehensible why men should want to reject corporate freedom.

In any event, the gift of the Stand-In Spirit compels the disciple to make manifest who Jesus is (v. 26). The disciple's sharing in God's freedom becomes effective in further sharing: "You are my witnesses" (v. 27). This is what the liberation church is all about: freedom in public space attested by the witness of the disciple. It is not a matter of clustering together in a secretive conventicle of piety, an esoteric mystery circle, or a beatnik commune. The witness of the disciple is public witness. Only in public witness to God's liberating work, searching out God's struggle for man's survival, may men glimpse the reality of true community. It is the stand-in, the resistance spirit, who draws men together. But he is only found where God is liberating today as he was liberating in Jesus. If we look for him in the secular church we look for him in vain, just as the organization church did in Jesus' day.

THE LIBERATION CHURCH—
THE IMPOSSIBLE POSSIBILITY   16:1–33

The "Impossible" Life   16:1–4

¹ "I have told you all this so that your trust will not be shaken. ² They will excommunicate you. In fact, the time is coming when anyone who kills you will think that he is serving God. ³ They will do this because they do not know the Father nor me. ⁴ I have told

*you these things so that when their time comes you may remember
that I told you of them. I did not tell you all this before, because
I was still with you."*

If someone asks you, "Where is the liberation church?
Is it at Sixth and St. Clair?" do not answer him. The liberation
church is an event as Christ joins the battle of the oppressed.
"Neither this man, nor his parents sinned. His blindness affords an opportunity to embody God's works" (9:3). It is
always a matter of Christ choosing where to embody God's
works. You cannot pinpoint the liberation church beforehand.
You only know it when you are there. Secular man does not
see it. The liberation church is always—where we do not expect it. There was more liberation church in Auschwitz than
in all the comfortable white churches of Hitler Germany still
singing "A mighty fortress is our God." It takes election to see
what is at stake. Wrote a black upon seeing the Jewish pageant,
"We Will Never Die":

> I am part of this:
> Four million starving
> And six million dead:
> I am flesh and bone of this. . . .
>
> I am part of this
> Memorial to suffering,
> Militant strength:
> I am a Jew.
>
> Jew is not a race
> Any longer—but a condition.
> All the desert flowers have thorns;
> I am bleeding in the sand . . .
>
> —Owen Dodson

For those who try to become Christians, insight into where
the liberation church is is hindsight. In order to become Christians we must begin with the church, the traditional, visible
church where the reality of the liberation church at best breaks
through only from afar like the rays of the rising sun. But
here my pen breaks to pieces. Deep down inside I know that
the liberation church has nothing visibly radiant about it:
"They will excommunicate you. In fact, the time is coming
when anyone who kills you will think he is serving God" (v.
2). Thus the life of the disciple becomes an "impossible" one.
He knows he must work for something other than the ecclesiastical establishment, and yet he must begin his work within
its bounds. Setting one's eyes on the liberation church within
the bounds of the secular church is immediately to invite
ostracism.

Few in Western civilization today would burn the disciple at a stake; social ostracism is just as effective. So the
disciple no longer has much opportunity for real martyrdom.
Society and church merely let him shrivel away.

It is here that the life of the disciple proves "impossible."
Trying to do theology, to do God, resurrection, and death
leads to an impasse. This is truly "Mission Impossible." It
turns out that all the things we said in Chapters 1–12 should
be *done*, can't be done. Doing theology is an impossible thing.
The attempt to apply the theological, Christological, and anthropological insights gained in Chapters 1–12 to the church
as reflected in Chapters 13–15 throws us into havoc and makes
us discover the plight of the disciple: "The more the Church
is the Church, he stands within it, miserable, hesitating, questioning, terrified. But he does stand within the Church, and
not outside as a spectator. His possibility is the possibility of
the Church, and the Church's impossibility is also his. Its
embarrassment is his, and so too is its tribulation. He is one

with the solidarity of the Church, because it is the lack of the glory of God which creates fellowship and solidarity among men" (Karl Barth). We are *not* invited more fully to ponder our lack of the glory of God, but to turn *away from ourselves* to God's glory. For *where we cannot do a thing* (15:5) the joy of discipleship begins. Where we cannot do a thing we discover God—doing his thing. What God is doing now becomes the primal theme of theology—now that we realize our inability to make of ourselves a significant theme. We have "cancer of the soul" (Philip Wylie). Just when we think we have been healed it breaks out again. And we have to go back to the divine cobalt treatment.

There is no way under the sun that we could liberate ourselves. God must liberate us. "Could my zeal no respite know, could my tears forever flow, All for sin could not atone; Thou must save, and Thou alone." I cannot liberate myself. I cannot liberate others. "If the Son liberates you, you will be free indeed" (8:36). If we do not feel a scare at this point—the divine scare over our inability for liberation—we will not grasp the awesomeness of God's liberation. "Watch out, a time is coming, in fact, it has already come, when all of you will be scattered, each to his own home, and will leave me alone" (v. 32). Our attempts at liberation stand under this judgment. We cannot watch with the Lord one hour! (Mt. 26:40) The disciple will disappoint himself, also in his theology, even his liberation theology. But the dead end here is also a beginning: "Only when the end of the blind alley of ecclesiastical humanity has been reached is it possible to raise radically and seriously the problem of God" (Karl Barth).

Liberation: Making Room for Freedom 16:5–15

[5] "Now I am leaving for him who sent me, but none of you asks, 'Where are you going?' [6] You are overwhelmed by sadness

because of what I have told you. [7] But I tell you the truth when
I say: It is to your advantage that I should leave. If I do not leave
the resistance counselor will not come to you. But if I go I will
send him to you. [8] When he comes he will uncover for the world
the real nature of sin, righteousness and doom. [9] He will unmask
sin by their not trusting me. [10] He will disclose my righteousness
by my going to the Father when you will see me no more. [11] He
will expose what doom is by proving that the ruler of this world
has been doomed. [12] I still have much to tell you, but you cannot
take it now. [13] When the Spirit of truth comes, he will lead you
into the full truth. For he will not speak of his own authority, but
he will share only what he hears, and he will anticipate the future
for you. [14] He will embody me, because he will take what is mine
and declare it to you. [15] Whatever the Father has is mine. This is
why I said that he will take what is mine and declare it to you."

Having grasped the impossible possibility of theology we
must now study utmost economy of language. Where the impossible possibility appears we can do no more than stammer-
ingly point to the reality that makes theology possible: God
as God.

So it was of advantage that the earthly Jesus would leave
his disciples (v. 7). Otherwise we might have been left with
the impression that everything in becoming a Christian hinges
on one human individual. In the sending of the Spirit as resistance counselor it becomes clear that God himself is the
subject of theology: the one who really does theology. Liberation having been embodied in Christ is now expanded by God
himself as universal empowerment. The Spirit was always present to man as was the Word. But he was not present as power
of making God concrete universally. Before Jesus, manhood
was not known as God's temple. Now the Spirit opens all men
to becoming the temple of God. God himself battles for wider
space among men, so that the freedom Jesus brought can become universally effective.

Making room for freedom is also always a matter of the disciple resisting the spirit of the system—society organizing itself without God. Sin is unmasked (v. 9)—this means man's fear of acknowledging unconcealment is exposed. Where the power of sin is curtailed there is space for freedom. Those who trust Jesus through the work of the Spirit share in a wider space—a growing corporate self.

In corporate selfhood men are confronted with true life: God's reality and man's true self. The Holy Spirit is the bond of union between God's reality and Jesus' selfhood. He declares Jesus' life righteous. Men now have a new opportunity to see the direction of their destiny (v. 10).

The increase in the corporate self is also an occasion for exposing doom. As long as men feel doomed they paralyze themselves and confine freedom. Those who reject freedom doom themselves. Where the corporate self prevails "the ruler of this world," the power of the system that confines, has been "disempowered." In fact, the ruler of this world is exposed as having had no real power in the first place (v. 11).

So the Spirit opens a new space for freedom. He leads mankind into full unconcealment. By concealing himself man always closes off the space for freedom and does not venture out into fuller freedom. The Spirit opens greater space for freedom as he discloses corporate selfhood in Jesus and imparts freedom for true selfhood among all who trust. Thus he never works in his own behalf, but for the liberation already embodied in Jesus (vv. 12 f.).

Jesus is present in the space for freedom the Spirit creates. The more the reality of Jesus is grasped in his present identification with the lost, the greater the space for freedom becomes. The Spirit will draw men more and more together in their common claim on freedom. A beginning was made among the first disciples (v. 14).

In receiving new space for freedom the disciple learns

what the future holds: ever new opportunities for freedom.
The entire Godhead is present in the future. The waiting of
the Father also belongs to the Son. And both are present in
the Spirit of waiting. It is thus that God's future becomes
more and more present (v. 13). Mankind is more and more
opened up for liberation, being offered ever new space for
freedom. Nothing could be more ultimate.

The Presence of the Liberator   16:16–24

16 "A little while and you see me no more, and again a little
while and you will see me." 17 Some of his disciples said to one
another, "What does he mean by saying, 'A little while and you
see me no more, and again a little while and you will see me,' and
'because I go to the Father'? 18 What is this 'little while' that he
is talking about? We do not know what he means." 19 Jesus knew
that they wanted to ask him; so he said to them, "Are you trying
to figure out what I meant by saying, 'A little while and you see
me no more, and again a little while and you will see me'? 20 Believe me, you will weep and mourn, but the world will rejoice; you
will be sorrowful, but your sorrow will be turned into joy. 21 A
woman in labor is in pain, because the time of birth is near. But
when the child is born, she no longer remembers her pain in her
joy that a child is born into the world. 22 Now you are sorrowful,
but I shall see you again and your hearts will rejoice. No one shall
take away your joy. 23 On that day you will not ask me any questions. Believe me, whatever you ask of the Father in response to
what I am he will give you. 24 So far you have asked nothing in
response to what I am. Ask and you will receive so that your joy
will be complete."

While Jesus did not stay with us as the earthly Jesus and
also not as the risen Jesus to be directly encountered we meet
him again in the Spirit who makes room for freedom. In the
Spirit Jesus "comes again," not as yet in full manifestation

for every creature to behold, but in increasing freedom. In his presence he offers men battling for survival their true destiny (vv. 16–19).

The pain of which Jesus here speaks involves the birth-pangs of the Messianic Age. As something new appears with the birth of every child, liberation as the really new grows out of the suffering of those who battle for survival (v. 21):

> I return the bitterness.
> It is washed by tears;
> Now it is a loveliness
> Garnished through the years.

It is in human suffering that the Spirit makes the liberator present, so that liberation continues to be called forth concretely. As a mother forgets her pain when she sees the newborn child, so also liberated man rejoices when he finds himself freed through audacious suffering.

"On that day you will not ask me any questions" (v. 23). We ask questions as long as we are spectators of life. But in identifying with the oppressed we come forth tempered by suffering. Sharing in corporate suffering, however, intensifies the human struggle. It does not give answers. The "answer" lies in the ability to resist in the struggle. Here one learns how to theologize with the hammer, God's hammer (Luther), that forges truth out of suffering. Questions are asked as long as one is not part of the struggle. But in audacious suffering unconcealment is acknowledged in truth—for here we learn that God himself suffers. In Jesus' presence in the Spirit the wretched of the earth are the crucible of the acknowledgment of unconcealment. Trusting God's unconcealment, the destiny of all things, we no longer need to ask questions. Their place is taken by prayer, prevailing response of those who battle for

survival with God on their side. Prayer will be fulfilled in keeping with the freedom embodied by Jesus: man finds complete
joy when he discovers God in his unconcealment sharing his
Son's battle among the truly oppressed (vv. 23 f.):

> I return it loveliness
> Having made it so;
> For I wore the bitterness
> From it long ago.

The Awesomeness of Liberation   16:25-33

25 "All this I have shared with you in figures of speech; the
time is coming when I shall no longer speak to you in figures, but
tell you in plain words of the Father. 26 On that day you will make
requests in response to what I am. I do not promise to ask the
Father for you, 27 for the Father himself loves you, because you
have loved me and trusted that I have my origin in God. 28 I have
my origin in the Father and have entered the world. Now I am
leaving the world again and going to the Father." 29 His disciples
said, "Now you are talking plainly and not in veiled figures of
speech. 30 Now we are certain that you know all things and no one
needs to question you. Therefore we trust that you have your
origin in God." 31 Jesus answered, "Now you trust me? 32 Watch
out, a time is coming, in fact, it has already come, when all of you
will be scattered, each to his own home, and will leave me alone.
Yet I am not alone because the Father is with me. 33 I have shared
this with you, so that in me you may have peace. In the world you
are anxious. But take courage. I have overcome the world."

Many times Jesus has used parabolic language to interpret himself. He spoke of himself as temple, bread, light, and
vine. Now the disciples feel he is using plain language (v. 29).

Jesus brings a unique relationship of man to God. This
much the Gospel has tried to make clear. But it apparently

had not become clear to the disciples how awesomely simple
the Gospel ultimately is. There ought to be no "fixation" on
Jesus. He is not a religious end in itself. As focus of concern
he "disappears" again in the reality of God: "I have my origin
in the Father and have entered the world. Now I am leaving
the world again going to the Father" (v. 28). Only for this
reason does he know all things (v. 30). This is not the knowledge of intellectual genius. It is the grasp of the heart of creation: liberation through audacious suffering with the oppressed. If the disciple understands this, instead of asking
questions he will find the answer in his struggle for freedom.

As simple as it sounds, this is the most difficult thing for
man to do. It does not come natural to man to give up his
fixation on success. It does not come natural to man to bracket
out his private selfhood. "Watch out, a time is coming, in
fact it has already come when all of you will be scattered, each
to his own home, and will leave me alone" (v. 32). Liberation
is such an awesome thing that even the boldest show fear
when the going gets rough. Man wants freedom, and yet does
not want it. It is not just a question of being timid, although
many of us are. It is a matter of sin—our inability to overcome our self-contradiction: "I do not understand my own
actions. For I do not do what I want, but I do the very thing
I hate" (Rom. 7:15). That is, we do want freedom, and yet
deny it in our action. We want to "do" God, resurrection, and
death. And yet we do the opposite. Why we do it is a "surd"
—there is no explanation for it in our good creatureliness.
Radical irrationality enters our being in the reality of sin. We
do what does not make sense. We sense we ought to be where
we are not. But we do not grasp that we ought to be where
the battle for survival goes on. "The revolutionary must . . .
own that in adopting his plan he allows himself to be *overcome of evil*. He forgets that he is not the One, that he is

not the subject of the freedom which he so earnestly desires, that, for all the strange brightness of his eyes, he is not the Christ who stands before the Grand Inquisitor, but is, contrariwise, the Grand Inquisitor encountered by the Christ. He too is claiming what no man can claim" (Karl Barth). And the claims run their course and defeat themselves. What has happened to the liberationists of the sixties, the occupiers of administration buildings, the sit-in heroes, and the red-flag-wavers? *Time* in 1971 notes the fast change in the radical voices: "Three years ago I might have said that 250,000 people must be able to stop the war, that someone must hear them and pay attention. I don't think the war can be stopped—by any of us." Another young voice in *Time*: "We Americans suffer from a tendency to hail what is one hundred percent, but nothing is ever one hundred percent, and life is absurd, and that is the way it should be."

The realization of our self-contradiction in view of liberation does not make us one hundred percent either—not one hundred percent blissful, not one hundred percent desperate. But we do begin to sense how awesome a reality liberation is. It is not in our power to attain. So we go on, haunted by anxiety, restless, ill at ease: "In the world you are anxious" (v. 33). We appear ephemeral when judged by God's liberation.

Over against our ephemeral gropings and aspirations appears the counterthrust of the Gospel: "Take courage. I have overcome the world" (v. 33). The overcoming here is not a matter of victory, but of resistance, of becoming immune to the world's power, to its totalitarian demands. The free man has had the strength to withstand the onslaught of evil. Here is a reality that breaks our straight-line logic of everyday existence. The sacred breaks through: a peace which passes all understanding. It draws us out of ourselves into a new world, so that we can think new thoughts and do new deeds. We cannot produce true freedom. Liberation is awesome—it is God's privilege: "I have overcome the world."

PRAYER FOR THE LIBERATION
CHURCH   17:1–26

The Reality of the Sacred   17:1–5

¹ *After these words Jesus raised his eyes toward heaven and said, "Father, the hour has come. Glorify the Son, that the Son may glorify you.* ² *For you have given him authority over all men to grant prevailing life to all you entrusted to him.* ³ *Prevailing life means to know you, the only real God, and Jesus Christ whom you commissioned.* ⁴ *I have glorified you on earth by completing the work you gave me to do.* ⁵ *Now, Father, glorify me in your presence with the glory which I had with you before the world began."*

In making liberation our burden we are trying to play God. Jesus' prayer makes clear what we have been struggling with all along: sacred reality. There is a reality that does what we cannot do. While God is not hidden to man, this does not mean that he is like man.

We have been told time and again that modern man has lost the sense of the divine. Secularity has revealed more and more the nonexistence of God. So it has become obsolete to argue with William James: "It is as if there were in the human consciousness *a sense of reality, a feeling of objective presence, a perception* of what we may call '*something*' there, more deep and more general than any of the special and particular 'senses' by which current psychology supposes existent realities to be originally revealed." There is also no point to appealing with Rudolf Otto to the sense of the *numinous:*

"When Abraham ventures to plead with God for the men of Sodom, he says (Gen. 18:27): 'Behold now, I have taken upon me to speak unto the Lord, which am but dust and ashes.' There you have a self-confessed 'feeling of dependence,' which is yet at the same time more than, and something other than, *merely* a feeling of dependence. . . . I propose to call it 'creature-consciousness' or creature-feeling. It is the emotion of a creature, submerged and overwhelmed by its own nothingness in contrast to that which is supreme above all creatures." We are not claiming with Otto that man has a general experience of the divine, or that he ought to have it. The point is: what happens to a man if he plunges into existence together with Christ? If a man tries to become a Christian by following Christ, he finally finds himself up against the prayer of Jesus. And even if modern man should have lost the sense for the divine, what does he do with the reality of the praying Jesus?

Jesus prays on the way to the cross where he will fully identify with the oppressed. In the reality of the cross men are radically confronted with God. Jesus had been authorized to share the ultimately real. In his identification with the lost it has become evident that the ultimately real is the mutual response between the Father and the Son. The struggle for unoppressed life in which Jesus prevails in communion with the Father is the core of the life that prevails. Knowing this God in the struggle of Jesus is to have eternal life. The cross is the center of the struggle where eternal life becomes concrete (vv. 1–3).

"I have glorified you on earth by completing the work you gave me to do" (v. 4). Only one man was able to say this. Here in one man's life is freedom. Now Jesus prays that freedom be sustained as the true reality of human life in which man can find a new direction of his destiny (v. 5). Here a dimension of reality breaks through that is not commensurate with secular experience. This is sacred reality which we should have recognized all along. It is not that we have been looking for sacred reality. We do not even care to look for it. But we have seen a man struggle together with the lost for their freedom. What kind of a reality is this?

It is not easy to talk about this reality today. Secular man seems to have shut his eyes to it. At best he experiences transcendence as historical *future*. But this is not what Jesus' prayer is all about. Confronted with this prayer we experience not just sheer creaturehood, but our radical profanity, the vulgarization of our life. We are so brutalized that we have no sense for God's glory. Not future or moral transcendence, but sacred transcendence, otherness, opposes our profanity. We are possessed by our desire to oppress. What liberates us is the breakthrough of a reality that is not brutal, but tender, struggling for the survival of the least among men where we are too insensitive even to look. We are not trying to reintroduce some need for religious feeling, or some general notion of religion. Let every man open his ears to Jesus' prayer! Here he will find an otherness that judges him and unconceals him, a glory that is not glamor, but verily ultimate reality.

The Experience of the Sacred   17:6–10

⁶ I have acknowledged who you are before the men you gave me from the world. They were yours, you gave them to me, and they have obeyed your order. ⁷ Now they know that whatever you gave me is from you, ⁸ for I have shared with them the words you shared with me. They acknowledged them and are convinced that I had my origin in you, and they have trusted that you commissioned me. ⁹ I pray for them. I am not praying for the world, but for those whom you gave me for they are yours. ¹⁰ All who are mine are yours and all who are yours are mine and I am glorified in them.

The sacred does not want to stay wholly transcendent. It is offered man as a gift in which to share. Every word of Jesus offered liberation. Through his word the sacred is still shared with man. As the first disciples acknowledged this liberating communication, they had to learn to live from beyond themselves. *"Verbum Dei malleus est conterens petras* (the word of God is a hammer, breaking the rocks), says Luther, following the prophet; this 'word' alone is capable of breaking the walls with which reason has surrounded itself. And it is in this that the function and meaning of 'God's hammer' consist . . . which breaks the trust man puts in his own knowledge and in the virtue founded on the truths furnished by this knowledge" (Shestov). It is in the word that we are enabled radically to turn away from our profanity—the word that mediates the intercession of him who first embodied freedom in new community (v. 9). It is the deed-word which overcomes the division we make between reason and life.

The sacred reality Jesus represents becomes concrete for the world in a new space for freedom among the disciples. God's freedom embodied in Jesus is to be experienced in new contexts of public space. The truth of God's communion with Jesus is experienced, however, only as the new community shares in the word that frees man from his bondage. Jesus does not pray for the world, because if "his own" incarnate God's reality they will become a leaven in the world.

Sacred Corporateness   17:11–23

¹¹ *I am no longer in the world, but they are in the world while I come to you. Holy Father, keep in accord with your reality those whom you have given me that they may be corporate as we are corporate.* ¹² *When I was with them I kept those whom you have given me in accord with what you are. I guarded them and*

none of them is lost except the son of perdition, for the event had to agree with the Scripture. [13] Now I am coming to you. But I speak these things in the world, so that they may have my joy fully in themselves. [14] I have shared your word with them, and the world has hated them because they belong to the world as little as I. [15] I am not praying that you take them out of the world, but that you protect them from the evil one. [16] They belong to the world as little as I. [17] Consecrate them in the truth. Your word is truth. [18] As you sent me into the world I have sent them into the world. [19] I now consecrate myself for their sake, that they also may be consecrated in the truth. [20] I am praying not only for them, but for all those who trust me because of their word, [21] that they may all be corporate. As you, Father, share in me and I in you may they share in us, that the world may believe you commissioned me. [22] I have shared with them the glory which you granted me, that they may be corporate as we are corporate. [23] May they be fully corporate, I in them and you in me, so that the world may recognize that you commissioned me and loved them as you loved me.

God—is different. He is costly love as prevailing response between himself and the Son sharing the struggle of the lost for survival. Jesus prays that this otherness of God be expressed in a new space of freedom among the disciples. It is thus that he witnesses to the sacred. It is not an abstract sacredness, but the otherness of corporateness audaciously involved in the human struggle. It is historical transcendence in the *present* suffering of the lost.

Corporateness does not mean organizational unity. Even if the church barriers are broken down, corporateness will not result as a matter of course. Since Jesus prays for willingness to do battle against the negativities of life, the disciples must be ready to acknowledge God's work among men where no other men even care to look. For Jesus, corporateness means surrender of the proud privacy of which Judas is a symbol (vv. 11 f.).

Judas shows how threatened the corporateness of the disciples is (*cf.* 13:21–30). It is not a matter of course that one persists in battling where God is doing his thing. It always depends on careful listening to Jesus' word, the mark of which is joy (v. 13).

The world organizing itself without God cannot stand the corporateness that is the doing of God's thing, neither in Jesus nor in his disciples, since it contradicts the law of success (v. 14). The disciples are always tempted to capitulate to society's pseudoreality, to mistake corporation bigness for corporate oneness. Time and again they have to be made aware of the doing of God's thing by God himself. Only thus will they be protected from society organizing itself without God (v. 15).

The disciples are being set apart from man's illusory reality as much as their Lord (v. 16). And yet time and again they must be consecrated in their ability to discern truth. It is not a matter of course that we recognize it. Only as we concentrate on the word that shares what God is doing are we able to be in touch with truth (v. 17).

It is never a matter of having the truth in pious isolation. The disciples are sent into the world as was their Lord. In his death he was most immediate to the world sharing the lot of the oppressed—having become an oppressed one himself. This is consecration in truth: that the disciple can see the free man doing God's thing on the cross (vv. 18 f.).

The first disciples will be followed by others who will have the same chance. The response between the Father and the Son is to be embodied in a growing corporateness. The church is to be more and more a sign to the world of what God does in his Son (vv. 20 f.). Through word and deed of the free man do the disciples have access to what God is doing: "I in them and you in me." Discipleship has relevance for the whole world as it reflects God's corporateness (vv. 21 f.).

"Where God is there is no law, there is freedom. And where freedom is not, God is not" (Shestov). It is in the corporateness between Father and Son, most forcefully expressed on the cross, that freedom manifests its true mettle. In the ever-renewed assumption of responsibility for corporateness freedom is most free. It commits itself to the audacious struggle for new life which includes the agony of the cross, but also joy (v. 13), and the "glory" (v. 22) of sacred freedom.

PRAYER AS CENTRAL RESPONSE TO THE SACRED   17:24–26

[24] Father, I desire that those whom you gave me may be with me where I am, to see the glory which you granted me because you loved me before the world began. [25] Righteous Father, the world has not known you. But I have known you, and these men realize that you commissioned me. [26] I have made known to them who you are, and I will make it known, so that they may share the love with which you loved me and so share in me.

The free man has been saying all these things in prayer, we should not forget, having been gripped by the sacred himself. He cannot bring off the things he has referred to "on his own." The renewal of the world in the costly love of the Father depends on the Son himself *being loved* (v. 26). It is here that the glory of God is to be seen (v. 24). And prayer is called for, so that we can focus in on his reality. Jesus himself climaxes his work by prayer. This is not the John A. T. Robinson prayer of a kindly give and take between persons. It is encounter with the transcendent sacred—a "hard rock" we cannot tamper with.

THE CHURCH AS LIBERATION CHURCH

As soon as we ask where we might find the church Jesus is praying for we are in a dither. The liberation church is not a matter of being realized here and there in beautifully visible groups. As soon as we begin to point to the holy few—be they the most nonviolent, the most just, the most peaceful Jesus freaks—we have surrendered our theological integrity. The point of Jesus' prayer is to draw us away from ourselves to the place where we can see God doing his thing, quiet, unobtrusive, inconspicuous—where we least expect it.

All the while the church is there in all its weaknesses and limitations, an earthen vessel indeed. We are not called to dissociate ourselves from it, to form a better church, but to point within it to God's liberation. For it is by grace that this earthen vessel is the place where God's liberation is remembered, known, and worshipped. The strange dialectic which makes for the essence of the church is exactly what we need to recapture when we speak of the church as liberation church. The church is never an end in itself. It always points beyond itself. Its task is to witness to transcendence, sacred corporateness as the heart of creation. Insofar as it does point to transcendence, God's involvement in the wretched of the earth, it is the liberation church, not the church already liberated and thus perfect, but people of God rejoicing in the mystery of what is coming toward them in the waiting of costly love.

Chapters 13–17 do not mediate to us a doctrine of the church. But they offer us a basic posture toward what is at stake in the existence of the church, the posture we must not lose sight of in our effort of being the church: the witness to what goes on as God's work beyond the church and in spite of the church. This posture dare not be organized as a separate church. It needs to pervade all of the church, so that the church as a whole become the liberation church. "Life together under the Word remains sound and healthy only where it does not form itself into a movement, an order, a society, a 'collegium pietatis,' but rather where it understands itself as being a part of the one, holy, catholic Christian church, where it shares actively and passively in the sufferings and struggles and promise of the whole church" (Dietrich Bonhoeffer).

It may be that the offer of liberation is something people do not even want. There may be no takers for it. The Grand Inquisitor thought that man did not want freedom. And yet there is the ache in us that as long as all men are not free we are not free ourselves. So the church is called to continue to witness to what transcends all men: the power that affords us the space to be free.

All we have said about the liberation church would remain an innocuous generality, however, if we would not indicate what it practically amounts to. Our references to black experience were not fortuitous. The mention of Jewish suffering by a black was also not by chance. God does not withdraw from the complacent, but he is present among them in judgment. In order to know God anew as costly love the complacent have to find God again where the pain is.

To admit that God struggles among the oppressed means to join the battle in opening up public space for freedom for those who have no access to it. Opening up white churches for black members makes little difference for those who suffer. The real point is to open up the jobs and better housing. On a wider scale it is granting unionization rights to *Chicanos* and self-determination to Vietnamese. The real corporate issue in the ecumenical movement is thus no longer the reunion of denominations, but the liberation of Christians who are at odds with one another because of color, social status, or different location.

Without changing the human self-image, however, nothing much will change in society. Here the task for the church as liberation church is crystal clear. Where Christians live contrary to the truth they know, the heresy has to be nailed down for all to see. The issue is not one of disliking a person of other color, but of taking color as an excuse for a master-servant relationship.

> Has the Church failed mankind, or has mankind failed
> the Church?
> When the Church is no longer regarded, not even op-
> posed, and men have forgotten
> All gods except Usury, Lust and Power.
>
> —T. S. Eliot

It is the false image of man that creates the false gods which needs to be destroyed. It needs to happen where these gods are at work. And they are exceptionally effective in the white church. It is not for us today to say where else they are also effective. It is for us to repent. In view of black suffering there can be no question as to where liberation needs to take place today. And there can be no question as to why the church needs to become the liberation church.

PART V

LIBERATED MANHOOD

"The knowledge of God—faith working through love—
is presented to men as the possibility which, though realized
at no particular moment in time, is, nevertheless, open to them
at every moment, as the new and realizable possibility of their
being what they are in God—His children—cast, as men of
the world, under judgment, looking for righteousness and
awaiting redemption, but under grace, already liberated" (Karl
Barth). As we come to the final phase of the Gospel we actually come to its first phase. The Gospel originally was the
Passion-Resurrection narrative. Only later did we get elaborate introductions. The Passion-Resurrection reality has been
built into the Fourth Gospel as a whole. Now we must consider it quite explicitly. We are not liberated. Jesus is. Only
through him can we grasp our liberation. For us liberation, in
terms of realization, is an eschatological reality—*futurum
aeternum.*

In reflecting on the church, if not before, we have realized that we do not achieve liberation. We have had to face
up to the tragic dimension of human life. "The tragedy of

225

man is that he can conceive perfection, but he cannot achieve
it" (Reinhold Niebuhr). This is what we must ponder more
fully now. In the free man we contemplate liberated manhood.
In ourselves we contemplate bondage. It has often been said
in recent years that modern man has come of age. But where
are the truly mature men? Are not the brash youth and the
cocksure middle-aged full of dishonesty, self-hatred, and despair? We are not the oppressed, by a long shot, we affluent
Christians, although we occasionally like to think we are. We
are the possessed—immature, dishonest, noncommitted, captive to evil powers competing for our loyalties. All the figures
around Jesus in the Passion story reflect our abysmal bondage.

REFUSING VIOLENCE   18:1–14

¹ After these words, Jesus went out with his disciples across
the ravine of the Kedron to a garden which he entered with them.
² Judas, who betrayed him, also knew the place because Jesus had
often met there with his disciples. ³ So Judas went there, taking
along the guard and temple police from the chief priests and
Pharisees with lanterns, torches, and weapons. ⁴ Jesus, knowing
everything that was going to happen to him, stepped forward and
asked them, "Whom are you looking for?" ⁵ They answered, "Jesus
of Nazareth." Jesus said, "I am he." Judas, who betrayed him, was
standing among them. ⁶ As he said to them, "I am he," they
stepped back and fell to the ground. ⁷ He asked again, "Whom
are you looking for?" They replied, "Jesus of Nazareth." ⁸ Jesus
answered, "I have told you that I am the man. If you are looking
for me, let these men go." ⁹ He said this that his word, "I have
not lost a single one of those you gave me," would come true.
¹⁰ Then Simon Peter, who carried a sword, drew it and struck the
High Priest's servant, cutting off his right ear. The servant's name
was Malchus. ¹¹ Jesus told Peter, "Put your sword back into the
sheath. Should I not drink the cup my Father has given me?"

¹² *Then the guard with its captain and the Jewish temple police arrested Jesus and bound him.* ¹³ *First they took him to Annas, the father-in-law of Caiaphas who was High Priest that year.* ¹⁴ *It was Caiaphas who had advised the Jews that it would be in their best interest if one man should die for the people.*

The contrast between Chapters 17 and 18 is harsh. We just listened to words of love. Now we hear of weapons (v. 3) and an ear cut off (v. 10). From reverence for life we move to violence. We delude ourselves about our true condition if we assume that we have no part in violence. We all share in the human attempt to force upon each other illusory reality in which violence is rampant.

It is not unimportant that violence stands right at the beginning of the Passion narrative, violence not committed by the world only, but by one who is a disciple. Man's sickness is strong. Our drive to assert ourselves, our pride, even sways the action of our discipleship. "There is no health in us." We said earlier, rebirth is the ability to identify with those who struggle for survival. It will be impossible, however, to take one's place at the side of the oppressed unless one's false pride has been broken. Liberation is a complex thing. We dare not play down the very personal dimension of the change that needs to take place in the encounter with the free man. We need to share in his crucifixion of eros, his radical surrender of pride.

The magnitude of sin is underscored by Judas' betrayal (vv. 2–5). Before we claim that we are also somehow oppressed, we need to admit that we are possessed, possessed by evil powers that control us. It is the free man who refuses to be possessed by evil. Openly he steps forward to face evil: "Jesus, knowing everything that was going to happen to him, stepped forward and asked them, 'Whom are you looking for?' " (v. 4). His way of battling evil is nonviolent. It is expressed in his rebuke of Peter, who had cut off the ear of a member of the arresting party (v. 11). Evil holds power only if it is fought on its own terms—which means by violence in its many forms. It has no power over the one who absorbs its blows. Jesus refused to retaliate. In its very attempt to destroy him evil manifested its impotence.

THE SELF-EVIDENCE OF TRUTH   18:15-24

¹⁵ *Simon Peter and the other disciple who was personally acquainted with the High Priest followed Jesus. The latter went into the High Priest's courtyard with Jesus,* ¹⁶ *but Peter stayed outside at the door. Then the other disciple who knew the High Priest went back and talked to the maid at the door and brought in Peter.* ¹⁷ *The maid asked Peter, "Do you not also belong to this man's disciples?" He answered, "No, I do not."* ¹⁸ *Since it was cold, the servants and the police had made a charcoal fire as they were standing about, and they were warming themselves. Peter stood among them, keeping himself warm.* ¹⁹ *The High Priest questioned Jesus about his disciples and his teaching.* ²⁰ *Jesus answered, "I have spoken publicly to the world. I have always taught in the synagogue and the temple where all the Jews usually meet; I have said nothing in secret.* ²¹ *Why are you questioning me? Ask my hearers what I taught. They know what I said."* ²² *After saying this, one of the police slapped Jesus in the face and said, "Dare you answer the High Priest that way?"* ²³ *Jesus replied, "If I have said something wrong, prove it. But if I spoke the truth, why do you hit me?"* ²⁴ *At this Annas sent him bound to Caiaphas, the High Priest.*

The story of violence continues with a slap in Jesus' face. Throughout the Passion narrative we have opportunity to contemplate our "possession" by evil. Self-contradiction has in-

delibly impressed itself upon the human soul. We do not respect the truth when we are faced by it. Even in our religious
best we fall short of giving due respect to the truth.

The ecclesiastical authorities prove this once more. In the
Gospel, ecclesiasticism time and again represents the defend-
ers of the status quo, illusory reality. Confronted by true manhood, ecclesiasticism does not know its obligation. Jesus had
always lived and taught openly before men (vv. 20 f.). The
light had always shone in the darkness (cf. 1:5). Why does
the organization church not understand the man who embodies the light? Religion, too, is possessed by evil.

The High Priest represents churchmen who refuse to acknowledge God's unconcealment, the self-evident in the life
of every man. Churchmen like all men refuse to acknowledge
the openness of true manhood. All truth can do here is to appeal to its self-evidence.

Man was so created that he could know true manhood in
himself. Confronted with true manhood in Jesus, every man
should be able to find his true self. And yet we continue to
deny what is most near to us.

NO SELF-LIBERATION
OF THE INDIVIDUAL   18:25-27

25 Simon Peter stood around warming himself. They asked
him, "Do you not also belong to his disciples?" He denied it, saying, "No, I do not." 26 One of the High Priest's servants who was
kin to the man whose ear Peter had cut off, said, "Did I not see
you in the garden with him?" 27 Peter denied that also.

The story of human evil still continues. Peter denies the
truth, too. Here is one who had grasped the meaning of the
light. And yet he reneges and relies on darkness. Peter was no

absolute coward. He had been ready to be hero in violence, to put up a fight when the enemies came to arrest his master (v. 10). But he was acting in terms of his prideful view of self-liberation. In terms of man's true self, there is no need to be violent in order to affirm liberation.

The moment truth appears defeated, with no glory of success, even the disciple is embarrassed. This truth is too un-assuming and modest. Is Peter not a disciple of this man? Most certainly not. Not of one who is a failure. At the moment truth does not succeed in battling evil; although it is unconcealed, it is veiled to the one who trusts in success.

At this juncture the radical attack of the Gospel upon man as a sinner is manifest once more. Man is a heel. He does not face the truth. Twisted and distorted, he cannot hope to liberate himself.

Today there are many gospels of self-liberation competing with the Gospel. Norman O. Brown, for example, promotes a change of man's relationship to himself. Man should acknowl-edge his animal body with its needs and desires. Returning to animal nature would be liberation. Since all of human history must be understood as aberration from man's original state, man must become one again in unity of spirit and body ac-cepting death and affirming life. The theme is related to Jesus' view that "he who finds his life will lose it, and he who loses his life for my sake will find it" (Mt. 10:39). The solution of the problem of identity for Brown is to get lost. What he seems to overlook is that in the Christian concern the losing of self is related to Christ.

The whole issue boils down to what we in fact *can* do. We are Peter. In trying to assert ourselves we don't get lost, but get more deeply caught in our self-contradictions and we remain afraid of ourselves. Norman Brown claims: "What is needed is . . . to change the human body so that it can become for the first time an organism—the resurrection of the body." Presupposed is our ability to remake ourselves. Repressions can be overcome and we can come forth a new animal. What needs to be looked at carefully, however, is the nature of the disease from which we are suffering. Brown himself says: "To miss the nature of the human disease is also to miss the nature of the cure." And from the Gospel perspective our disease is not repression so much as possession, subservience to forces we cannot control. Peter is not remaking himself, but is getting more deeply enmeshed in unmaking himself. However, while Peter is not liberating himself, something is going on in history that is liberating him.

What we are saying seems a gross oversimplification. And yet we need to understand that the Gospel wants us to see that our liberation is already taking place, so that we do not have to think ourselves back to our primal state in order to arrive at a more perfect state. It is exactly the problem of our self-liberation that is taken out of our hands. The liberating is being done *for us*.

Modern man has painted himself into a corner as far as liberation is concerned. He senses that he can be liberated, but he also realizes more fully the disease of history. With Freud, we can fathom the murky depths of our soul or with Norman O. Brown examine Western civilization as a history of disease. But the despair and the frustration we find there may ultimately overwhelm us unless we notice men who are getting lost in resisting the world in Jesus' name: in joining the battle for survival among the lost. Here a liberation takes place that overpowers despair and frustration.

Jesus resisting evil while struggling together with the lost and becoming one of them already embodied liberation. We cannot say, this is all there is to it. God's liberation in the Incarnation is a great mystery. But in the struggle of the black

and the Indian and the *marginales* of South America today
we have an analogy of the context in which liberation was first
embodied. It can help us understand what we are missing in
our complex Freudian schemes of self-liberation. As long as
Peter refuses to be known as a friend of a wretched man called
Jesus of Nazareth (vv. 25–27) he is not free. We are not sug-
gesting that liberation takes place completely outside ourselves
(*extra nos*). But it antecedes and transcends our efforts at self-
liberation. To be liberated we need to get "with it"—to get
involved in what is already going on as the liberation of man
among the oppressed.

NO SELF-LIBERATION IN POLITICS   18:28–40

28 Then they took Jesus from Caiaphas to the Governor's
residence. It was early morning now. They did not go into the
residence themselves, so that they would not be religiously unclean
and could eat the Passover. 29 Pilate went out to them and said,
"What charges do you bring against this man?" 30 They answered,
"If this man had not committed a capital offense, we would not
have brought him before you." 31 Pilate said, "Take him and judge
him according to your law." 32 The Jews told Pilate, "We are not
allowed to execute anyone." Thus the words of Jesus came true
which indicated how he would die. 33 Then Pilate went back into
his residence, called Jesus and asked him, "Are you the king of
the Jews?" 34 Jesus answered, "Is this your own idea or have others
suggested it to you?" 35 Pilate retorted, "Am I a Jew? Your own
people and the chief priests have turned you over to me. What is
your offense?" 36 Jesus answered, "My kingship does not originate
in this world. If it did, my servants would fight to keep me from
being arrested by the Jews. But now my kingship does not originate here." 37 Then Pilate said to him, "So you are a king?" Jesus
answered, "You use the word 'king.' I was born and came into the
world to bear witness to the truth. Everyone who shares in the

truth listens to my voice." [38] *Pilate said to him, "What is truth?"*
On saying this, he went out again to the Jews and told them, "As
for me, I find no charge against him. [39] *You have a custom that*
I release one prisoner at the Passover. Do you want me to release
the king of the Jews?" [40] *They all shouted, "Not him, but Bar-*
rabas!" Barrabas was a robber.

While the state commits itself to the administration of
justice, this does not exclude frequent usurpation of its commitment. We must admit of corporate as much as of individual self-contradiction.

Jesus gets a fair hearing from the state. He is brought to
death not in consequence of Pilate's attempt to administer
justice, but as a result of his surrender to what seems expedient. Again man's being possessed by evil is inescapably clear.

In stating the facts of the case the state is just: "I find no
charge against him" (v. 38). Not entirely bereft of the light,
it is able to acknowledge truth up to a point. As an attempt
of ordering human life the state is an instrument by which
God's light touches man. But the free man confronts the state
with the full light of truth (v. 37). Pilate's question shows
the predicament of the state. "What is truth?" (v. 38). The
state is subject to truth, and yet cannot measure up to it. Even
if individual man were moral, society is immoral. The power
play between contending groups cannot escape sin.

In the midst of immoral society stands Jesus as king—the
king of truth. The kingdoms of this world, albeit distortedly,
proclaim that man must serve a king. But they do not bring
forth true kingship—which is waiting on man.

"'Everyone who shares in the truth listens to my voice"
(v. 37). Those who can stand unconcealment can also accept
the kingship of the free man. If we realize how deeply we are
steeped in self-deception, we may be able to take the first step

toward unconcealment. For a moment Pilate is struck by the truth. But he does not acknowledge it. And so the state tergiversates and finally surrenders to the whim of the people: "Do you want me to release the king of the Jews?" (v. 39).

If we take man's basic disease into account, his being possessed, we realize that ambiguity and compromise are of the essence of politics, the realm of conflicting desires over public issues. Ideologies which imply that man must also liberate himself in the public realm and not only in his private responsibilities mistake the central issue. Herbert Marcuse is probably the most illustrious antipode of the more privately oriented Norman O. Brown. In Marcuse's thought a return to primordial beginnings is not called for. Rather, man must find new societal structures that are nonrepressive. The approach is based on the proposition that the coming revolution will "be liberating only if it [is] carried by the non-repressive forces stirring in the existing society." Here a new elite will have to chart the future, no longer the proletariat of Karl Marx, but a new intelligentsia with the sensibility of nonrepression. It could be argued against Marcuse that people cannot be liberated from above. But the crucial question is whether there is a liberated elite at all. Once more, the nature of the human disease must be faced squarely.

This is not the place to give elaborate evaluations of Norman O. Brown and Herbert Marcuse. The point of mentioning both is simply to raise the question of the nature of the human disease. Man is ultimately not free to see his radical bondage to evil. He indeed has virtues. And yet in "the moment of truth" they turn out to be splendid vices. Judas, Peter, Pilate . . . There is a Judas in every one of us, a Peter, and also a Pilate. We botch our best insights and achievements. So God himself goes into the darkness of death to take upon

himself the consequence of human oppression and possession
and to transform it.

We can learn from both Brown and Marcuse. Liberation
is indeed: getting lost. Liberation is indeed: finding nonrepressive structures. But getting lost is ultimately a matter of identifying with the lost, and finding nonrepressive structures is
ultimately a matter of identifying with the oppressed—finding
liberation operative among the very people caught in repres-
sive structures.

LIBERATED MAN   19:1–6

¹ *Then Pilate took Jesus and had him flogged.* ² *The soldiers
made a crown of thorns, put it on his head, and threw a purple
robe around him.* ³ *They came up to him crying, "Hail, king of the
Jews!" and they slapped his face.* ⁴ *Pilate stepped out again and
said to them, "Look, here I am bringing him out again to you to
let you know that I find no charge against him";* ⁵ *and Jesus came
outside, wearing the crown of thorns and the purple robe. Pilate
said to them, "Look here, the man!"* ⁶ *When the chief priests and
the temple police saw him they shouted, "Crucify! Crucify!" Pilate
replied, "You take him and crucify him yourselves. As for me, I
find no charge against him."*

Jesus is now nearing the cross—together with God. Regardless of how much the Judas, Peter, or Pilate in us denies
the truth, God does his thing. There is a divine determination
about the Passion narrative that curtails human evil, so that it
cannot steal the show.

How did God get into this suffering in the first place?
It was because of Jesus' audacious identification with the
wretched of the earth. Someone might wonder, is God alive
only to the extent that we are poor and oppressed? If so, what

happens to his presence when we are liberated and become affluent? We need to remember that God went into the darkness of death *because* he had been identifying with the lost. And because of this identification he became a lost one himself. "God chose what is weak in the world to shame the strong" (I Cor. 1:27).

This does not mean that Judas, Peter, and Pilate have no place in the Gospel story. God identified with the oppressed all the more effectively to convict the possessed. Obviously just as Bonhoeffer wanted us to talk about God at the center of life and not at the periphery, so we too must talk about God at the center of our political and social life and not just at the periphery. And yet we must never forget that God is the one who first of all was radically embodied at the periphery, outside the city wall on a cross, and who still goes outside the walls of suburbia to seek what is lost. It is a harsh word, but nonetheless true to God's presence in Jesus: "Those who are well have no need of a physician, but those who are sick" (Mk. 2:17).

God is certainly not alive only to the extent that we are poor and oppressed. But the affluent possessed often try to kill him and say that he is dead. He is always where the rich and the religious do not expect him, on the other side of the tracks, seeking to save what is lost where they do not even care to look.

He stands before Pilate because of his identification with the lost. Pilate does not know who Jesus is in truth. But he senses part of the truth, touched by its self-evidence: "Look here, the man!" (v. 5). Merely a man! How can one find wrong in a man who wants to be no more than a man, who is open about his origin and his destiny?

Churchmen attack him because he moved himself into close proximity to God. What he claimed was that man's aspirations and hopes are fulfilled when he accepts his true selfhood. Man is free when he is battling together with the lost for survival. This is what Jesus is "all about." Pilate seems to have had a faint inkling of it. But the churchmen are blind to it: "Crucify! Crucify!" (v. 6).

That the state finally also fails to stand up for the free man proves how incapable man ultimately is of accomplishing liberation. Said Pilate, "You take him and crucify him yourselves" (v. 6).

Here stands liberated man—to be crucified. He is liberated because he does not want to be more than he is: man. He does not want to transcend himself, whether backward into the tribal past or forward into the superman future. He is liberated man because evil has no power over him. "Look here, the man!" As this man he stands in the way of state and church. Even if he does not have much space for freedom left, he is free—because God is still his space for freedom.

CAESAR AS ONLY KING   19:7–16

⁷ *The Jews answered, "We have a law, and by that law he must die, because he claimed to be the Son of God." * ⁸ *When Pilate heard this he felt even more uneasy. * ⁹ *He went back into his residence and asked Jesus, "Where are you from?" Jesus did not answer him. * ¹⁰ *Then Pilate said to him, "You will not talk to me? Do you not know that I have power to release you or to crucify you?" * ¹¹ *Jesus answered, "You have no power over me, unless it is granted you from above. Therefore the one who turned me over to you has the greater sin." * ¹² *From that moment Pilate tried all the more to release him. But the Jews shouted, "If you release him, you are not Caesar's friend. Any man who pretends to be a king is against Caesar." * ¹³ *When Pilate heard this he brought Jesus out and sat down on the judgment-seat at the place called The Pavement or, in Hebrew, Gabbatha. * ¹⁴ *It was about noon on the day of preparation for the Passover. Pilate said to the Jews, "Here is*

your king." ¹⁵ *They shouted, "Take him! Take him! Crucify him!"*
Pilate said, "I am supposed to crucify your king?" The chief priests
answered, "We have no king but Caesar." ¹⁶ *Finally Pilate turned*
him over to them for crucifixion. Then they took Jesus.

There is always a contention in church and society as to
who the liberated man really is. Freedom is usually attributed
only to the powerful. How can Jesus measure up to this expectation?

He had claimed: "I and the Father are one" (10:30).
The loyal churchmen could not approve of it (v. 7). Since
for them God was utterly transcendent, Jesus seemed to be
blaspheming. But he did not view himself as God. He was well
aware of the real nature of power, that it comes from "above,"
from God (v. 11), and that he too had to receive power from
"above." Just because he did not lay claim to any power of his
own was he liberated.

Once more the truth is denied. Facing the crowd, Pilate
wonders: was he supposed to crucify their king? The churchmen answer: "We have no king but Caesar" (v. 15). To say
this is to forget that Caesar is not truly king. In answering
Pilate the churchmen should have thought about "what it
means to be a king and what to be a man" (Pascal). Whenever we absolutize loyalty to "Caesar," we show ignorance of
the true nature of power. Making "Caesar" absolute is to surrender our freedom.

THE FREE MAN AS KING   19:17–22

¹⁷ *He went out carrying the cross himself to the Place of the*
Skull, as it is called, or, in Hebrew, Golgotha. ¹⁸ *There they cruci-*
fied him with two others, one on the left, one on the right, and
Jesus between them. ¹⁹ *Pilate had a sign made to be fastened to*
the cross. It read, "Jesus of Nazareth, the King of the Jews."

²⁰ *Many Jews read it because the place where Jesus was crucified was close to the city. The sign was written in Hebrew, Latin, and Greek.* ²¹ *The chief priests of the Jews said to Pilate, "Do not write, 'The King of the Jews,' but rather, 'He said, I am the King of the Jews.' "* ²² *Pilate answered, "What I have written, I have written."*

Jesus has now been nailed to the cross. Pilate's sign on the cross, "Jesus of Nazareth, the King of the Jews" (v. 19), contradicts the churchmen's self-proclaimed loyalty to Caesar. Pilate did not openly acknowledge Jesus as King of kings. But inadvertently he witnessed to him as king of his people, as true man. Jesus is king because of his freedom. Faced with Jesus, men are invited to recognize their own freedom. Even the Roman state, represented by Pilate, finally submitted to the meaning of the inscription on the cross. After the Edict of Milan, "slaves gained a right to eventual freedom, and criminals were no longer to be branded on the face 'because it is fashioned'—ordained the Emperor, anticipating Dante—'after the similitude of heavenly beauty' " (Charles Williams).

Outside the city wall, on Golgotha, the Place of the Skull, it became manifest how fully God had identified with the oppressed. He was now an oppressed himself. Once we truly see the cross we can never forget *truth forever on a scaffold*. Liberation is here not at all a matter of discovering one's animal nature or of belonging to an intelligentsia elite. It is taking up the burden of life with those who are denied their freedom.

LIBERATED MAN IN DEATH 19:23–42

²³ *The soldiers, when they had crucified Jesus, took his clothes and divided them into four parts, one for each soldier. They also took his robe which was without a seam; the whole length was*

woven in one piece. [24] So they said to each other, "Let us not tear it, let us cast lots for it and see who gets it," so that the event would fit the Scripture, "They have divided my clothes among them, they gambled for my clothing." This is the way the soldiers acted. [25] Standing near Jesus' cross were his mother with her sister Mary, Clopas' wife, and Mary Magdalene. [26] Jesus, seeing his mother and the disciple whom he loved standing close by, said to her, "Woman, he is your son," and to the disciple, "She is your mother." [27] From that hour the disciple took her into his house. [28] After this, Jesus, knowing that everything was complete, said, "I thirst," so that the event would agree with the Scripture. [29] A bowl filled with sour wine was standing there; so they soaked a sponge in it, put it on a spear and held it to his mouth. [30] After Jesus had taken the wine he said, "It is complete." His head fell forward, and he gave up his spirit. [31] The Jews asked Pilate to have the legs of the crucified broken and their bodies taken down, so that they would not remain on the cross over the Sabbath, for it was already the day of preparation, and that Sabbath was an especially great day. [32] The soldiers went out and broke the legs of the first man who had been crucified with him and also of the second. [33] But when they came to Jesus and saw that he was already dead they did not break his legs. [34] However, one of the soldiers pierced his side with a spear, and immediately blood and water came out. [35] The man who saw it witnessed to it, and his witness is true. He knows that he speaks the truth, so that you also may trust. [36] This occurred so that Scripture and event would agree, "No bone of his shall be broken." [37] Another Scripture text says, "They shall look on whom they have pierced." [38] After this, Joseph of Arimathea who was a disciple of Jesus—but secretly for fear of the Jews— asked Pilate for permission to take Jesus' body. Pilate agreed. So Joseph went and took his body away. [39] Nicodemus, the one who had first visited him by night, also came there, bringing a mixture of myrrh and aloes which weighed about seventy pounds. [40] They took Jesus' body and wrapped it in linen strips, using the spices according to the Jewish burial custom. [41] At the place where Jesus had been crucified there was a garden and in it a new tomb in *which no one had been buried as yet.* [42] *Since it was the Jewish day of preparation and the tomb was rather close by, they laid Jesus there.*

The outward facts of Jesus' death, as the Gospel relates them, are well known and need no special commentary. What concerns us is the meaning of this death. Why did this young man, perhaps not even thirty, have to suffer a violent death? The Fourth Gospel does not offer us a doctrine of atonement in its Passion narrative. But the entire Gospel is a commentary on the death. The meaning of the death is woven through all the strands of the Gospel.

Jesus embodied God on the cross. As embodiment of God, Jesus' life is "substitutionary"—acknowledging for all men what they ought to acknowledge as the heart of creation: God's identification with the struggle for survival among the oppressed. This is man's true selfhood. God's reality, his transcendent freedom, is the ground of man's self.

Man's whole dilemma is his belief that liberation is a goal still to be achieved—and to be achieved by himself—while liberation in principle has already occurred. "It is complete" (v. 30). The cross is the moment when liberation is consummated in history. From this moment on all that is called for is to apply its reality to history, to draw out its implications, to make it universal.

That Jesus' legs were not broken points out once more that he is the true Paschal Lamb (vv. 31–37). According to Exodus 12:46 no bone of the Paschal Lamb was to be broken. As the Paschal Lamb, Jesus suffered the beating and ridicule inflicted upon him. He did not strike back. Thus evil was defeated. Man's liberation, however, does not begin on the cross. It begins with Jesus' first act of obedience. The cross seals it.

Jesus fully shares in the human lot. While soldiers take

his clothes and gamble for his robe (vv. 23 f.) he is intensely concerned about those closest to him (vv. 25–27). He suffers deeply (vv. 28 f.). Nothing gives us the impression that he was not sorely tempted to succumb to the onslaught of evil. And yet he carries out his work without surrender to the power of evil.

He dies outside the city wall, so that others would be empowered to be free to identify with the lost. Because of his liberation men are no longer in bondage. Because he prevails in the corporateness of God, mankind is offered eternal life which will be underscored once more in the story of the resurrection. Good Friday ends with the tomb. Jesus radically shares in man's lot (vv. 38–42).

This man is liberated because evil holds no power over him. Having rejected to act on its terms, he stands outside its influence and is not possessed by it. Among men he is the one who is not possessed. This has become God's very embodiment. Evil has no part in God. While he himself has become an oppressed, he radically refuses to become possessed. And so he really *does* death with evil holding no sway.

And what of the possessed? The human story lends itself to much agonizing over evil, to a fascination with evil and its psychoanalysis. And yet there is no need whatever to plunge into the catalogue of infinite sins. In view of the cross, evil turns out to be an opportunity for good. Our faults and vices are a *felix culpa*, a fortunate fall. Our evil is God's opportunity for liberation. So we need not carry the burden of sin, we need not wax melancholy over it, we need not become desperate studying our neuroses. We are invited to ponder God's audacious suffering for our sake in order that we might become free. The word of the cross on our sin is: *felix culpa*, fortunate fall!

It is a distinctive characteristic of the Christian faith that it points us beyond ourselves if we want to find freedom. This does not at all mean that we should sin, so that grace may abound. What it does mean is that we must lose ourselves in order to find ourselves in the new selfhood that affords us true freedom: the selfhood of the man on the cross.

LIBERATED MAN IN RESURRECTION 20:1-31

¹ On Sunday morning, Mary of Magdala went to the tomb very early while it was still dark. She noticed that the stone had been removed from the tomb. ² At this she ran to Simon Peter and the other disciple whom Jesus loved and told them, "They have taken the Lord from the tomb, and we do not know where they have laid him." ³ So Peter and the other disciple headed for the tomb, ⁴ running together. The other disciple, however, outran Peter and came to the tomb first. ⁵ He looked in and saw the strips of linen lying there, but did not go in. ⁶ Then Simon Peter, who was close behind him, arrived and entered the tomb. He saw the strips of linen lying there, ⁷ but the piece of cloth which covered Jesus' head was not with the linen strips; it was rolled up in a place by itself. ⁸ Then the other disciple who had reached the tomb first also went in, and he saw and believed. ⁹ Until then they had not understood the Scripture that he must rise from the dead.

¹⁰ The disciples returned home again. ¹¹ But Mary stood outside the tomb, weeping. As she wept she looked into the tomb ¹² and saw two angels in white sitting there, one at the head and one at the feet where the body of Jesus had lain. ¹³ They said to her, "Woman, why are you weeping?" She answered, "They have taken away my Lord, and I do not know where they have laid him." ¹⁴ After saying this she turned and saw Jesus standing there, but she did not know that it was Jesus. ¹⁵ Jesus asked her, "Woman, why are you weeping? Whom are you looking for?" Since she thought he was the gardener, she said, "If you have carried him away, sir, tell me where you have laid him, and I will take him away." ¹⁶ Jesus said to her, "Mary!" She turned to him and said

in Hebrew, "Rabbuni," which means teacher. [17] Jesus said, "Touch me no more, for I have not yet gone to the Father. Go to my brethren and tell them: I am going to my Father and your Father, my God and your God." [18] Mary of Magdala went to the disciples and told them that she had seen the Lord and what he had said.

[19] On the same Sunday in the evening, when the disciples were meeting with the doors closed for fear of the Jews, Jesus entered and stood among them saying, "Peace be with you!" [20] When he had said this, he showed them his hands and his side, and the disciples were glad to see the Lord. [21] Jesus said again, "Peace be with you! As the Father commissioned me, so I commission you." [22] Then he breathed on them and said, "Receive the Holy Spirit! [23] If you forgive men their sins, they are forgiven; if you say they are unforgiven, they remain unforgiven."

[24] Thomas, called the Twin, one of the Twelve, was not with them when Jesus came. [25] So the disciples told him, "We have seen the Lord!" But he said, "Unless I see the mark of the nails in his hands and put my finger into the marks and my hand into his side, I will not trust." [26] A week later the disciples again were gathered inside, and Thomas was with them. The doors were closed. Jesus entered, stood among them and said, "Peace be with you!" [27] Then he said to Thomas, "Put your finger here and look at my hands. Take your hand and place it in my side, and do not doubt, but trust." [28] Thomas replied, "My Lord and my God!" [29] Jesus said, "You trust because you have seen me. Happy are those who have not seen and yet trust!"

[30] There are many other signs Jesus performed in the presence of his disciples which are not written in this book. [31] These, however, have been recorded, so that you may trust that Jesus is the Christ, the Son of God, and that in trust you may have life in accord with his selfhood.

Jesus had been taken from the cross and laid into the tomb. But soon it was found empty (vv. 1 f.). Upon hearing the news two apostles take to their heels to verify it. Mary had been right. The tomb *was* empty, except for the linen strips and the piece of cloth that had covered Jesus' head (v. 7). The disciples initially did not know what to make of Mary's message: "Until then they had not understood the Scripture that he must rise from the dead" (v. 9). At the sight of the empty tomb the idea of the resurrection dawned upon one of them: he "saw and believed" (v. 8).

When pondering Jesus' resurrection we should keep in mind that, according to the Gospel tradition, the first human beings who became aware of it were caught by surprise. They had not expected it. Even had Jesus referred to his resurrection beforehand, as the Gospel claims he did (*cf.* 2:19–22), it apparently had not made much of a dent on them. Today, after the emergence of the modern world view, the resurrection is no less a puzzle. Strange supernatural events simply do not occur in the modern world regardless of whether the world is viewed as ruled by the rigid laws of cause and effect or not. Any modern man will puzzle about the resurrection: could it have happened? A dogmatic assertion that the resurrection is an event of revelation or a revealed truth will not really come to grips with the modern question. It even makes light of the puzzlement Jesus' disciples themselves found in the cross and the empty tomb.

Richard R. Niebuhr has suggested that we reexamine "the nature of historical causality and redefine it, if necessary," in order to demonstrate that reason and resurrection are not incommensurable. His basic thesis: "History is its own interpreter, and . . . the resurrection event, as it is reflected in the New Testament, epitomizes the historical event itself while the resurrection tradition illuminates the nature of historical thought." Niebuhr believes that the resurrection "must contain elements historical reason can recognize." But while

it may be instructive to learn that in "the resurrection of
Christ the spontaneity, particularity, and independence of historical events rise to the surface in a single eruption," it is
difficult to see in what sense Jesus' resurrection epitomizes the
historical event as such. There are specific aspects of the resurrection which raise the question in what sense it is an historical event. Does it also epitomize the conquests of Alexander
the Great, the horrors of Adolf Hitler, the space feats of the
astronauts, or the assassination of John F. Kennedy? We
should not try to generalize about the resurrection too much.
It may prove to have analogies to the spontaneous character
of other historical events. But it also has its very own character
and uniqueness.

The empty tomb alone did not evoke the resurrection
faith. It was Scripture that suggested the resurrection idea (v.
9). It is likely that the primitive church was reminded of passages such as in Psalm 16:8–11. Moreover, the idea of resurrection was popular in Jesus' day. Many Jews believed in some
future resurrection, the Sadducees being the one exception.
Jesus' disciples applied the concept to one whom they had followed and whose tomb had become a puzzle to them. He had
died and had been buried. But his life prevailed. No longer
was he with them as before. And yet he was still with them.

Whatever is implied in Jesus' strange words to Mary,
"Touch me no more" (v. 17), Jesus does not tarry with her
for an exchange of intimate information on the *how* of the
resurrection. He sends her to his disciples with the message
that his rising from the dead involves fuller communion with
God: "I am going to my Father and your Father, my God and
your God" (v. 17). During his life he had witnessed to divine
corporateness, but within the limitations of finite existence
and on the hither side of the grave. Now his sharing in divine
corporateness had become lasting. His life had not vanished.

The disciples receive from him the commission he had

received from God (v. 21). So they are being empowered to call men to share in God's liberation. Jesus had been commissioned to free men. He had exposed man's sin as unwillingness to be free. Now God as Holy Spirit himself makes Jesus' work prevail among men. He opens up new space for freedom among the disciples. Where sin is forgiven freedom has elbow-room. Under the image of the resurrection the disciples grasp the continuing presence of his power to set men free. And in the Holy Spirit, as the power of freedom, they experience the continuing presence of the resurrected one.

After the resurrection the disciples represent Jesus' liberating work. They cannot embody God the way Jesus did. They are sinful. And yet they can witness to freedom, since they have been empowered by the Holy Spirit (v. 22) who is its power. The Holy Spirit is God himself making Jesus' freedom prevail (cf. 15:26 f.; 16:14). In the Holy Spirit the reality of Jesus before God is unconcealed. He not only teaches the disciples and makes them remember the teaching and work of Jesus; he also makes them resist the onslaught of evil (cf. 14:25 f.).

The presence of the Holy Spirit, however, does not undo the epistemological problem of the resurrection, which existed from the beginning as the Thomas incident proves (vv. 24–29). Could the resurrection have happened? Thomas is not rebuked for his epistemological doubt. He was made to experience that liberated man prevails. The marks of Jesus' radical waiting on man remained indelibly real beyond the tomb (v. 27). In fact, God himself was known in Jesus' prevailing life: "My Lord and *my God*" (v. 28).

So Thomas had the privilege of experiencing the pristine presence of Jesus as risen. He was even able to touch him. Communion with him who embodied freedom is truly communion with a man and not with an idea.

Jesus, however, had to tell Thomas: "You trust because

you have seen me. Happy are those who have not seen and yet trust" (v. 29). The word pertains to all who become disciples after the pristine resurrection experience. The trust it requires is not some vague "faith in faith." It is confidence in freedom. It is not belief in some mythological feat, but certainty of what resists the power of death. It is readiness to face the neighbor eternally, friend and foe, and together with him, God.

As the cross says that *evil* has no power over the free man, the resurrection affirms that *death* has no power over the free man. Jesus is thus the liberated man in the ongoing resistance against the forces that seek to destroy human life.

The resurrection is the radical witness to prevailing freedom from death and prevailing freedom for communion between God and man and man and neighbor. It speaks of God's waiting on man prevailing against death. Jesus did not vanish because he embodied freedom. The disciples had no other concept with which to respond to the overpowering experience of his prevailing reality than *resurrection*.

We are not invited to give assent to the bare facticity of a resurrection event, but to have our wills changed by it. While we ourselves did not witness the pristine presence of Jesus as risen we are invited to trust the testimony of the first witness: "This is the same disciple who witnesses to these things and who recorded them. We know that his witness is true" (21:24). The reality of the resurrection cannot be buttressed by science. The "objective" historical fact is nothing but the empty tomb. We should not deceive ourselves about this situation. But then we are also asked to become involved in the power of prevailing freedom—remembered by the disciples under the image of the resurrection. The resurrection story is a summons to increase our resistance against the destructive power of death, so that we too become willing to face God and neighbor forever. In this sense the resurrection of Lazarus already prefigured Jesus' resurrection.

The free man, however, is the resurrection in person (*cf.* 11:25). His life, liberated from the power of death, embodies what the prevailing life over death means: the ironclad law of man's view of nature and history no longer pertains. Resurrection says: death was unable to silence the free man. The disciples continued to hear his voice, guiding and illumining them. He continued to promise them a new direction of their destiny.

In applying to him the concept of resurrection, the disciples, facing the fact of the empty tomb, interpreted resurrection nonecclesiastically, contradicting the resurrection dogma of the ecclesiastical authorities. Now the resurrection was no longer viewed as a sheer mythological event at the end of history. Tied to the person of Jesus, it pointed to prevailing life in history as well as beyond history. Apart from this nonecclesiastical interpretation we cannot hope to understand the resurrection event.

Jesus did many signs in his public activity. The Fourth Gospel presents a selection in order to clarify in what manner the man Jesus is the Christ, the Son of God. It wants to show in what sense Jesus transforms the hopes for the Christ. He is the man who in joining the struggle of the oppressed embodied true selfhood. Thus he was also the Son of God. Those who trust him share God's reality in his freedom and thus also prevailing life (vv. 30 f.).

In sum, the resurrection indicates in what way one man is already liberated man. In him the eschaton reaches into history. For us who are still struggling in history, resurrection is empowerment with liberated manhood, so that we resist the power of evil and death more forcefully and battle for unoppressed life. Resurrection does not remove us into a never-

never land of painless bliss without suffering, but it makes us struggle with suffering and death in order to turn them into something creative. It is not a matter of triumphalism, but of realism, the realism of making life prevail.

RESURRECTION AND HISTORY   21:1–25

[1] Later on Jesus showed himself again to the disciples, at the Sea of Tiberias. This is how it happened. [2] Simon Peter, Thomas called the Twin, Nathanael from Cana in Galilee, the sons of Zebedee and two other disciples of Jesus were together. [3] Simon Peter said to them, "I am going fishing." "We will go along," they replied. So they left and got into the boat. That night they caught nothing.

[4] When morning came Jesus stood on the shore, but the disciples did not realize that it was Jesus. [5] He said to them, "You caught nothing?" They answered, "No." [6] He said, "Throw the net on the right side of the boat and you will catch something." That they did, and they were unable to pull it in because of the big catch. [7] At this, the disciple whom Jesus loved said to Peter, "It is the Lord!" When Simon Peter heard that it was the Lord, he slipped on the tunic he had taken off and jumped into the lake. [8] The other disciples came to shore in the little boat. They were not far from land, only about a hundred yards, and they dragged in the net full of fish.

[9] On landing they noticed a charcoal fire with fish and bread on it. [10] Then Jesus said to them, "Bring some of the fish you have caught." [11] Simon Peter stepped into the boat and dragged the net ashore filled with big fish, a hundred and fifty-three of them. Although there were so many, the net did not tear. [12] Jesus said to them, "Come and have breakfast." None of the disciples dared to ask, "Who are you?" They realized that it was the Lord. [13] Jesus came forward, took the bread and gave it to them, also the fish. [14] This was the third time after his resurrection from the dead that Jesus appeared to the disciples.

¹⁵ After breakfast Jesus said to Simon Peter, "Simon, son of John, do you love me more than these?" Peter answered, "Yes, Lord, you know that I love you." Jesus said to him, "Feed my lambs." ¹⁶ For the second time Jesus said to him, "Simon, son of John, do you love me?" He answered, "Yes, Lord, you know that I love you." Jesus said to him, "Shepherd my sheep." ¹⁷ For the third time Jesus said, "So you love me, Simon, son of John?" Peter was sad that Jesus asked the third time, "So you love me?" He said, "Lord, you know everything. You know that I love you." Then Jesus said to him, "Feed my sheep. ¹⁸ Believe me, when you were young you used to dress yourself and go where you pleased. But when you are old you will stretch out your hands, and someone else will dress you and carry you where you do not want to go." ¹⁹ He said this to indicate by which death Peter was going to glorify God. ²⁰ Then he added, "Follow me." Peter turned and saw the disciple whom Jesus loved following. He was the one who at the supper had leaned toward Jesus' shoulder and had asked, "Lord, who is the one that will betray you?" ²¹ When Peter now saw him he asked, "Lord, what about him?" ²² Jesus said, "If I want him to remain until I come, what's that to you? You follow me." ²³ The word was passed on to the brothers that this disciple would not die. But Jesus had not said that he would not die. He only told Peter, "If I want him to remain until I come, is that your business?"

²⁴ This is the same disciple who witnesses to these things and who recorded them. We know that his witness is true. ²⁵ There are many other things which Jesus did. I suppose, if they were all recorded the world could not hold the books that would be written.

After the pristine resurrection experience, history did not come to an end. There was no universal resurrection. Time continued. Those who had shared in the resurrection presence of the free man went back to work. Some went fishing. In their daily work, Jesus made them again aware of his presence. He appears to his disciples in the fishing boat as well as in the quiet of the Upper Room, in the factory as well as in the sanctuary. His presence informs human life with new freedom.

The miraculous catch of fish (vv. 4–8) points to Jesus' freedom in his continuing presence. Where men seem to adjust to the inevitable, he makes them chart a new course of freedom. Life in obedience to his freedom fulfills man's need beyond his highest expectations.

After the draught of fish the disciples are invited by their Lord to breakfast near the shore. He acts as the host who offers bread and fish (v. 13). The sharing of the food is a reminder of the feeding of the five thousand (*cf.* 6:1–14) and the Last Supper (*cf.* 13:2 ff.) and points to the Messianic meal which was traditionally understood as the consummation of God's communion with his people (*cf.* Is. 25:6). The purpose of the life of the disciple is to share in the life of the liberated man. The sharing of fish and bread by Jesus in his continuing presence affirms that this is the liberated life beyond death. In fact, what man is in the sharing of bread and fish through Jesus, he will be forever. There is no greater "heavenly" glory than communion with the free man. Herein God is already shared in history. Either this life in communion with the free man will prevail or there will be no eternal life. "Corporeality is the end of God's ways" (Oetinger).

The history of mankind goes on. Peter is told: "Feed my lambs" (v. 15). He receives the specific task of leading the disciples in sustaining freedom. This is more difficult than fishing. It will bring suffering. Jesus hints at his death, the death of a martyr (vv. 18 f.). Although the disciple cannot repeat Jesus' sacrifice, he might nonetheless have to suffer persecution and death for the sake of freedom. Jesus requires radical discipleship: "Follow me" (v. 20). Suffering and violent death may well be part of it. It may come quickly if a man truly identifies with the oppressed.

As history goes on the disciple may begin to puzzle about his new responsibilities in history. Why should he not focus on the risen Lord alone? There is the strange presence of the other disciple. "What about him?" Peter wonders (v. 21). Jesus' answer is his last word in the Fourth Gospel in its present form. It is somewhat mystifying: "If I want him to remain until I come, what's that to you? You follow me" (v. 22). What is clear in Jesus' word is the mandate of discipleship, which involves corporate selfhood. Unclear is the remaining until Jesus comes. Does it mean that Jesus promised the disciple he would not die? The Fourth Gospel apparently does not think so (v. 23). In any event, the disciple must wait for the universal manifestation of Jesus' freedom. We all live under the eschatological proviso of liberation still to be acknowledged universally.

"There are many other things which Jesus did. I suppose, if they were all recorded the world would not hold the books that would be written" (v. 25). Many words and deeds of Jesus have been recorded in the Fourth Gospel. They all call attention to prevailing freedom. We humans squander life, blinding ourselves to its eternal value. The Gospel declares: the point of human life is resistance to death. We are summoned to choose: either to prevail in response to God's freedom or to doom ourselves to eternal oblivion.

Only in the experience of freedom does resurrection make sense. In freedom we share in prevailing life. The resurrection invites us to experience our true selfhood, a radical awareness of prevailing corporateness and communication, so that we may serve God in openness and discover the new direction of our destiny. *Deo servire libertas*—to serve God is freedom.

PART VI LIBERATION IN THE LIGHT OF THE FOURTH GOSPEL

The readings in the Fourth Gospel are an experiment in a new form of Christian theology. Paul Klee liked to quote a fellow artist: "Drawing is the art of omitting." Today theology too must understand itself as an art of omitting. We tried to lift out the most salient features of contemporary theology as the ideas of the Fourth Gospel impinged on our contemporary experience. We will briefly sketch in conclusion the core issues as they shape up for the development of a liberation theology. Crucial for our understanding of liberation became the tension between the present and the future as it pervades the Fourth Gospel.

ESCHATOLOGY AND HISTORY

The relationship between the present and the future in the Fourth Gospel is often viewed as the difference between realized and final eschatology. Raymond E. Brown finds a useful example of final eschatology in the apocalyptic view of

Albert Schweitzer, who claimed that "in speaking of the coming of the *basileia* Jesus was speaking of that dramatic intervention of God which would bring history to a conclusion." [1] He sees the opposite pole represented by C. H. Dodd, who holds "that Jesus proclaimed the presence of the *basileia* within his own ministry, but without the apocalyptic trimmings usually associated with the event."

According to Brown, the Fourth Gospel seems to present the most advanced form of realized eschatology in the New Testament. Here the disciples see God's glory. The judgment is now. Eternal life is a present possibility. But does this mean that there is no apocalyptic element in the Fourth Gospel? Brown discovers also indications of a future coming, a resurrection of the dead, and a final judgment (5:28 f.; 6:39 f., 44, 54; 12:48). If these indications exist, how are they related to the so-called realized eschatology of the Fourth Gospel?

Brown believes that in "Jesus' own message there was a tension between realized and final eschatology. In his ministry the reign of God was making itself manifest among men; and yet, as heir of an apocalyptic tradition, Jesus also spoke of a final manifestation of divine power yet to come. . . . The passages in John that treat of apocalyptic eschatology are a remembrance that this theme is found in Jesus' own preaching." For systematic theology, the juxtaposition of these two strands is felicitous. While some biblical scholars give the future priority and others emphasize the present, it is important for systematic theology that neither present nor future appears to the exclusion of the other. If the "future" of the future appears less stressed in the Fourth Gospel, this is because it is less concrete. The "presence" of the future is more central insofar as the Fourth Gospel is crucially concerned about the concrete. In terms of principle, eschatology is never absolutely realized, but embodied, as we said. The point is well articulated in the words: "The hour is coming, and now is" (5:25). What now is, is still coming. And what is coming, already reaches into the present.

Systematic theology must learn to work with the dialectic between the two. Jürgen Moltmann has wondered as regards the relationship between the present and the future: "Does the present determine the future in extrapolations or does the future determine the present in anticipations? Is there a third factor in which present salvation-in-faith and not-yet-present salvation in hope can be meaningfully united?" [2] The Fourth Gospel may provide us with a clue for answering the question. Here the present and the future appear for some to contradict each other. In one instance the present takes priority over the future. In another instance the future determines the present.[3] We are probably confronted here with perspectives that complement each other in their difference. There can be no meaningful final eschatology without its anticipations in Jesus Christ, and there can be no meaningful embodied eschatology without the prospect of the final consummation.

What actually creates the forward movement of history, however, is the power of liberation that in Jesus Christ encompasses present and future as a "third factor." The movement of history is not set in motion primarily by human extrapolations, but by God's constant unlocking of the present through liberation. It is also not merely determined by the past. Says Jürgen Moltmann: "Only when the world itself is 'full of all kinds of possibilities' can hope become effective in love." [4] From the perspective of the Fourth Gospel, it is God's liberation that fills the world with all kinds of possibilities and enables man to hope.

As soon as the issue of eschatology has been put on this

level, the nature of history itself becomes clearer. History is not primarily a matter of recollection in turning to the past in faith, or of turning to the future in hope, but of God's liberation breaking into the present through the coming of Jesus Christ. History is thus always created by what opens man up in giving him freedom.

The problem of eschatology, while not solved in the Fourth Gospel, is focused on the anthropological issue of man's inability to appreciate either God's presence or God's future. Already early in our readings we were compelled to stress man's self-deception, his blindness to the reality of God. It is not that man cannot grasp God because full liberation has not as yet occurred, but because he does not care for God's liberation in the first place. So the lack of appreciation for both present and future liberation brings man under judgment. He does not acknowledge God from whatever angle he is approached by him—be it the present or the future. The rejection of eschatological truth makes man all the more inexcusable in terms of the Fourth Gospel.

GOD'S UNCONCEALMENT

The debate on revelation in twentieth-century Protestant theology has been confounded by the fact that revelation was understood as disclosure of something that is hidden not only in fact, but also in principle. As we have seen, however, God is not hidden in principle. And in fact he is hidden only because man blinds himself to him. It is man's sin that hides God. The presence and future of God always reach man. The real trouble is that man does not acknowledge it.

"Seeing God" is nonetheless a possibility of liberation. From God's side nothing stands in the way of seeing him.

But only the one who with his entire being responds to God's unconcealment really sees him. This total response took place in the man called Jesus. And through him also the disciple can see God. But it is a mediated "seeing": "Anyone who has seen me has seen the Father" (Jn. 14:9). The disciple shares in Jesus' seeing of God. It remains for the disciple a seeing "in part," focused in the liberation Christ brings.

So it should be clear why we cannot accept the way in which the problem of revelation has been formulated in twentieth-century Protestant theology. Jesus Christ is not God's act of self-revelation, but the acknowledgment of his unconcealment. God working together with the man who acknowledges his openness to his creation labors toward a fuller opening up of the world to its destiny. Man is now able to see himself in a new way. He can understand life more fully. He can walk toward the openness of God. But this is merely the effect of the acknowledgment of God's openness in Jesus Christ and need not be called an act of revelation.[5]

In terms of the Fourth Gospel, God is the light that illumines man's darkness. He always reaches into man's experience and struggles with him in judgment and grace. Nevertheless, although man may be *aware* of the presence of the light, he may not understand it at all.

So we must try to grasp the reality of God where it is first of all acknowledged: in the life, death, and resurrection of Jesus Christ. Here we learn that God is not found where we might expect him, in the temple, in the sanctuary, or in the pious conventicle, but where the pain is: in audacious suffering in the battle for survival.

Even where man only raises the question of survival is God at work. It is in view of this *awareness* that the theological enterprise begins to make sense. It is merely an awareness, however, not a preunderstanding.

What happens to a dream deferred?

> Does it dry up
> like a raisin in the sun?
> Or fester like a sore?
> Does it stink like rotten meat?
> Or crust and sugar over—
> like a syrupy sweet?
>
> Maybe it just sags
> like a heavy load.
>
> *Or does it explode?*
>
> —Langston Hughes

Does the reader need to be reminded that this is a poem about Harlem? As simple as it may now seem, this was the hardest thing for me to notice: how God's unconcealment and Harlem go together. God's unconcealment is most "obvious" where it is not obvious at all in terms of the criteria of greatness and power. The discovery of the presence of God where the pain is, is impressed on us by the biblical story. And yet it is not at all easy to acknowledge that this is the case. It is even more difficult to find its truth in concrete contemporary situations. The scales covering our eyes as regards the biblical witness persist also as regards God's unconcealment in our historical experience.

POLITICAL THEOLOGY AS
NEW INTERPRETIVE FOCUS

We said in the Introduction that our interpretation of the Fourth Gospel would offer a response to the emerging political theology of our day. We now need to address this point more fully. It is a complex task to describe how theology originates in a particular historical experience. It is never a matter of sheer repetition of biblical ideas. The work of theology is always at least bifocal. Besides the biblical matrix as a focus there is also the focus of the contemporary situation. While the past cannot be changed the present still is changing, and changing swiftly. The unchanging Gospel must always be translated into the changing present. Here a major aspect of the interpretive or hermeneutical problem emerges.

The contemporary situation is so multifaceted, vast, and complex that it is impossible for theology to address itself to it as a whole. A choice has to be made as to where the focus of the theological work actually is found. In a sense, the choice is being made for us by the situation itself. Of course, an individual theologian may decide that he wants to concern himself with a particular facet of the contemporary situation that personally interests him. But he can do so only at his own peril. The result may turn out to be very privatistic. What the theologian needs to do if he wants to be responsible is to discover where the church is already being touched by the cutting edge of life.

It appears that in the American church today the focus is more and more on the political dilemmas in which we find ourselves, the hurt inflicted in the power struggle over public issues and in the exploitation bolstered by political power. Why are people still in bondage? What is the church still contributing to man's unfreedom? Where is the church itself in bondage? These are questions impressed upon theology by the church, whether theology likes it or not.[6]

In response to these queries, political theology is emerging as a new interpretive focus, a center around which a new theological understanding is gradually being developed. By interpretive focus we do not mean an interpretive or hermeneutical principle which would inform much of theological construction as a consciously accepted hypothesis determining the shape of theological enterprise as a whole, so that issues of a political nature would become dominant *in principle*. And we certainly do not mean by interpretive focus *the* hermeneutical norm that would determine the actual *content* of the developing theology. There is a measure of disagreement on these points in theological circles today. Some regard political theology as having already attained the status of an interpretive principle and some would even wish to use it as the interpretive or hermeneutical norm. We want to indicate that while in our perspective the whole enterprise of political theology in America is still in a somewhat amorphous stage, it has at least attained the status of a prelude as regards the total theological enterprise. It is unmistakable that the questions of political power, group loyalty, or national prestige are strongly influencing the basic quality of church life today. So we wish to speak of an interpretive focus.

The worst thing that could now happen would be that political theology were understood as invitation to developing a Christian ideology for this or that political task. What political theology can help us to understand is why religious people still exploit their neighbor. We must see ourselves time and again in the mirror of the Christ event, so that we realize how much we continue to conceal ourselves. The shaping of an ideology would probably afford us a new opportunity for hiding behind a front. Much of our exploitation of the neighbor is due to our placing between ourselves and him an ideology according to which we want to mold him. Ideology continues exploitation because it does not let us see the neighbor as he is. It approaches him in terms of what he is expected to be in our utopistic schemes. It is especially the idea of revolution today that dare not again become the beginning of a new Christian ideology. What it can do is to provide a master-image for the change that is the fabric of modern life. We must be open for this change. But the liberation to openness does not basically originate in revolution. It springs from the encounter with the open man. Only in openness to oneself and the other as first acknowledged by Jesus Christ can we hope to participate creatively in the so-called revolutionary processes shaping modern man.

LIBERATION THEOLOGY

The discoveries we made in the biblical matrix of thought have influenced our concern for political theology as new interpretive focus. And the concern for political theology triggered new questions addressed to the biblical matrix of thought. It was in this context of reflection on theological principles that we developed our readings as an outline of Christian theology. Political theology as new interpretive focus was constantly present in our deliberations. We concentrated especially on the freedom-bondage syndrome in contemporary American experience.

Within the structures of our society we not only become interdependent as human beings, but also interfere with one another immediately curtailing one another's freedom. Throughout the past decade many have tried to alleviate the interference. The civil rights struggle was by and large one great effort by many well-meaning people to make room for freedom, so that everyone would have enough space to be human. But in the process events occurred that pulled us only deeper into the mire of hate or mutual interference. The more we tried to improve, the more difficult relationships became. The gargantuan idealism of Christians who understood themselves as servant church ended up in the stark realism of the militant church, the *ecclesia militans*: the church in conflict with itself.

So, running through the present conflict in society and church there is an increased yearning for liberation, for being freed from interfering with one another, from being master and slave. The yearning is expressed in many ways, by young and old, by people in all walks of life. It has been beautifully expressed by Felix Cavaliere in a lyric, widely known through a recording by the Fifth Dimension, where he observes how men everywhere just want to be free. This yearning is not at all a merely selfish thing. It is not just freedom *from*, it is also freedom *for*. It is often quite clearly understood in terms of the coinherence of all men, a hope for a time when in the whole land no man is living in pain. But when will there be such a time? So concomitant with the increased yearning for liberation comes the realization, at least for some, that liberation is not our thing. We can do various things to overcome certain aspects of the captivity in which all of us are caught. We can put new laws on the books. We can put up new buildings for the poor. But the spiral of dissatisfaction seems to grow with every new law and every new building. Why? We never rest satisfied with our best accomplishments because we want perfection. "Man's reach is always beyond his grasp" (Reinhold Niebuhr).

The importance of liberation theology on the very primal level lies in its new stress on the difference between the perfect and the sinful, the absolute and the finite. The major impression one often gets from recent American theology is that we humans are expected to play God. It is supposed to be *our* task to revolutionize society, to reform the church, and to renew the mind. As a consequence, we are more and more bereft of the basic Christian experience: that man can only live by grace. From the perspective of the Fourth Gospel, the basic human disease is for man to think that he must carry the world on his shoulders and must heal himself.

Once we grasp the basic Christian experience we will also see that it does not leave us paralyzed, but enables us to become agents of liberation in the world. It will always issue, however, in contingent balances of power, relative improvement, finite progress. A grasp of our limitations will make us all the more willing to risk everything in making life more human—after receiving the power of liberation. We do not wish to downgrade the concrete possibilities of liberation, but would like to make its dynamics unmistakably clear, so that true liberation can occur.

Lerone Bennett, Jr., states the concrete issues of liberation quite succinctly: "A philosophy of liberation requires a frank appraisal of the institutions and policies of the white communities. A philosophy of liberation also requires an advance program of economic democracy. Racial integration requires economic integration. And this, in turn, requires a recognition that the race problem cannot be solved without profound structural modifications in 'America,' without real changes in the tax structure and the relations between the public and private sectors, without redefinition of all values and a redistribution of income and power." All these things also become the concern of a new liberation theology. In fact, they are already the concern of the churches, as a recent report of the United Church of Christ indicates: "The theme of 'liberation' is appropriate for the United Church of Christ in its attack on white racism in the 1970s. As a predominantly white denomination in the United States, we need to be aware that as white Christians we are a double minority in terms of the world's population. The vast economic and military power in the hands of this 'white minority' constitutes a serious 'minority' problem for the world's peoples. 'Liberation' from the burdens of excessive power is also a demand upon white church members to disassemble those racist institutions they cannot change and to redirect their resources to support the oppressed peoples of the Third World." Theology's task is to articulate what the dynamics of liberation are. It is not that we are discovering a theme for the church. But we are trying to state in what way it can function effectively. The next step will be to show how liberation theology offers specific suggestions for the solution of our political dilemmas.

Initially, however, liberation theology is interested in radically witnessing to the power of liberation, the grounds on which the goals of liberation can be tackled sanely, with a measure of effectiveness. This calls for stressing the core point of the Fourth Gospel once more: *we* cannot generate the power of liberation—God liberates.

AUTHOR'S NOTES

INTRODUCTION

1. Thomas J. J. Altizer and William Hamilton, *Radical Theology and the Death of God* (Indianapolis: Bobbs-Merrill, 1966), 28.

2. Thomas J. J. Altizer, *The Gospel of Christian Atheism* (Philadelphia: Westminster, 1966), 15.

3. James H. Cone, *Black Theology and Black Power* (New York: Seabury, 1969), 71.

4. John B. Cobb, Jr., "Speaking About God," *Religion in Life*, 36:1 (Spring, 1967), 28–39.

5. Schubert M. Ogden, *The Reality of God* (New York: Harper & Row, 1966), 58–70.

6. Schubert M. Ogden, "Theologian of Open Catholicism," *Christian Advocate* (September 7, 1967), 12.

7. Schubert M. Ogden, *The Reality of God*, 41.

8. Leslie Dewart, *The Future of Belief* (New York: Herder & Herder, 1966), 175–185.

9. Harvey Cox, "Afterword," in Daniel Callahan (ed.), *The Secular City Debate* (New York: Macmillan, 1966), 199 f.

10. *Essential* Works *of Descartes* (New York, 1961), 59.
11. *Ibid.*, 20.
12. *Ibid.*, 21.

PART VI LIBERATION IN THE LIGHT OF THE FOURTH GOSPEL

1. For this and the following see Raymond E. Brown, *The Gospel According to John* (Garden City, New York: Doubleday, 1966), cxii ff.

2. Jürgen Moltmann, "Antwort auf die Kritik der Theologie der Hoffnung," in Wolf-Dieter Marsch (ed.), *Diskussion über die "Theologie der Hoffnung"* (München, 1967), 209.

3. This has led to rather contradictory interpretations of Fourth Gospel eschatology. Lodewijk van Hartingsveld, *Die Eschatologie des Johannesvangeliums* (Te Assen, 1962), 154, claims that affirmations of realized eschatology are possible only on grounds of affirmations of final eschatology. Joseph Blank, *Krisis* (Freiburg, 1964), 353, asserts just the opposite: without an eschatological presence there is no eschatological future. There seems no point in trying to merge these two views. Rather, we must see that in the Fourth Gospel they complement each other.

4. Jürgen Moltmann, *Theology of Hope* (London: SCM Press, 1967), 92.

5. Long after the idea of God's unconcealment was formed in my thought I encountered an observation of Daniel Callahan in "The Relational Nature of Theology," in Dean Peerman (ed.), *Frontline Theology* (Richmond, 1967), 169: "I am increasingly skeptical of any talk of a 'hidden God.' To put it more precisely I am doubtful that Christians can continue to have their God a hidden God and yet at the same time continue to talk about him as if he were quite visible. . . . I am actively exploring the plausible hypothesis that the whole concept represents the Christian's special way of coping with the threat which the patent absence of a personal revelation from God normally poses. How much

better, as a psychological device, to posit a hidden God (which is compatible with any facts at all) than to do away with belief altogether. . . ." On account of a similar argument, on the basis of the Fourth Gospel, I arrived at the idea of God's *unconcealment*. We must give up the idea of a *principally* hidden God.

6. I have tried to give a fuller account of these questions in "Political Theology," *The Christian Century*, 86:30 (July 23, 1969), 975–978, and in "The Political Gospel," *The Christian Century*, 87:46 (November 1, 1970), 1380–1383. See also my essay, "Political Theology in the American Context," *Theological Markings*, 1:1 (Spring, 1971), 28–42.

INDEX

N.B. This Index covers only names and topics in the Introduction and Part VI, "Liberation in the Light of the Fourth Gospel." Themes and topics in Parts I through V will be found in the subheadings for these sections in the Table of Contents.